BEST TRUTH

BEST TRUTH

INTELLIGENCE IN THE INFORMATION AGE

BRUCE D. BERKOWITZ AND ALLAN E. GOODMAN

YALE UNIVERSITY PRESS/NEW HAVEN AND LONDON

Designed by Mary Valencia.
Set in Bell Normal and Futura type.
Printed in the United States of America.

Library of Congress Cataloging-in-Publication Data

Berkowitz, Bruce D., 1956–
Best truth : intelligence in the information age /
Bruce D. Berkowitz and Allan E. Goodman.
p.   cm.
Includes bibliographical references.
ISBN 0-300-08011-5 (alk. paper)
1. Computer security.   2. Intelligence service–
United States.   I. Goodman, Allan E., 1944–   .
II. Title.
QA76.9.A25B48   2000
005.8–dc21   99-39390

A catalogue record for this book is available from
the British Library.

The paper in this book meets the guidelines for
permanence and durability of the Committee on
Production Guidelines for Book Longevity of the
Council on Library Resources.

10 9 8 7 6 5 4 3 2 1

To Judy, Mary Alice, and Rebecca;

Collette, Danielle, George, and A. J.;

and to the memory of William Colby

A time for silence

and a time for speaking . . .

A time for war

and a time for peace.

—Ecclesiastes 3:1–8

CONTENTS

PREFACE

Calendars are arbitrary, so we avoided the temptation to call our book a plan for "intelligence in the new millennium." But facts are not arbitrary, and the fact is that U.S. intelligence faces a new era, dramatically different from any it has faced previously. To remain effective, it must change.

Many experts agree. During the past decade, U.S. intelligence officials have labored to identify new intelligence requirements rearrange organizations, and introduce new technologies. Yet, even though the intelligence community has tried to reform itself, so far it has not succeeded. The reason is that fixing U.S. intelligence has less to do with posting requirements, moving organizations, and adopting technology, and more to do with rethinking the intelligence process itself.

This book is, in effect, a manifesto for intelligence in the Information Age. The Information Revolution is not just about cheaper communications or faster computers. The Information Revolution is also changing how people *use* information. As a result, organizations such as the intelligence community must change their modi operandi in order to provide it. The Information Revolution is bringing into question many of the basic principles about how intelligence is "supposed to work." To adapt, the intelligence community must abandon many of these principles, replacing them with a new approach.

We began planning this book about six years ago. Our earlier study, *Strategic Intelligence for American National Security*, focused on how to plan intelligence programs more efficiently and more effectively. This reflected the most significant problems the intelligence community was then facing. At the time, the key failing of U.S. intelligence was that intelligence consumers—the ultimate judges of whether intelligence is useful—did not have enough influence in planning. Also, programs were planned in a haphazard manner, often seeming to evolve with a life of their own.

Some of the ideas we (and others) discussed at the time have since become the conventional wisdom. For example, today the intelligence community boasts that it uses "mission-based" planning—intelligence consumers indicate what they need, and intelligence planners design programs aimed specifically at meeting those needs. This may seem like an obvious way of doing business today, but bringing about the reforms to implement such a process required many years and much effort. Unfortunately, almost as soon as the intelligence community adopted a more rational approach to planning, the world changed. Obviously, the end of the Cold War changed the "what" that U.S. intelligence is supposed to monitor. But the "how" has changed even more.

If one theme runs throughout this book, it is *intelligence is information*. To understand intelligence issues and problems, it helps to look at what is going on in the world of information as a whole.

The Information Revolution is shaping every aspect of the world economy and politics. So it is little wonder that the intelligence community, which deals almost exclusively with the collection, analysis, and dissemination of information, finds itself at the center of a revolution as well. The problem is that the concepts on which U.S. intelligence is organized and operates are anything but revolutionary. The most charitable thing to say about them is that they are familiar relics from another era.

As one might expect of a "manifesto," we have tried to be provocative, and illustrative rather than exhaustive. This book tries to show where the old concepts fail, and proposes some alternatives. The reader may notice that many of our examples come from industry and the commercial sector. This is intentional. Intelligence must be thought of as one part in a tsunami of change that is overtaking the world of information. These changes will inevitably affect intelligence, and intelligence specialists must understand them.

Consider some of the developments in information technology and information services that have taken place in just the past ten to fifteen years. Widespread use of cellular phones and faxes. Nearly universal adoption of "point and click" computer software systems. The Internet and the World Wide Web. CNN, MTV, the breakup of the Bell System and the resurgence of communications conglomerates. Data links capable of transmitting the entire body of information known in the age of Jefferson in minutes. GPS, ISPs, ATMs, VCRs, and DVD. And so on.

Recent developments in information technology are remarkable. But the changes that are taking place in how information is managed, produced, and consumed may be even more significant. Not only is "mission-based" planning for intelligence no longer good enough— today, no centralized planning can adequately anticipate mission needs, let alone identify and assess all of the alternatives for meeting them. A centrally controlled, centrally managed intelligence system misses the most important lesson of the twentieth century: Sometimes the invisible hand is better. Create the conditions in which people and organizations have the incentive to innovate, and they will.

Similarly, "objectivity" in intelligence is no longer good enough. Today we know that the process of providing facts and judgments is more complex than in the past, and different. Information consumers want facts when they are available, and they expect this information to be objective. But they do not accept summary judgments blithely.

We also know today that, in many cases, the truth is simply unknowable and the future depends on "unknown unknowns" and "mysteries." In these cases, policy must be made in an environment of uncertainty. Decisions depend more on judgment calls than on simple facts. The people to make these calls are officials, who are selected precisely to make such judgments and who can be held accountable for their decisions. Officials may choose their favorite guru, and they may want to know as much about a situation as is possible. But, in the end, such decisions are based on judgment rather than pure analysis, and it is important not to confuse the two.

In sum, in the Information Age the meaning of "best truth" has changed. The best truth is one that is delivered in a way that meets the needs of individual users. It draws on all of the available sources of information and expertise, wherever they may be. And, in the Information Age, we have a better understanding of the limits of even the very best truth one can find.

Unless the intelligence community adopts fundamental changes, it will not be able to provide the kind of information U.S. officials need to address the national security threats that lie ahead. Unfortunately, the hardest thing in the world to do may be to change the practices of an established organization. Large organizations such as the intelligence community, unfortunately, usually do not adopt great changes until they make great failures. Most intelligence failures, by definition, happen by surprise. Both of us started our careers in the Central Intelligence Agency—an organization created largely because of an intelligence failure, Pearl Harbor. We would like to upset conventional wisdom now in order to avoid such surprises in the future.

While we were writing this book, the Central Intelligence Agency celebrated its fiftieth birthday. Many commentators observed that, as a creature of the Cold War, the CIA needs to find its place in the new era. An equally important issue was largely overlooked: Can an organization that has fifty years of culture, history, and sheer inertia adapt?

Much of what has occurred in international relations since the end of the Cold War and the fall of the Soviet Union has defied the best efforts of experts to categorize and forecast. The United States has not yet framed a strategy, let alone a national consensus, to deal with the problems that have arisen. Academic theories of international relations provide little help. The state system today is characterized, above all, by the declining power of governments. Indeed, the modern state is part of an ever-expanding network of changing players—most of whom are not sovereign countries—cooperating and competing with each other in any number of dimensions.

During the Cold War, theories about world politics mainly focused on national power and how nations interacted. These theories rarely considered that militarily powerful states—such as the Soviet Union—might disappear completely. They paid little attention to players in world politics other than states. Consequently, at each step in the unraveling of the superpower conflict, the usual reaction of government analysts was either psychological denial or dumbfounded confusion. Intelligence agencies need to be even more far-thinking about the possibilities for politics, economics, and social events today than during the immediate post-Cold War era. Rethinking the intelligence community may be the most important task for national security in the twenty-first century.

Many people assisted us during the research and writing of this book. We would like to thank the following individuals for conversations, comments, and contributions: Morton Abramowitz, Madeleine K. Albright, Martin Anderson, Christopher Andrew, Richard Arenberg, Les Aspin, Charles Battaglia, Richard Betts, Henry Bienen, Stephen W. Bosworth, Zbigniew Brzezinski, Hodding Carter III, Jimmy Carter, Chester Crocker, Drew Cukor, Kenneth Dam, Arnaud de Borchgrave, Brewster Denny, I. M. Destler, Carol Evans, Robert Gallucci, Adam Garfinkle, Robert Gates, Toby Gati, Leslie Gelb, Michael Graff, David Gries, Richard Haass, Morton Halperin, Lee Hamilton, Owen Harries, Rita Hauser, Jim Hoagland, Jane Holl, Samuel Huntington, Loch Johnson, Stanley Karnow, Richard Kerr, Anthony Lake, Brian Latell, Arjen K. Lenstra, Richard Leone, Richard Leopold, Paul Leyland, Mark Lowenthal, Andrew Marshall, C. William Maynes, Dave McCurdy, Walter McDougall, Donald McHenry, Walter Mondale, Theodore Moran, John Negroponte, David D. Newsom, Matthew Nimetz, Janne Nolan, Joseph S. Nye, Jr., Phyllis B. Oakley, Kevin O'Connell, Earl Ravenal, Condoleezza Rice, Jeffrey Richelson, David Rosenberg, Henry Rowen, Richard Rumpf, Howard Schaffer, Daniel Schorr, Elaine Sciolino, Brent Scowcroft, Gaddis Smith, Britt Snyder, Theodore Sorenson, Harry Soyster, Arlen Specter, George Tenet, Gregory Treverton, Stansfield Turner, Arturo Valenzuela, John Voll, Rod von Lipsey, John Walcott, William Webster, Tim Weiner, Clifton Wharton, Albert Wheelon, R. James Woolsey, Casimir Yost, Philip Zelikow, Robert Zoellick, and Mortimer Zuckerman. A handful of others asked not to be identified. We thank them, as well.

John H. Hedley and the staff at the CIA Publications Review Board, and James Wolfe at the Senate Select Committee on Intelligence were helpful in completing the security review of the manuscript. Naturally, neither this review nor our acknowledgments above imply any endorsement or verification of fact.

A special note goes to Frank B. Horton III and Thomas Rona. Both were great supporters and encouraged us throughout the project with comment and insight. We and many others will miss them.

We also were saddened during our writing by the loss of William Colby. Colby was a remarkable man who stood across two eras. Along with so many men and women of his time, Colby had a sense of duty, a desire for challenge, a taste for adventure, and a love of freedom.

Colby and his contemporaries fought two wars—a world war and a cold war—and left the world better than they found it.

Yet Colby was also a man of the new era that we are just beginning to appreciate. He understood the changing world and the new threats facing Western democracy. Even more significant, Colby understood that it was both possible and essential for intelligence organizations to operate in a manner consistent with American values. If changing a culture is one of the hardest challenges for an organization, seeing beyond one's own culture is one of the hardest challenges for an individual. Colby rose to that challenge. The intelligence community will be fortunate if it succeeds in doing the same.

ONE
THE PROBLEM: PROVIDING INTELLIGENCE IN A CHANGING WORLD

In this book we present a new paradigm for intelligence. In doing so, we question many long-accepted ideas about how an intelligence organization should function. In their place, we propose several new ideas about how to plan intelligence programs, manage intelligence organizations, perform analysis, and serve intelligence consumers.

When Sherman Kent wrote about intelligence some fifty years ago, the first thing he felt obliged to do was explain to his readers just what he was talking about. Kent, a veteran of the Office of Strategic Services during World War II, was one of the "founding fathers" of U.S. intelligence and was writing specifically for national security specialists. Even so, he thought he needed to make clear that "strategic intelligence" did not refer to the kind of mental abilities that psychologists tried to measure. Rather, he explained, intelligence is "knowledge which our highly placed civilians and military men must have to guard the national welfare."[1] Kent's study, *Strategic Intelligence,* became one of the most significant books in its field—a primer on the use of information to support government activities intended to protect U.S. national security.

Much has changed since Sherman Kent wrote. Kent himself might have been surprised to discover that today one out of seven of "our military men" are not men, and that, in a test of free association, as many people would likely link the word "intelligence" with "CIA" as with "IQ." These, of course, are just two indicators hinting at the enormous changes that have taken place in the world of national security since the U.S. intelligence community was established in the early years of the Cold War.

On the surface, the intelligence community has changed enormously, too. Today's intelligence organization charts bear little resemblance to those of fifty years ago. Some of the technology now used in intelligence was scarcely imaginable when the intelligence community was established. And there has been a seemingly endless stream of commission reports, Congressional investigations, and think-tank studies proposing changes for organizing and operating the intelligence community. Many of these proposals have been adopted.

What has not changed, though, may be the most important thing of all: our basic idea about how intelligence is supposed to be produced and the role intelligence is supposed to play in the decision-making process—or, as A. B. Darling, the first historian of the Central Intelligence Agency put it, how intelligence is supposed to perform as "an instrument of government."[2] As will become clear, many of the old assumptions no longer apply. Consequently, this book offers a new approach. Three factors are especially important in shaping this new paradigm.

The first factor is the changes that have taken place in the subject matter that intelligence must cover. Some of these subjects resemble the political, military, or economic issues that intelligence has traditionally covered, but with a new twist. For example, during the Cold War we worried about the growth of Soviet military forces; today we are concerned about the growth of Chinese military forces. Many of today's intelligence topics, however, are quite different from those that concerned us previously, such as the global environmental, demographic, and financial forces that can now threaten the welfare of Americans.[3]

The second factor consists of the changes that are underway in both information technology and how people use information. In fact, this "Information Revolution" may be the single most important factor affecting intelligence today. Intelligence is, above all else, about collecting and analyzing information, and the intelligence community is, above all else, an information service designed to do just that. No aspect of society and the economy is changing as quickly as the world of information, and the intelligence community is affected by virtually every one of these changes.

The third factor consists of recent trends in U.S. domestic politics and American attitudes toward intelligence. These developments are important because the intelligence community does not operate in a vacuum. It depends on political support for funding. Public opinion is critical in determining which kinds of intelligence operations are acceptable, and which are not.

INTELLIGENCE AND THREATS IN THE POST-COLD WAR WORLD

Since the end of the Cold War, public officials, national security experts, and foreign-policy opinion leaders have struggled hard to find a new idea to replace the concept of containment as an organizing principle for thinking about national security matters. For the intelligence community, finding this idea is important because it identifies the main players in world affairs and defines the main threats to the United States from abroad. In effect, it answers the first question of any intelligence officer: Who we are supposed to be watching and why do we need to worry about them?[4]

Saying that the fall of the Soviet Union "created a vacuum" in national security policy is good shorthand, but it barely captures the full impact of the situation on how American officials think about intelligence and the relationship between intelligence and national security policy. For virtually all of the fifty years of the Cold War, national security planning was a relatively straightforward, even routine process. No one attending meetings at the White House, Pentagon, or CIA needed to debate first principles. Everyone understood where the threat lay, and everyone understood the strategy that the United States had adopted to counter it: containment. U.S. leaders assumed that the most important factor shaping global affairs was the threat of Soviet expansion. They believed that the Soviet Union was driven to expand its control over the world for both historical and ideological reasons, and that only solution was a strategy that combined military, political, and economic measures.[5]

People still debate whether this view of the Soviet threat was realistic, but having a common, consistent view of the threat did simplify intelligence planning. Each organization within the national security establishment—the military services, the State Department, agencies involved with international economic affairs—had a defined mission to achieve the overall objective of containing the Soviet Union. The task for the intelligence community was to support these organizations with information about the Soviet threat. (The intelligence community also had an operational assignment—covert operations—which had its own requirements for information but was part of the overall strategy of containment.)

Because the Soviet threat was predominant and enduring, intelligence planning became predictable and incremental. Intelligence questions usually involved issues with two or three decades of history behind them. For example, the intelligence community continually analyzed the Soviet strategic missile force. So the specific issue of concern in the 1970s might have been determining the number of SS-9 intercontinental ballistic missiles the Soviet Union would deploy, and the problem in the 1980s might have been determining the number of warheads the SS-9's successor, the SS-18, could carry.[6] But the basic issue was the same: What is the effective size of the Soviet missile force, and what is its destructive capability?

In other words, the questions were evolutionary, not revolutionary. As a result, it did not matter if the analysts working on the problem were usually the same. In fact, experience was almost synonymous with expertise. The same was true for other fields: Soviet foreign policy, Soviet weapons production, the Soviet economy, Soviet political developments, and so on. And because developments in other parts of the world were also viewed through a Cold War lens, the same was true of most other issues, too. The Middle East was a scene of conflict between U.S. clients, Soviet clients, and countries that vacillated in between. Europe was a question of how to keep NATO functioning smoothly and estimating the degree to which maintenance of Eastern European satellites augmented or detracted from Soviet capabilities. Japan was a question of whether the U.S.-friendly Liberal Democrats would remain in power, and whether the government would boost its defense spending to assist the United States in containing the Soviets and their proxies in Asia. The fundamentals of each field rarely, if ever, changed radically. The sources of information and methodologies for analysis changed incrementally, too.

Without such a robust organizing concept like containment, it is hard to plan national security programs, operations, budgets, or even justify the continued existence of certain organizations. Little wonder why many U.S. officials and foreign policy specialists have tried to postulate a new theory explaining global affairs in the post-Cold War era. Several theses have been floated. Each assumes (sometimes implicitly) that a new type of actor will replace the Soviet Union as the primary threat to the United States. Each thus implies a new "who we should be watching" for the intelligence community. Some of the theories include:

Ethnic Conflict

In the summer of 1993 Harvard professor Samuel Huntington caused a stir among foreign-policy aficionados with an article he published in *Foreign Affairs*. The article (later expanded into a book) proposed that the Cold War, and, for that matter, all conflict since the French Revolution, was just a facet of a more enduring and global struggle among Western European culture and seven other major cultures—as Huntington put it, "Confucian, Japanese, Islamic, Hindu, Slavic-Orthodox, Latin American, and possibly African." Conflict supposedly occurs at "fault lines," where the edges of each culture rub against one another. Huntington argued that the resulting "clash of civilizations," is, in fact, the traditional driver of global competition, and that, with the Soviet Union gone, it would again become the main factor in global politics. The threat to the United States in this situation is that we could find ourselves ensnared in the resulting conflicts. Recent crises in the Balkans—a region of persistant conflict located at the crossroads of the Western European, Slavic, and Islamic worlds—may be the best example.[7]

Religious Conflict

A second view has proposed that future conflict will result from friction among religious groups, or between religious nationalists and secular governments. Most writers who have warned about religion-driven conflict have focused on the threat presented by Islamic fundamentalists. Yet there are many other religious sects, cults, and movements that could trigger conflict, such as Hindu nationalists in India, Jewish extremists in Israel, and the Fulan Gong in China. The threat to the United States, according to this view, is that religious groups could undermine the governments of some of our allies, or that religious zealots might engage in global terrorism.[8]

Economic Conflict

Beginning in the late 1980s, many factors mixed together to raise fears of "economic warfare." One was that, as the Cold War ended, traditional war suddenly seemed obsolete. John Mueller, a professor at the University of Rochester, argued, for example, that war was no longer "useful" because in the modern age its costs almost always exceeded any benefit a country could hope for by winning. Francis Fukuyama, a scholar then at the RAND Corporation and now at George Mason University, went even further, proposing that conflicts between ideologies and nations had played out, liberal democracy had won, and that the world was witnessing "the end of history." All that was left was to compete for market supremacy.[9]

At about the same time, the United States seemed to be falling behind Japan and the emerging tigers of the Pacific Rim. Some Western writers began to argue that trade, technology, and military capability were tightly linked. Some Japanese writers began to agree, in effect confirming the West's worst fears.[10] The proponents of this idea warned that economic competition and trade conflicts would replace the military standoff between the Soviet Union and United States as the main international concern of U.S. leaders. A former director of central intelligence, Admiral Stansfield Turner, even suggested that trade and economics were now the most important dimensions of national security.[11]

Warnings of a "competitiveness gap" lost some credibility during the 1990s, when the Japanese bubble economy burst and, later, when Asia was rocked by a monetary crisis. But by that time economic warfare had become a mainstream political issue. Candidates as diverse as Pat Buchanan, Ross Perot, and Bill Clinton all ran on trade-oriented foreign policy platforms, and countering the threat of trade wars was firmly cemented as part of the U.S. national security agenda.

Nineteenth Century-Style Geopolitics

Yet other experts believe that, with the Cold War over, the world will revert back to the situation that prevailed before the world wars—lots of countries, roughly equal in power, all competing for an advantage, with no single country able to dominate. John Mearshiemer, a professor at the University of Chicago, was one of the first to write along these lines. In 1990, just after the Berlin Wall fell, Mearshiemer wrote an article in *The Atlantic* about how we would soon miss the simple days of the Cold War, when politics was easy to understand because superpower confrontation could be painted in black and white: us versus them. He warned that the United States was about to find itself in a maelstrom of competing powers, where alliances were complex, interests were diverse, and deterrence was difficult.[12]

NGOs and NSAs

These abbreviations stand for "nongovernmental organizations" and "nonstate actors." They include many different types of groups. Some are benign; some are sinister. Terrorist and international criminal organizations qualify, as do multinational corporations like AT&T and IBM, international financial institutions like Chase (and the rogue BCCI), and nonprofit groups like Greenpeace and Amnesty International. The essential point is that national governments are no longer the only players on the world scene—or even the most important. Who is more significant to Western economic development and security, Portugal or Microsoft? Who is the greater threat to peace, Paraguay or Hezbollah? In a recent listing of the 150 largest economic entities in the world—as measured by GDP or annual revenue—97 were companies or transnational agglomerations (for example, the loose financial networks of ethnic Chinese scattered throughout East Asia) rather than countries.[13]

Indeed, as early as the 1970s political scientists observed that nation-states were being eclipsed on the international stage by other actors.[14] Sometimes they saw this as good and necessary, as when international organizations worked together to protect the environment. Sometimes analysts saw this as a threat, such as when the Mafia in its Italian, Japanese, and Russian variants undermined national economies and government institutions. In any case, it seems clear that, if we only considered formal, duly recognized governments, we would be at a loss to explain much of what is going on in the world that could threaten the welfare of the United States.[15]

Each of these views of the post-Cold War world and its main driving forces implies a different set of missions and priorities for intelligence—and, consequently, a change in the way intelligence professionals organize and do their work. If you think the problem is ethnic unrest that could threaten U.S. allies and spill over into our neighborhood, you hire analysts who can tell the difference between the Cradle of Civilization and the Arc of Crisis. If you think the main problem is economic warfare, you recruit agents and infiltrate computer systems in order to collect data to expose industrial spies.

So, whom should the intelligence community be watching, and what threats should it be worried about? The answer is *all of them, potentially.* Each proposed paradigm seems valid in certain situations, but none explains all of the threats the United States faces today. And that is exactly the point. Today many different types of actors can be players in world affairs, and thus threaten American interests. The reason each of the theories described above seems to have some validity is because each does, sometimes.

As a result, there are a greater number and variety of targets for intelligence to watch. Also, as we will see, threats can appear and mutate much more quickly today. In sum, the problem for intelligence planners is not simply that potential threats are different or greater in number, but that the nature of the threat environment has changed fundamentally. It is important to understand this phenomenon, because it results in a profoundly different kind of intelligence problem than what the U.S. had to deal with during the Cold War. Several factors are responsible for this development.

First, *it is easier today for groups other than national governments to organize themselves effectively and directly threaten sovereign states.* Modern information systems are an important factor driving this trend. In the past, broadcasting and news networks were expensive to operate and thus limited in number, so national governments could control much of the media. Now nonstate actors have their own capabilities, which they can use to mobilize and organize supporters. As Thomas Friedman observes, "Where globalization comes into the story is that it weaves together and diffuses revolutions in science, computing, miniaturization and telecommunications in a way that enables smaller and smaller groups and individuals—no matter where they live—to reach farther and farther around the world, faster and faster, cheaper and cheaper. For those with good intentions it empowers them to shape their own world or to participate in the global economy more than ever. But for those with bad intentions, or antipathy to the U.S., it empowers them to lash out more forcefully than ever."[16]

Recall how opponents of the Shah in 1979 used cassette tapes and boom boxes to rally people in the streets of Tehran with recorded speeches by the Ayatollah Khomeini. Today such information technology is more advanced and even more readily available. For example, in the early 1990s the Zapatista National Liberation Army used the Internet to organize itself, plan operations, and publicize its activities and positions to the world.[17] A few years later, opponents of Serbian ruler Slobodan Milosevic evaded the government's efforts to shut down their newspapers and radio stations by moving their operations to the World Wide Web. Listeners could download Radio B-92's broadcasts off its home page.[18]

Not only is the new technology cheap and readily available; it is also hard for government authorities to interdict effectively. When the Peruvian government tried to suppress radio broadcasts by the Tupac Amaru guerrillas, for example, the group took to the Internet, setting up a decentralized network that funneled propaganda into Peru from abroad. One site, it turned out, was operated by sympathizers on the computer system at the University of California, San Diego. A Peruvian official acknowledged that there was no way to stop the "broadcasts" without bringing down the country's own telecommunications network. "We can't very well cut phone lines and confiscate computers," he said.[19]

Richard Rosecrance, a professor at the University of California, Los Angeles, calls this the emergence of the "virtual state."[20] In elaborating on the political consequences of this phenomenon, Jessica Mathews, then a senior scholar at the Council on Foreign Relations and now president of the Carnegie Endowment, went further by noting that

Widely accessible and affordable technology has broken governments' monopoly on the collection and management of large amounts of information and deprived governments of the deference they enjoyed because of it. In every sphere of activity, instantaneous access to information and the ability to put it to use multiplies the number of players who matter and reduces the number who command great authority. The effect on the loudest voice— which has been government's—has been the greatest. . . . Above all, the information technologies disrupt hierarchies, spreading power among more people and groups. In drastically reducing the cost of communication, consultation, and coordination, they favor decentralized networks over other modes of organization. In a network, individuals or groups link for joint action without building a physical or formal institutional presence.[21]

This trend toward networked, decentralized global actors is not just academic abstraction. It already has created problems for U.S. intelligence. In August 1998, for example, the United States carried out a cruise missile attack against an Afghanistan base used by terrorist leader Osama bin Laden. Yet many critics questioned whether the strike yielded any results. Although the Zhawar Kili camp was linked to bin Laden, his organization did not have a single central headquarters. It was a network organization in the purest sense. Its assets were scattered in banking accounts around the world. The organization consisted of numerous loosely linked cells. The network could operate independent of a fixed infrastructure because members often used satellite telephones to communicate with each other. And, possibly most notable of all, the leader was not a citizen of any country; bin Laden, born in Saudi Arabia, had been stripped of his citizenship and expelled because of his terrorist activities.[22]

The point is, because people can organize themselves and operate efficiently independent of the national government, they do so.[23] The resulting proliferation of potential players and the surfacing of the emotions and societal forces that motivate them inevitably increase the intelligence community's target set.

Second, *there are more incentives for groups other than nations to gel as actors, and fewer reasons why they should not.* With the end of the Cold War, the main external threat to many nations has disappeared. But in the case of many countries, the absence of Moscow's heavy hand or the threat of external intervention in response to internal disorder or conflict has invited old conflicts to arise that are now tearing them apart. This seems to explain much of what happened in Yugoslavia. Tito was able to keep the Balkan states together in part because every ethnic community was concerned about the Soviet threat next door. Similarly, the Soviets would never have permitted Czechoslovakia to split; it would have compromised Warsaw Pact defense planning and would have provided an undesirable example for the Soviet Union's own fractious components. But, when the Cold War ended, the Czechs and the Slovaks found it extraordinarily easy to go their separate ways.[24]

Third, *military technology, much of it advanced, is more widely available*. Again, this is a trend that has been underway for some time, but it does seem that today the proliferation of destructive technology is reaching critical mass. As the overall level of technology available in the world has grown, so has the potential for making weapons, including weapons of mass destruction. The process for making chemical weapons ("CW") such as nerve gas is similar to the process for manufacturing insecticide; when you have mastered one, you can usually do the other. The biological weapon ("BW") threat is an even greater problem, because the kinds of equipment used to manufacture BW agents are, in fact, the same as that those used to manufacture certain pharmaceutical products. As Defense Secretary William S. Cohen observed in a 1997 study, the widespread existence and availability of these weapons gives "disproportionate power . . . [to] regional aggressors, third-rate armies, terrorist cells, and even religious cults."[25] Chemical and biological weapons experts have been aware of the impact of these weapons on regional balances of power for some time, but it was not until the Aum Shinrikyo, a Japanese cult group, used nerve gas in a terrorist attack on the Tokyo subway system that the general public appreciated the problem.[26]

Yet, if the proliferation of weapons of mass destruction is disturbing, the availability of conventional weapons is absolutely staggering. Experts estimate, for example, that the Soviet Union and other countries have manufactured over 35 million Kalashnikov automatic rifles, the weapon of choice of international terrorists. One credible estimate claims that there are 1.5 million Kalashnikovs scattered around Mozambique alone. Such weapons can fire hundreds of rounds per minute, providing even a lone terrorist the capacity to inflict considerable destruction in an urban setting.[27]

Ironically, at the same time deadly technology is improving, the targets are becoming softer. Modern societies, and especially democratic, market societies, depend on delicate interconnected networks of transportation systems, communications systems and data bases. These networks are often highly vulnerable to attack by a foreign power or terrorist group. As a result, there are many more potential targets that can be attacked in many more ways. This complicates the problem of planning intelligence even further.

Taken together, these trends define an especially difficult problem for intelligence organizations: the "instantaneous threat." During the Cold War, threats required time to materialize. A new Soviet missile might require four or five years from the time analysts first detected an unfamiliar weapon designation on purloined planning documents to the time the missile was operational. In between, the intelligence community could follow the missile's development, design, and testing. Similarly, the Soviet Union's policies and its relationships with its allies usually evolved slowly. This gave the intelligence community time to develop and validate its sources and methods. Not so today. Because groups can organize and metamorphose so quickly, and because the means of destruction are so readily available, a threat can emerge literally overnight. Given the right conditions, a splinter faction could potentially break off from a terrorist organization, organize and develop a plan for action, gain access to advanced weapons, and be prepared to strike directly at the United States in a matter of days.

So, while defining the "post-Cold War paradigm for world politics" may seem like an arcane exercise in academic abstraction, the issue has very real consequences. Should we, for example, expect intelligence to monitor just potential adversary states? Or should the mission be expanded to include all of the nonstate actors that can pose threats to American security? Do we put a higher priority on supporting U.S. military forces, or do we try to detect industrial espionage against U.S. corporations that could be just as threatening to our armed forces over the long term? The answers to these questions are critical in deciding the kinds of intelligence resources we buy, and how we expect the intelligence community to operate.

THE INFORMATION REVOLUTION AND INTELLIGENCE

The second factor that will shape intelligence is at least as important as the first, and possibly more: the Information Revolution. This "revolution" refers not just to the rapid advancements underway in information technology, but also to the changing ways people use information.

Technology and the Information Revolution

The basic technology trends behind the current Information Revolution can be summarized in three phrases: growing capabilities, falling costs, and greater connectivity. It is impossible to overstate the improvements that occurred in information technology during the last third of the twentieth century.

In 1965, Gordon Moore, then director of research at Fairchild Semiconductor, was asked to give a speech on the future development of integrated circuits. Moore, one of the true pioneers of the modern computer industry, reviewed the enormous progress that had occurred in electronics. He predicted these trends would continue, and that the number of transistors that could be put on a single microprocessor would double every eighteen months for the foreseeable future. Moore later went on to co-found Intel Corporation, the computer chip giant, and played a large role in making his prediction come true.

Transistors are the switching elements in a microprocessor—the parts that enable a processor to count—and the performance of a microprocessor is directly tied to the number of transistors it contains. So, in effect, Moore was predicting that the capacity and processing speed of microprocessors would grow exponentially over time, like compounded interest in a savings account. Figure 1.1, which charts improvements in the performance of Intel's own personal computer microprocessors, shows how Moore's prediction proved correct.[28]

This principle seems to apply to many information technologies, and not just microprocessors. Tomorrow's technology will have a multiplier effect as it builds on today's technology. So the capabilities of information systems do not just improve over time; they improve at an accelerating rate. This principle is so fundamental to the usefulness of information technology that it has become known as "Moore's Law." The flip side of Moore's Law is just as important, though. As information technology improves, the cost of a given amount of capability decreases exponentially. And, sure enough, as Figure 1.2 shows, the cost of information systems (in this example,

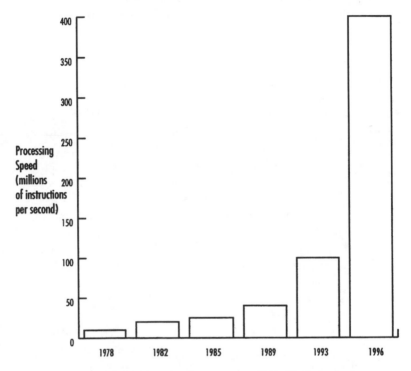

Figure 1.1. Trends in Capabilities of Intel Microprocessors, 1978–1996. Source: Intel.

hard disk drives) has indeed fallen like a rock. The storage capacity that a dollar would buy in 1988 cost less than a penny ten years later. Anyone who has gone shopping for a computer knows these trends all too well. The system you buy today will almost always cost less next month.

The growth of communication capabilities is somewhat harder to measure because these capabilities depend as much on network interconnections as on the speed or capacity of individual components. Even so, one can point to some general indicators of the improvements that have been made. For example, using the breakup of the Bell system as an approximate starting point, one finds that the vol-

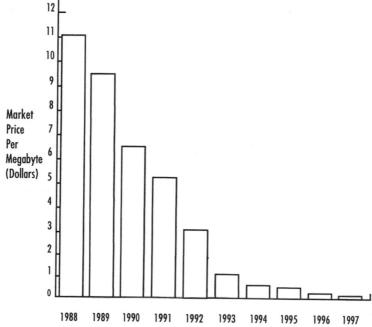

Figure 1.2. Trends in Prices for Hard Drive Data Storage, 1988-1997. Source: Disk Trend, 1998.

ume of interstate telephone calls increased threefold, while the cost of the average interstate telephone call dropped by about 60 percent.

But a more interesting measure lies not in just the volume of traffic, but in the growth of opportunities to form networks. Consider the explosion in the number of registered Internet domains, the "@" in an e-mail address. As Figure 1.3 shows, the growth in domains is proceeding at an exponential pace. In March 1997, Network Solutions, the Virginia-based company that assigns Internet domains, announced that it had recorded its one millionth commercial ("dot-com") domain. (The honor went to Rebecca and Steven LaBlance, owners of Bonnie View Cottage Furniture in Potoskey, Michigan. "We figured this would help our business grow," Mrs. LaBlance observed.)[29]

From the perspective of an information service such as the intelli-

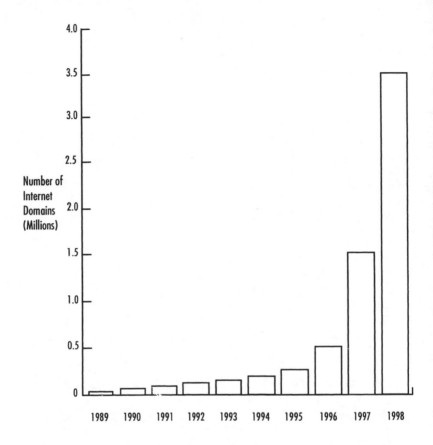

Figure 1.3. Trends in Numbers of Registered Internet Domains, 1989–1998. Source: Network Solutions, 1999.

gence community, the growth in interconnectivity is at least as important as the growth in processing capability. As the number of users in a network grows, the number of potential opportunities for users within the network to interact—exchange information, collaborate, and so on—grows exponentially. With this in mind, Robert Metcalfe, the inventor of Ethernet and the founder of 3Com Corporation, has proposed the networking counterpart to Moore's Law—Metcalfe's Law, which states that the value of a network increases exponentially with the number of new users that join it.[30]

What is more, the effects of these trends are not restricted just to the computer on the desktop. They permeate virtually every electronic device. Everything from satellite sensors to cash registers to transportation control systems has become more powerful, more sensitive, and more accurate because, buried deep in the bowels of the device, there is some microprocessor or memory chip supporting it. And, as the technology gets better, the existing technology filters down to more routine applications. Some guidance sensors used in missiles and aircraft today, for example, have a supporting chip that is derived from the Intel 486 processor—the heart of the most advanced personal computers of the mid-1990s. As a result, the data from the sensor is extensively processed before it ever gets to the main computer in the vehicle's guidance system. Similarly, the solid state memory in a two-hundred-dollar fax machine manufactured today is approximately equal to the entire memory contained in a top-of-the-line computer of just ten years ago.

Such progress in information technology has led, in turn, to changes in how information systems are designed and how they are used. Some of the more significant trends with particular relevance to applications in the intelligence community include.[31]

Decentralization
Rather than having a large number of users depend on a small number of centralized sensors or data processing facilities, new low-cost, high-capability sensors, microcomputers, and stand-alone work stations make it possible for many users to have their own dedicated data systems.

Tailored Systems
Because information systems have become so inexpensive, it is not only possible to give individual users their own data processing equipment, it is also possible to tailor this equipment to the specific needs of each user (often by using custom or customized software, rather than modifying the data processing equipment itself).

Networking
High-efficiency communications links and software make it possible to link these smaller systems together via the Internet and local area

networks (LANs). Individual users can share and exchange data, often without the need for a central processing facility.

Distributed Operations

When companies and organizations began installing the first LANs, some wags noted the irony: After replacing centralized mainframe systems with personal computers on the grounds of efficiency, the same computer jocks were recentralizing by connecting all of the PCs together in a network. The critics missed the point. The new networks, unlike the old mainframes, allow users to share data and processing tasks, but require them to do so only to the degree that it is efficient. Moreover, the networks are fluid, allowing relationships among users to change as required—something the old mainframe architectures never did.

The Impact of the Information Revolution on Technology for Intelligence

It is always hard to predict technology developments, but already we can anticipate some information technologies that are likely to have a dramatic effect on how people generate, disseminate, and use intelligence. A few of the more promising examples include:

Cellular and High-Data Rate Satellite Communications

Several companies—Iridium and Globalstar are the best known—have introduced communication systems consisting of fifty or more satellites in low earth orbit (LEO). Essentially, these systems operate like space-based cellular phone systems, so that one can telephone anyone, anywhere, using a hand-held receiver. Some companies hit a rough patch when the market for these systems developed more slowly than expected (Iridium in particular received a lot of press about its financial troubles). But the basic technology is sound and will likely be around in one form or another.

Other satellite systems, such Astrolink and CyberStar, are designed to operate in the more traditional geosynchronous orbit and serve as giant data pipelines. These systems, which just began to enter service in the late 1990s, enable anyone with a medium-sized dish antenna to receive a gigabyte of data in under a minute. Yet other systems, like Teledesic, plan to combine the no-lag communications of LEO satellites with broad-band data volume. For intelligence operatives, all of this means it will be easier than ever to be in direct contact not only with collectors in the field but with policymakers on the move, who may be working from the field as well.

Small, Low-Cost Reconnaissance Satellites
Some of these may cost as little as $100 million and weigh less than fifteen hundred pounds—less than a tenth of the cost and size of current systems.[32] The cost of some of these new satellites is low because they use components from the satellites being built for the new LEO communication systems. Mass production reduces unit costs. In addition, all of the latest reconnaissance satellites benefit from the general decline in cost for information technology. The new small intelligence satellites will not always have the capability of their larger brethren. But because they will be less expensive, individual agencies will be able to afford them, and they will be able to tailor them to their specific needs.

Versatile, Adaptable, and Smaller Sensors
Currently, designers are required to make many tradeoffs when designing sensors—range versus sensitivity, spatial resolution versus spectral resolution, area coverage versus resolution. Improvements in microprocessors and the sensors themselves are making some of these tradeoffs less constraining to deal with. So, for example, it is now possible to design imaging sensors that can both detect small objects and divide their images into narrow spectral bands. This could enable one to distinguish, say, a tank from a satellite or aircraft, and also determine whether it is metal (that is, a real tank) or plastic (a decoy). Policymakers will thus have less of a need for photo interpreters and be able to make decisions based on what they can see with their own eyes rather than having to take on faith the interpreter's judgment that a dark blotch on a grainy picture is, in fact, a particular weapon or platform.

Universally Available, High-Capability Encryption Software
Commercial programmers have already written encryption software that is, for all practical purposes, unbreakable.[33] Most government of-

ficials have realized that banning this technology is impractical, and at least some versions of these "super ciphers" will inevitably be widely available. This will make signals intelligence harder, but it will offer other opportunities that will benefit the intelligence community. For example, it will be easier to transmit sensitive intelligence data over commercial lines. And it will be much easier for intelligence agencies to distribute their products, as well as for individuals and organizations within the intelligence community to communicate with each other.

Adaptive Software

Currently, developing signatures, breaking codes, and processing many types of intelligence data is a time consuming process requiring massive data bases. New self-generating software will streamline the process and make information systems more flexible. For instance, a sensing system might be able to learn how to recognize specific types of objects after repeated encounters. It will also be harder for opponents to spoof or deceive technical collection systems.

GPS on a Chip

The Global Positioning System uses an orbiting satellite constellation as a reference point to enable users to determine their location anywhere on earth within a few feet. A GPS receiver is essentially a radio receiver integrated with a computer. With mass production and miniaturization, an entire GPS receiver can be manufactured as a single integrated circuit. Simply put, it will be possible to determine the precise location of almost any object to which one can gain physical access. If one can attach such a GPS receiver and and a radio transponder to the object, it will be possible to track its location precisely, possibly in real time.

Biosensors

These devices will be capable of detecting the presence of even a few atoms or molecules of a substance.

Small, Inexpensive Drones Tailored for Specific Users

Drones (or "UAVs," for "unmanned aerial vehicles") don't have the glamour of satellites, but they often have significant advantages as data collection platforms. Besides being much less expensive than a satellite, drones can fly under clouds and loiter around a target (one reason why U.S. military forces relied on UAVs so heavily in the Balkans). The latest UAVs range from large, long-range systems that can loiter over a target for hours or even days, to ultra-small, disposable systems that resemble Frisbees and can be tailored for individual users. The benefits will be similar to those resulting from small, cheap satellites—an even larger number of individual users will be able to afford their own tailored collection system.[34]

Super Workstations and Personal Data Assistants
Already, electronic pocket datebooks come equipped with four or five megabytes of memory—more than the typical desktop computers of just a few years ago. This will accelerate the growing capability of individual intelligence users to collect and store more data and do more of their own analysis.

The Information Revolution and Intelligence Consumers
The Information Revolution is not only about hardware and software, but also about behavior and culture. The explosion in information technology developments has changed how society and individuals use and interact with information. Specifically:

- People have come to expect information on demand. They often prefer to be in direct contact with whatever sensor or human reporter is collecting information for them. If they cannot be in direct contact, they at least expect to know how their information is being gathered so that they can assess its credibility and accuracy for themselves, and so that they can make adjustments.
- "Channel surfing" is more than a cliché. It describes how people consume information today. In an age of media conglomerates, thousand-channel cable services, and the Internet, people usually have many sources of information from which to choose. Information consumers quickly change channels, switch stations, or cancel their cable service if they are dissatisfied with the quality of the support they receive or if they doubt its content.
- Partly because of the greater availability of information, and partly because of the general decline in deference to institutions, people are reluctant simply to accept "wisdom" from authority figures. People often prefer to

evaluate data themselves, or have experts they trust do so on their behalf. Even at the highest levels, policymakers can now function as their own analyst in ways and at a depth that was not possible only a few years ago.

To appreciate the changes that have occurred in information resources since the intelligence community was first established, picture the typical American college in the 1940s. This was the environment in which Sherman Kent, William Langer, and many of the other founding fathers of the analytical side of the U.S. intelligence community first worked. It was also their reference point when they developed paradigms for how intelligence organizations ought to function to support policymakers. Look at a handful of college catalogues from the period, and an interesting detail falls out: the way people measured the quality of a college or university at the time. Most of the prestigious institutions boasted about how many volumes—books, journals, and original papers—their library held. (Harvard's library took honors with 5,274,618 volumes in 1949, making it the envy of other institutions.) At the time, libraries were literally storehouses of knowledge, just as, say, silos were storehouses of grain. So, the more knowledge, the better the institution. The same rule implicitly applied to the faculty. The best way to interact with someone was in a face-to-face conversation, so the quality of the college was linked to the number of knowledgeable faces one might encounter on campus.

In short, when the modern intelligence community was established—and, with it, the basic organizational framework for the agencies and departments that remain with us today—information was scarce, expensive, and considered authoritative when provided by organizations with accepted credentials. Now, try to fast-forward fifty years. The first thing you notice is that you cannot "fast-forward" because in the 1940s people still listened to phonographs. Tape cassettes did not hit the market until the 1960s. Perhaps fifteen or twenty years from now, the expression "fast-forward" will seem as quaint as "sounds like a broken record," when recording tape is replaced by solid state, random-access memory cartridges. It is not just that we have better technology now than in 1949. The more interesting lesson is that even our metaphors, the shorthand of memory and expression, have a hard time keeping up. The way in which people think and use information is also considerably different. Today's top universities do not boast only about their libraries, but about their "connectivity," and how their students can reach their professors and access the Internet without leaving their dorm rooms.

The most important impact technology has on intelligence will be in how decision makers themselves interact with information. Policymakers will expect tailor-made information. Specialized intelligence will become just one part of this (and, continuing a trend that has been underway for some time, this intelligence will represent a smaller and smaller part of their total information support). Policymakers will increasingly become, as Nicholas Negroponte has put it, "the senior analyst on their core account."[35] The challenge for the intelligence community is whether it will be able to adapt to the Information Revolution. Two questions are critical. Will the intelligence community be able to adapt to the changing ways society in general consumes information? And will it adopt management practices that permit it to make maximum advantage of the new technology?

Here, again, is where the traditional intelligence paradigm not only fails us, but threatens to stand in the way of progress. Traditionally, intelligence officials automatically assumed that both their information and their technology was better than that available in the "outside world." In the Information Age, this will often be an invalid assumption—the commercial sector will frequently have technology superior to that of government-bound intelligence organizations, and it will almost always be better in developing products and services, and delivering them quickly to users. In some cases, the commercial sector will also have better information. In this new environment, the challenge for intelligence officials is to understand how best to leverage the capabilities of the commercial sector, and concentrate on those specific areas in which it has a comparative advantage. The old paradigm is ill-suited for doing this.

INTELLIGENCE AND AMERICAN ATTITUDES
The third factor that will affect the ability of U.S. intelligence to support national security policy in the post-Cold War era is domestic politics and public attitudes. The old paradigm of intelligence is out

of step with changes that have taken place in politics and attitudes. For example, the traditional paradigm, reflecting the security-at-any-price mind set of World War II and the Cold War, assumed that the government had vast amounts of money to throw at intelligence problems. One could expect that the intelligence community would be ready and able to fund almost any good idea that was proposed. This is no longer true. Today intelligence organizations must work within finite—and often tight—budgets.

The old paradigm also assumed that the intelligence community could operate in isolation, with minimal oversight, and that politicians and the public would accept whatever it did in good faith. This assumption, too, is obviously no longer true. To the contrary, today intelligence organizations can expect extensive political oversight and a good deal of public skepticism. They will need to justify secrecy in every case they request it. This situation has been developing for two decades (since the Church Committee hearings of the mid-1970s), and intelligence officials have acknowledged the need to adapt. Yet they will be unable to adopt the changes that are required if they remain bound by the traditional model of intelligence, with its roots in a culture of secrecy and isolation.

Intelligence and the Budget
Ultimately, U.S. intelligence capabilities will depend on the federal budget. Like any other government activity, intelligence programs are shaped by the budget knife and the budget ladle. A cynical view of how policy is made? Listen to a conversation at the Pentagon or in Langley about an intelligence program; odds are that the sharpest words will have dollar signs attached. Even a record of success does not guarantee an intelligence program immunity from budget cuts. One is reminded of a recent case, in which intelligence officers being driven to the White House to receive a presidential award for supporting U.S. diplomats in Bosnia were told en route that the Office of Management and Budget had recommended eliminating their budget![36]

Since the end of the Cold War, popular support for spending on national security has declined. By the late 1990s, such support had fallen to its lowest point since the end of World War II.[37] So, even if requirements for intelligence do grow significantly, the United States will not be able to spend more for it. Quite the contrary; it is more likely that the intelligence community will have to stretch smaller budgets even further. If it is to cope, it must learn how to plan, manage, and acquire technology—mainly information technology—more effectively.[38]

To understand why this is so, one needs to understand the current U.S. intelligence budget and the role technology plays in it. Intelligence spending is officially classified (whether or not to reveal the budget is itself a recurring issue in intelligence reform debates), but a substantial amount of information is publicly known. In 1997, the director of central intelligence announced the total annual funding appropriated for intelligence activities at the time—approximately $27 billion.[39] According to press reports, about half of this money is for the National Foreign Intelligence Program (NFIP), which supports users throughout the national government. The other half is spent on Tactical Intelligence and Related Activities (TIARA) programs, which provide direct support to military commanders.[40]

The 1996 Commission on Intelligence Roles and Capabilities provided what many accept as an accurate approximate guide to the main cost centers for spending on national intelligence programs.[41] These figures are mainly consistent with those previously reported in the press and suggest the following:

- The National Reconnaissance Office (NRO), which is responsible for developing, procuring, and operating national imagery and signals collection satellites, has the largest share of the national intelligence budget at about $6.2 billion and employs about a thousand people.
- The National Security Agency (NSA), which is responsible for intercepting and deciphering communications intelligence, runs second at $3.7 billion and employs about thirty-eight thousand people.
- The CIA, despite the intense publicity it receives, is third at $3.1 billion and has a work force of seventeen-thousand people, and is approximately 50 percent smaller than it was during the 1980s.
- The Joint Military Intelligence Program (JMIC, national intelligence programs operated by the Department of Defense, such as the Defense Intelligence Agency and the intelligence arms of the army, navy, and air force) is fourth at about $2 billion and nineteen-thousand people.

In other words, most of the budget is devoted to hardware. Roughly two-thirds of U.S. spending on national intelligence programs goes to two agencies, the NRO and NSA—or, to oversimplify, a space program and a data processing program. Moreover, although the CIA is best known for its analysts and operators, much of its budget has historically also been devoted to technical systems (for example, the U-2 aircraft, reconnaissance satellites such as CORONA, and the CIA's precursor of the SR-71, OXCART). Much of the $2 billion cited for DoD-managed national intelligence programs is allocated to a number of sea-, land- and space-based collection systems. And, as one would expect, most of the money devoted to TIARA programs (by inference, $14–15 billion) goes to hardware such as various radars, unmanned aerial vehicles, aircraft-mounted imagery pods, etc.

So, despite efforts to "streamline" and "consolidate" intelligence organizations, any impact from eliminating redundant personnel will inevitably be quite small. The money spent on staff pales before the amount of money spent on hardware. Eliminating people (either inside the intelligence community or contracted from outside) may make for good sound bites, but will not save much money. The intelligence community's success in dealing with limited budgets will mainly depend on how well it develops, acquires, and operates technology in the Information Age.

Public Opinion and Intelligence

At the same time public support for spending on national security programs has diminished, public support for the intelligence community in particular has faded, too. Consider the following barometer.

In 1956, the top film about the world of intelligence was *The Man Who Never Was,* a true World War II story in which the British Secret Intelligence Service hoodwinks the German army, saving thousands of lives during the invasion of Sicily. All the intelligence officers portrayed were brilliant, dedicated, and heroic. Nine years later, in 1965, the top film about intelligence starred Richard Burton playing Alec Leaman in John LeCarre's *The Spy Who Came In From the Cold.* In this true-to-life story of Cold War espionage, intelligence professionals are still portrayed as brilliant and dedicated, although

Leaman and all around him have few illusions about being heroes or being appreciated by the society outside.

Soon the movies were casting the intelligence professionals as the bad guys. For example, in 1975's *Three Days of the Condor,* Robert Redford plays Joe Turner, a low-level CIA analyst—"I just read books," he says. Turner uncovers an operation that goes sour and finds himself pursued by his own colleagues, who would rather kill him than chance his compromising a secret operation. By 1991, Oliver Stone's *JFK* purported to reveal long-hidden "historical facts" demonstrating that the CIA was responsible for the Kennedy assassination, the war in Vietnam, and, indirectly, Watergate. In an opinion poll taken that winter about half the Americans surveyed believed that the Central Intelligence Agency "might have been involved in a conspiracy to assassinate President Kennedy."[42]

Films and other artifacts of popular culture are, of course, imperfect indicators of prevailing attitudes. Yet it is fair to say that no other government organization has been the subject of as much controversy for as long a time as the intelligence community. Many institutions in America have gone through a bad patch or two, but most seem to turn around. Dysfunctional organizations get fixed, disappear, or gradually become irrelevant and ignored. For example, the disastrous failed hostage rescue operation at Desert One in 1980 focused attention on the low morale and declining readiness capabilities of the post-Vietnam War U.S. military. The *Challenger* disaster in 1986 led to self-reflection and reform throughout NASA.

The intelligence community, on the other hand, seems immovable. A review of the press shows that at least one agency within the intelligence community was the subject of a scandal or investigation virtually every year for the past two decades.[43] Indeed, the most remarkable feature about the continuing controversy over U.S. intelligence is simply that it has gone on for decades and has not yet been resolved. Why not?

One reason is that, up to now, efforts at "intelligence reform" have been mainly reactions to specific cases in which the intelligence community has failed in its mission or performed improperly. Rarely has reform been aimed at understanding the basic mission of intelligence and how it must adapt to changes in the larger society, economy, and global environment.

Thus, three basic premises about intelligence today and in the future underlie our conception of a new paradigm. The first premise is that intelligence policy can and should be analyzed like other areas of public policy. The government releases more information about intelligence organizations and operations than ever before. There may be some specific facts that need to be secret, but most of the things that make intelligence organizations succeed or fail can and should be discussed openly. The corollary of this argument, though, is that we should expect the intelligence community to work at least as well as other parts of the government.

The second premise is that the U.S. intelligence community is, above all else, an information service. Because information is the essence of intelligence, the intelligence community could—and should—be affected by the Information Revolution more than any other part of government. When we consider how the Information Revolution is changing other parts of society and the economy, it becomes clear that nothing less than a total rethinking of intelligence and its relationship to U.S. government decision making is likely to be adequate. Many of the ideas we present here may seem conceptually and organizationally radical. Yet, in fact, much the new technology that is at the heart of the Information Revolution is already being adopted by the intelligence community. What has not occurred is the change in thinking that needs to take place in order to take full advantage of this technology. This thinking needs to consider both the technology itself and changes in the ways people consume and interact with information today.

The third premise underlying our paradigm is that intelligence can be reconciled with American democracy. Secrecy and deniability may be necessary for some intelligence operations. Even so, the aim should be to limit the requirements for secrecy and deniability to the lowest level possible. In the cases that remain, the required compromises should be no greater than in other cases where most people are willing to accept a less-than-perfect democratic process for the sake of other essential interests, especially those involving American national security.

The need for a new paradigm for intelligence can be seen from several different perspectives. In Chapter 2, after surveying previous efforts at reform, we consider how the process of planning intelligence resources—both personnel and technology—must adapt in order to cope with the Information Revolution and a world of varied, rapidly changing threats. In Chapter 3 we examine the issue that logically follows from the first: Once one has the resources, how does one organize and manage them effectively in the new environment? In Chapter 4 we consider how this new environment affects the intelligence analysis process itself. In Chapter 5 we consider the implications of this environment for covert action, a subject that is technically separate from intelligence, but closely related to intelligence policy. Finally, in Chapter 6 we examine the culture of intelligence and how it must change if U.S. intelligence is to be effective in the Information Age.

TWO

PLANNING INTELLIGENCE RESOURCES IN THE INFORMATION AGE

Most experts agree that U.S. intelligence needs reform. During the past several years at least a half-dozen reports, totalling more than a thousand printed pages, have been issued by official and unofficial organizations on how to improve U.S. intelligence performance.[1] These groups have, by our count, issued recommendations for more than *two hundred* specific measures. Some of these recommendations have been adopted. Yet, for the most part, these studies have had remarkably little effect on the basic nature of how the intelligence community operates. This is because such studies have rarely questioned our basic assumptions about how intelligence should be produced and how it should be provided to the consumer.

Marginal reform is not enough. Intelligence is information. As we have seen, few technologies are improving as fast as information technology, and no part of our society is changing faster than the way we deal with information. Moreover, requirements for intelligence are growing—and changing in fundamental ways. The intelligence community must adopt a new approach and a new culture that not only keeps up with these changes, but also takes advantage of them.

PREVIOUS APPROACHES TO INTELLIGENCE REFORM

Recent efforts to reform the intelligence community have mainly concentrated on three strategies: streamlining to improve efficiency and effectiveness; reorganizing to improve responsiveness; and redefining roles and missions to make better use of available resources. As we will see, one reason why reform efforts have failed is that they have not addressed the root problem: How does one plan and produce intelligence in the post-Cold War, Information Age environment?

Improving Efficiency

Several recent reform efforts have been devoted to developing ideas that will save money and improve customer service. One was carried out as part of Vice President Al Gore's National Performance Review (NPR), the Clinton administration's "reinventing government" initiative. Part of the NPR focused on the intelligence community. The NPR offered twenty-one proposals for improving service—for example, establishing an "intelligence ombudsman" to serve as an "impartial observer, facilitator, and commentator" on behalf of intelligence consumers.[2]

If the NPR evokes a sense of "been there, done that," it should. In reality, the NPR (in its third iteration at this writing) is just the latest in a long line of public administration studies presidents have commissioned in the name of cutting red tape and saving money in the federal government. Harry Truman seems to have begun the practice in 1949 when he appointed former president Herbert Hoover to head a commission to investigate proposals for improving efficiency in the executive branch. (Although today he is remembered mainly as the president who preceded Franklin Roosevelt, Hoover enjoyed a legendary reputation as an administrator following his work as head of U.S. relief and recovery aid programs to Europe after World War I.) Dwight Eisenhower authorized a second Hoover Commission in 1955. Similarly, Richard Nixon appointed the Packard Commission, headed by David Packard, founder of the Hewlett-Packard Corporation. Jimmy Carter tried to implement the notion of zero-based budgeting, in vogue in the business world at the time. The Reagan administration established the Grace Commission, led by W. T. Grace, whose company had reportedly thrived through effective restructuring.[3]

Many of these reviews, like the NPR, had a section examining the intelligence community. In each case, these commissions usually found ways to make the intelligence bureaucracy work better. In each case, the intelligence community dutifully promised to review the recommendations and thanked the commission for its input. Eliminating "waste, fraud, and abuse" (the catchphrase of the 1980s) and creating "common sense government that works better and costs less" (NPR-speak) are worthy goals in an intelligence organization, just as anywhere else. But it is hardly the kind of reform the intelligence community needs to prepare it for a rapidly changing world and even more rapidly changing technology.

Reorganization

The second approach to reform has been reorganization. Indeed, the first official study on reorganizing the intelligence community began the day after the community was organized. In all, the Congressional Research Service has identified about two dozen specific proposals for reorganizing the intelligence community by the executive branch, Congress, and official commissions since 1947.[4]

Reorganization in recent years has usually been aimed at making intelligence organizations more responsive to the needs of intelligence consumers. For example, one of John Deutch's highest priorities while director of central intelligence (DCI) was to create the National Imagery and Mapping Agency, or NIMA. Maps and imagery analysis are vital to U.S. military forces today, and providing this support is a bigger challenge than ever. When the United States was concerned mainly with just the Soviet Union, mapping and imagery analysis programs could concentrate on a single (although, admittedly, large) target. Unfortunately, the intelligence community was ill-prepared to cover targets outside the Soviet Union.

These weaknesses were exposed in 1986, when the United States carried out an air strike against Libya in retaliation for a terrorist attack. U.S. military planners were unable to create digital maps quickly enough to program cruise missiles for the strike, so the United States instead had to rely mainly on manned bombers. Two aircraft were lost. A few years later, during Desert Storm, military commanders complained that the intelligence bureaucracy was slow in providing satellite imagery to assess bomb damage after U.S. air strikes.[5] NIMA was intended to combine several organizations into a single agency: the Defense Mapping Agency in DoD, the National Photographic Interpretation Center in CIA, a unit at the National Reconnaissance Office, and some smaller organizations.[6] Deutch believed centralizing all mapping and imagery analysis into a single unit under one chief would improve service.

Actually, centralization in the name of intelligence reform is a tradition as old as reform itself. Usually officials centralize offices after an intelligence failure, hoping that reorganization will prevent responsibilities from slipping between the cracks. For example, after the Japanese attack on Pearl Harbor, investigators discovered that bits and pieces of information warning of the strike had existed throughout the military services and State Department. The problem, they said, was that the United States lacked a central organization responsible for pulling the various threads together.[7] This failure became part of the justification for creating, logically enough, the Central Intelligence Agency—just as NIMA was a response to the failures in the Libyan raid and Desert Storm. Reorganization is also often intended to save money.

As successive DCIs have entered office and rearranged the boxes on the organization chart, the effects have resembled tidal cycles under the influence of the moon. For example, Stansfield Turner, DCI under Jimmy Carter, reorganized the CIA's Directorate of Intelligence from a geography-based organization (offices covering Europe, the Soviet Union, the Far East, etc.) to an issue-based organization (offices covering politics, economics, military developments). Turner also renamed the directorate the "National Foreign Assessment Center." Four years later, Ronald Reagan's DCI, William Casey, changed the organization and its name back to more or less its earlier form. Lately the trend has been to create special "centers" to support high-priority post-Cold War missions. In many respects, this is a reversion to an issue-oriented organization. Presumably, when the next crisis in China or the Middle East erupts, we will go back to geography as an organizational motif.

Are any of these organizational schemes better than the others? In truth, an argument can be made for almost any organizational structure. It depends on the immediate situation. An organization will usually be organized effectively for one type of problem, less effectively for others. Similarly, centralizing an organization may improve efficiency by eliminating redundancy. But such "excess capacity" is often what allows an organization to meet requirements that are not important now, but which may become important in the future. Or, to use the modern parlance, an organization that has been "right sized" for one assignment may be utterly "wrong sized" for another.

In a world in which requirements for intelligence are constantly changing, it is unlikely that organizational fixes will lead to genuine reform. No single scheme can meet the rapidly changing demands for information and improvements in the means for producing it.

Setting Roles, Missions, and Priorities

A third approach to intelligence reform has been to review intelligence priorities, roles, and missions—that is, what the intelligence community is supposed to do and who in the community is supposed do it. This was the main assignment of the Aspin-Brown Commission. It was also the focus of the Clinton administration's own intelligence policy. The president described it in a speech at the CIA in the summer of 1995. Much of the speech was essentially an unclassified version of Presidential Decision Directive 35, which the president signed earlier that year. PDD-35 set guidelines for U.S. intelligence planning. The president observed that, while requirements for intelligence are growing, budgets are tight. Therefore, he said, the intelligence community must be "selective" in choosing targets. The president said that his national security team would set clear priorities. PDD-35 defined the intelligence community's priorities as: supporting military operations; analyzing political, economic, and military developments in hostile countries; and monitoring "trans-national threats," such as proliferation, terrorism, and drug trafficking.[8]

Administration officials described the policy as though it were a Brancusi sculpture; what was not there was even more important than what was. PDD-35 was supposedly a breakthrough because it made tough choices about where to concentrate scarce resources. The directive specifically identified targets that the U.S. intelligence community would not collect against—"Tier 4 countries"—because they posed virtually no threat to U.S. national security.[9]

But, like other formulas for intelligence reform, priority-setting exercises are not really new, either. Similar plans have gone under different names over the years—Key Intelligence Questions, National Intelligence Topics, the DCI's Top Ten List, and so on. In this particular case, PDD-35 simply codified the outcome in the latest phase in a longstanding tug-of-war between civilian and military intelligence users. Defense officials have always wanted to insure that they could use intelligence systems when they needed them (especially reconnaissance satellites and other technical collection systems). They also wanted to insure that these systems had the capabilities needed to support military operations. Civilian foreign policy officials have always resisted such an emphasis. They worry that, if the military has overriding priority, they will be unable to meet their own intelligence needs. They also fear that collection systems designed to meet all of DoD's requirements will be too expensive to build in adequate numbers, and that their cost might crowd out other intelligence programs.

Historically, the balance has shifted back and forth. President Clinton's speech suggested that, at least for now, the military is prevailing. A presidential directive making military intelligence the highest national intelligence priority is, in effect, a brute-force solution to ensuring that U.S. military forces get the intelligence they need. Unfortunately, there is a danger in concentrating intelligence reform on setting roles, missions, and priorities. It will likely skew U.S. intelligence planning, leaving the United States poorly prepared for new or different threats it may face in the future.

For example, one reason U.S. military commanders could not get adequate support in Desert Storm is precisely because U.S. intelligence programs had focused so heavily on another—and no less vital—mission for twenty years: monitoring whether the Soviet Union was complying with strategic arms control agreements. Superpower relations hinged on arms control, and the intelligence community planned accordingly. Unfortunately, systems that could detect small changes in Soviet ICBM silos were ill-suited to searching the Arabian desert for Scuds. If we assign top priority to providing intelligence to military forces today, it will inevitably come at the expense of other missions that could prove at least as important. In this case, some officials fear that the emphasis on military support is eroding the intelligence community's ability to analyze political and economic developments.

An example of the problem appeared in a 1996 interview between Assistant Secretary of State Toby Gati, then director of the State Department's Bureau of Intelligence and Research, and a *New York Times* reporter. Gati said that, partly because U.S. intelligence was focusing so much on detecting North Korean preparations for a military invasion, she was not getting adequate information on North Korea's political instability and collapsing economy—precisely the factors that could lead to an invasion.[10] Similarly, in 1995 the administration had proposed closing CIA stations in Africa in the name of setting tough priorities, only to see those priorities change a few years later, when ethnic conflict in Africa resulted in hundreds of thousands deaths and required a major U.S. relief effort.[11]

The point is that no single set of intelligence priorities is likely to remain valid for long today. Central planning by the intelligence community and setting priorities through a presidential directive carries many of the same problems that would occur in, say, central planning of the national economy through a presidential directive. The problem is just too complex and conditions change too often for a single, codified solution. Also, information technology is changing at an unprecedented rate, so that more data about more of the world is becoming available to policymakers generally. The intelligence community needs an operating concept that permits it to redirect and refocus its efforts as quickly. The traditional approach to intelligence management cannot keep up, and this is a key reason why changing the paradigm for intelligence planning is so important.

The traditional approach to reform—efficiency studies, streamlining, and adopting ever more ambitious efforts at prioritization and planning—sends a message. It implies that there is nothing wrong with a traditional, centralized intelligence system (recent reformers prefer to say "integrated") and operational culture that better management could not fix. Unfortunately, such reform is likely to produce a more efficient, smoother-running intelligence community perfectly optimized for the intelligence consumer of . . . 1950. It will fail to meet the expectations of modern information users and it will be unable to adapt to the rapidly changing, rapidly emerging national security threats we can expect in the future.

Indeed, recent reform efforts themselves suggest just how out of step the intelligence community is with the wider world of information services. Consider how long "intelligence reform" has taken. Many officials began to push for an overhaul of the intelligence community when the Cold War ended in 1991. Little happened until 1994, when the public uproar over the Aldrich Ames espionage case created an opening. Even so, Congress and the White House took more than a year to negotiate an agreement to create an investigating commission, and the Aspin-Brown Commission required another year to complete its study.

Then, when the Clinton administration, the Senate, and the House tried to translate the recommendations into action, the result was gridlock.[12] The administration proposed creating a second deputy director of central intelligence (DDCI), so that one would manage the CIA and the other would oversee planning for the intelligence community as a whole. The administration also proposed having the DCI concur in appointments of certain State Department and Defense Department intelligence officials. The Senate intelligence committee wanted to increase the DCI's power even further by giving him authority to approve funding for NSA, NRO, and NIMA—in effect, letting the DCI control part of the Defense Department budget. And, rather than doubling the number of deputy directors, the Senate proposed adding three new "assistant DCIs," a measure recommended by the Aspin-Brown Commission. The Senate would have created one assistant DCI for collection, one for analysis and production, and one for administration.[13] Meanwhile, the House intelligence committee wanted to reorganize the entire intelligence community, creating consolidated agencies for signals intelligence, imagery, human-source intelligence, and logistics. The House also directed the intelligence community to build smaller, less expensive satellites.[14]

The results were what one might expect from such a mix of politics and bureaucracy. Intelligence officials lobbied to protect their turf. The House and Senate committees that oversee defense spending refused to give the DCI greater authority over DoD agencies. The Senate managed to get its proposed assistant DCIs into the final bill, only to have the administration promise not appoint them. The administration and the Senate opposed the House's small satellite plan; the final bill authorized a commission to study the concept.[15] So, after nearly four years of debate, hearings, and legislation, intelligence reform amounted to . . . NIMA.

Now, compare this to "reform" in the commercial world of information services. In the early 1990s, companies such as CompuServe, Prodigy, and, in particular, America Online created a booming industry in "online services." These services allow computer users to access data bases, download electronic versions of newspapers and magazines, and take part in "chat rooms." Microsoft decided to create its own online service, the Microsoft Network (MSN). Microsoft set up a new division to manage MSN. It signed up scores of "content providers"—companies that would locate sites on the new service. Many industry experts thought Microsoft might even dominate the online industry.

Then, in spring 1995, just as Microsoft was about to introduce MSN—a project representing an investment of millions of dollars—Microsoft's management decided that the market had changed. In 1993, The National Center for Supercomputing Applications had released Mosaic, the first graphical browser for the Internet. About a year later, Netscape Communications began offering the first commercial version of the browser. With the resulting explosion of the World Wide Web, online services began to seem obsolete. Individuals could use programs like Mosaic and Navigator to access the Internet directly, and companies could maintain web sites on their own servers rather than on online services. Internet use was growing at exponential rates. Microsoft concluded that the real opportunity was no longer in online services, but in offering—some would say controlling—access to the Internet itself. Indeed, Microsoft decided that it was so far behind such competitors as Sun Microsystems and Netscape—six to ten months!—that it needed to take drastic action. So the company scrapped its plans for MSN and developed a new strategy.

Microsoft reinvented itself—not in the NPR sense of adopting new management tricks, but by changing its concept of what kind of company it was and its entire business strategy. Microsoft's business had always been selling software. Its cash cow was Windows, at the time the operating system used in about 90 percent of all personal computers. Under the company's new strategy, though, its traditional software business became just the means toward an objective, which was exploiting the Internet. Indeed, Microsoft began giving away its traditional product—software—in the form of Internet Explorer, a direct competitor to Netscape's Navigator.[16]

To execute its new strategy, Microsoft began to buy up entire companies that had Internet expertise (for example, one, Vermeer, had developed software that simplified the process of creating a web site; another, WebTV, had developed technology that was supposed to make the Internet even easier to use). Microsoft also formed partnerships with media giants such as Dow Jones and General Electric. In exchange for promoting Explorer, Dow Jones agreed to give the electronic version of its *Wall Street Journal* free to subscribers to the revamped Microsoft Network. General Electric, through its NBC subsidiary, agreed to create a news service with Microsoft, MSNBC. When necessary, Microsoft licensed technology from other companies; Internet Explorer, for example, was based on a version of Mosaic developed by Spyglass. Finally, Microsoft redesigned almost all of its own software products so that users could link to the Internet almost without even realizing it.[17]

The most remarkable thing, though, was how quickly all of this took place. At the time, Microsoft had annual operating costs of $3.9 billion and twenty thousand employees—slightly larger than the annual budget and staff of the CIA.[18] Yet the entire process of transforming Microsoft required just one year. Microsoft was so successful that by 1998 it had captured more than half the market for browser software and became the target of a highly publicized antitrust suit by the Justice Department and over twenty state attorneys general.*

The point of this story of how Microsoft adopted a new paradigm is not that Bill Gates is a genius and intelligence officials are idiots. The point is that the intelligence community needs to move just as quickly and innovate just as creatively. The underlying problem that prevents it from doing so is that its model for planning intelligence is an artifact from an earlier age. Even the name "Central Intelligence Agency" is reminiscent of the New Deal era, when large, powerful, national bureaucracies were the accepted way of getting things done efficiently. When the CIA was established, the notion of a centralized bureaucracy for intelligence was at least as reasonable as a centralized bureaucracy for, say, rural electrification. In addition, when the intelligence community was established, information technology was

---

* Even so, by the time the government presented its case, the information industry had turned upside-down yet again. America Online, supposedly made obsolete by the World Wide Web, transformed itself in a strategy no less impressive than Microsoft's. It used its massive customer base to become the most-used portal to the Internet. The strategy was so successful that AOL was able to buy Netscape in 1998. Meanwhile, Microsoft faced a new challenge in the development of Linux, a public domain operating system that some companies touted as an alternative to Windows.

expensive and centralization offered economies of scale. (Remember "time sharing" and waiting for "off-peak rates" with the computer system in the basement?)

And that is the fundamental problem with so many of the recent proposals for intelligence reform. Most are based on concepts from another age. Appointing an "intelligence ombudsman" and identifying national intelligence priorities would be a great step forward—if one wanted an intelligence organization that worked like the Norwegian socialist bureaucracy of the mid-twentieth century. But such reforms will do little to enable the intelligence community to make the kinds of deals, form the partnerships, and adopt the technologies that enabled Microsoft to turn itself around. They are unlikely to enable the intelligence community to work at the pace of organizations such as 3Com, Yahoo!, and News Corporation. And they are unlikely to keep the intelligence community's thinking at the leading edge of innovation, in the manner of MIT's Media Lab or the Santa Fe Institute. Today, intelligence reform should describe what a twenty-first-century intelligence service should look like.

AN ALTERNATE APPROACH TO REFORMING INTELLIGENCE PLANNING

Return to first principles and ask why we need an intelligence community at all. That is, why we do we need a government-funded, government-managed organization to collect and analyze information for national security? Most information U.S. officials use is, and always will be, from open sources. The reason for an intelligence apparatus is to find and interpret information concerning national security that the government needs, but cannot obtain from the media or from other commercial sources. This information generally falls into the following categories:

- Expertise and information on subjects that the private sector will not cover adequately because it would be unprofitable;
- Information that the private sector will not or cannot collect because it would be too technologically demanding;
- Information that the private sector should not, cannot, or will not collect because of legal constraints or risks; and
- Tailored products providing this specialized information (combined with other sources, as appropriate) to U.S. officials.

Many organizations are ready to provide information. The question for intelligence planners is: What types of information can be provided only by the intelligence community? When the question is put this way, it soon becomes clear that one is aiming at a moving target. In the Information Age, the private sector keeps getting better, and at an ever-faster rate. Thus, the intelligence community needs to be capable of changing continuously, too. Indeed, the intelligence community's ability to change its focus may be the most important feature for intelligence planning in the Information Age—much more important than any single set of priorities.

To see this graphically, consider Figure 2.1. The pyramid represents the world's "technology base"—the body of knowledge about technology that exists at a given moment in time. This pyramid grows taller over time as more technology is developed, with the newest, most advanced technology at the top levels, and proven, mature technologies at the bottom. The diagram also shows which technologies the government is most active in developing, and where the private sector predominates.[19]

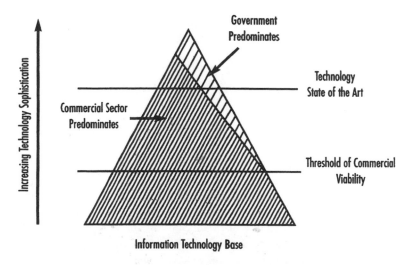

Figure 2.1. Relationship and Comparative Advantages of Government and Commercial Technology Sectors

In addition, there are two thresholds that define three categories of technology. The upper threshold defines the "state of the art," or the most advanced technology that is reliable enough for practical use. Technology above this threshold may seem promising, but is unproven and risky. The lower threshold defines "commercial viability." Technologies below this threshold are sufficiently cheap, reliable, and well-understood that they can be routinely used in profitable applications. The middle sector is transitional technology. Technologies in this sector may be reliable and effective, but too new for companies to believe they will be profitable.

Now, note where the government predominates in the development and use of technology, and where the private sector predominates. The government's role is much smaller overall than that of the private sector, but concentrated at the more advanced levels. This reflects government's comparative advantage. Companies in the private sector must show profits. New, advanced technologies often fail or are so costly that a company cannot get a return on its investment. This is why companies in the private sector tend to shun the absolute "cutting edge" technologies.

Government organizations, on the other hand, can throw money at a project with less pressure from the bottom line. They do not require immediate profits, cost-effectiveness, or (assuming taxpayers cooperate) even efficiency. This is why most of this technology is developed or operated under government-funded programs. Sometimes government organizations carry out this research themselves, and sometimes the work is contracted out. In either case, though, when technology is risky and profits slim, it is usually the government that pays the bills.

Yet once a technology reaches the point at which it can be used to make a profit—the bottom level of the pyramid—the private sector really excels, and government can scarcely compete at all. Corporations have more capital and mobile labor, and the market ruthlessly eliminates those who are inefficient. Competition forces corporations to levels of efficiency that government agencies rarely achieve. This is why if a government organization is active at this level, it is usually because someone is protecting or subsidizing it.

The middle sector is a gray area, where technologies are known to be practical, although the marketplace has not yet demonstrated that they are commercially viable. This middle sector is where venture capitalists and investment bankers look for opportunities to bring new products and services to market. Government agencies can compete here, too, because there are still significant risks and uncertainties that hold back private companies. Over time, the pyramid grows higher (along with the two thresholds) as new technologies emerge. The base of the pyramid, consisting of mature technology, grows broader. Technologies which previously only government organizations could exploit and develop become less expensive, more reliable and, in time, commercially viable.

The net result is that many technologies that were available only to the intelligence community ten or twenty years ago are commercially available today. Consider computers capable of high-level code breaking, for example. As recently as ten years ago, such systems were called "supercomputers" and only a handful existed—and most of them resided at the NSA. Today, such computing capability is commonplace.[20] Yet supercomputers are just one example. Technology is becoming more powerful, cheaper, and widely available in virtually every sector of every industry that deals with information. If anything, the trend is accelerating—recall Moore's Law.

This trend in information technology capability has had a parallel effect on information services. Consider human-source reporting, for example. Commercial information services are rapidly expanding to meet new demands and new opportunities. Because it is easier to collect, process, and broadcast information, it is also possible to create commercial news services that concentrate on more specialized topics and serve narrower audiences. Witness the growth of CNN, CNBC, and even MTV.

The results are readily apparent. In earlier years the only way to have a person on the scene to report from places such as Rwanda or Tadjikistan was to put a foreign service officer or CIA operative there. News media and area studies were still relatively primitive. Also, because the Soviet Union was so hard to penetrate, the intelligence community was often the only source of eyewitness information. Now Christiane Amanpour can cover Sarajevo, Baghdad, and Kabul in real time. Indeed, if our experience in teaching graduate seminars is any indicator, a junior-level international journalist is likely to have better foreign language skills, foreign contacts, and experience living abroad than an intelligence officer at a similar point in his or her career.

A similar pattern appears in the world of intelligence analysis. Consider economic intelligence. In its early days, the CIA was one of a handful of organizations that could provide foreign economic analysis. It often had unique data and expertise. Now, many organizations gather and analyze economic information from around the world—Dow Jones, McGraw-Hill, Dun & Bradstreet, to name a few. Indeed, today there are even analysts who analyze the analysis of other analysts. Companies such as First Call survey forecasters who cover specific industries to determine the prevailing consensus for future developments in each economic sector and most major companies.

Because information technologies and services are improving so quickly, the intelligence community will never keep up if it depends on an annual planning process to decide which functions it will transition to the commercial sector. Rather, the intelligence community must shift its focus constantly. This process should make intelligence organizations "off-load" responsibilities to the commercial sector automatically as private companies become capable of handling them. The intelligence community must continuously move on to the next frontier of technology or knowledge that the private sector has yet to fill. Fundamentally, one of the greatest challenges for reforming intelligence planning is designing a process that enables intelligence organizations to adapt to changing conditions without anyone making a deliberate decision to do so.

THE ADAPTABLE INTELLIGENCE ORGANIZATION

How adaptable is intelligence planning currently? Consider this: The intelligence community presently operates some collection systems whose original designs date from the early 1970s, when Americans were balancing their checkbooks with Bomar Brains.* Today Bomar is long gone and forgotten, and consumers keep track of their spend-

---

* For Gen-X readers and younger, Bomar was one of the largest makers of pocket calculators in the 1970s. The Bomar Brain was its most popular model; think of it as a Palm computer for the polyester and disco generation.

ing with personal computers and personal finance software like Quicken. Admittedly, the intelligence community has upgraded its collection systems over the years, but something unusual must be going on for an organization to cling to quarter-century-old information technology.

One reason why the intelligence community cannot deal effectively with the Information Revolution is that intelligence requirements and the intelligence community's comparative advantage are both fluid, but traditional bureaucracies are static. In addition, intelligence organizations have developed organizational dogma and have carved out turf for themselves in the budget. Once in place, they can be remarkably difficult to dislodge. The fact that these organizations often operate at a classified level further insulates them. As a result, the intelligence community may be locked into technologies, collection operations, and analytical methodologies, even when new and possibly better ideas come along.

Ironically, many of the recent "reforms" could make this problem worse. For example, the trend to reduce costs and improve responsiveness by consolidating agencies can narrow the base for new ideas and increase the tendency to adopt dogma. Similarly, if mission priorities are codified in national policy, then the technologies that the intelligence community buys will likely be overly specialized. Experience suggests that any such system will be used for a completely different mission a few years from now. For example, each of the three most expensive space systems operated by the intelligence community in the late 1990s was being used for a mission other than the one originally used to justify its development—which is exactly what one should expect with information technology. Fine tuning the intelligence infrastructure to support one particular user or mission will limit the flexibility that has invariably proved necessary in the past.

If the current approach to reform is likely to fail, what is the alternative? In the fast-paced world of information support, it will be hard for the traditional planning process to keep pace. That is why the intelligence community needs fundamentally new approaches to organization and management. An ideal intelligence planning process would meet several criteria.

First, and most importantly, an ideal intelligence planning process would better capture the priorities of intelligence users. In general, the process should link decisions on spending to intelligence users, and the span of this link should be as short as possible.

Further, such a process would minimize the intelligence community's fixed investment in hardware and personnel. This might reduce the taxpayer's burden, but that is really a secondary concern. The main reason is to improve the intelligence community's flexibility. The ability of the intelligence community to stay on the leading edge of technology suffers when intelligence officials must worry about writing off expensive equipment or laying off tenured staff.

Finally, such a planning process would freely allow intelligence users to draw on the commercial sector whenever it had capabilities they required. If intelligence consumers could use a commercial substitute whenever they found one that met their needs, intelligence managers would have more opportunity (and incentive) to concentrate on those highly specialized areas in which government has a comparative advantage. Moreover, an ideal planning process would accomplish all of these things seamlessly, without anyone having to make a deliberate decision.

Reaching this ideal in practice may be impossible, but clearly some approaches are closer than others, and traditional intelligence planning methods are hardly in the ballpark. Figure 2.2 shows in highly simplified form how the process for national intelligence programs currently works. (The details change over time, but the basic process has remained the same.)

First, the intelligence community develops formal priorities for intelligence. These priorities are codified in presidential policy documents (such as PDD-35) or in intelligence community planning documents (currently called Strategic Intelligence Reviews, or SIRs). Responsibility for drafting SIRs lies with the DCI's issue coordinators, a group selected from top intelligence community managers, analysts, and representatives from the Joint Chiefs of Staff and the Defense Intelligence Agency. At any one time, there are about eighteen to twenty issue coordinators. They meet with high-level intelligence consumers to identify their intelligence needs. According to a recent study by the House Intelligence Committee, the issue coordinators meet with over a hundred of these high-level consumers.[21]

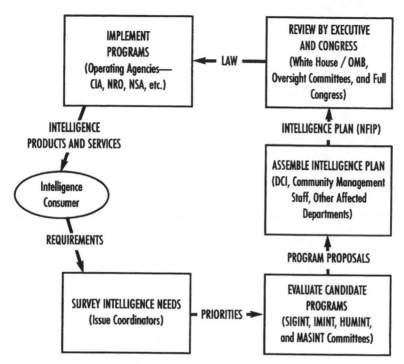

Figure 2.2. Traditional Intelligence Planning Process

After requirements are documented, they are used by the "Int Committees" to review proposed intelligence programs for the director of central intelligence.* The committees match these programs to the documented priorities, while also considering other factors, such

---

* The term "Int Committee" is derived from intelligence jargon: "SIGINT" is signals intelligence, "HUMINT" is intelligence collected by humans (i.e., intelligence officers, military attachés, and diplomats), "IMINT" is imagery, and "MASINT" is intelligence on the measurement and signatures of objects. So there is a committee for each "int." Each committee is comprised of representatives from agencies that have a stake in its decisions, and each resides in the predominant agency in the discipline: the NSA for the SIGINT committee, the NRO for the IMINT committee, the CIA for the HUMINT committee, and the DIA for the MASINT committee.

as cost-effectiveness, redundancy to protect against failures or losses of systems, and so on. When finished, each committee sends its recommendations to the DCI's Community Management Staff, which integrates them into a single package—the National Foreign Intelligence Program (NFIP). The NFIP then goes to the Office of Management and Budget, where it is coordinated and integrated with the rest of the president's budget. (As noted previously, "national" intelligence programs account for about half of total U.S. intelligence spending. The other half, comprising tactical intelligence programs for the military services, is developed as part of the overall defense budget.)

Oddly, the process reminds one of how the Soviet Union developed its Five Year Plans. Soviet officials drafted prioritization statements to reflect consumer preferences and investment requirements. They then evaluated proposed economic programs, and allocated resources accordingly in the Five Year Plan. Indeed, more than one wag has observed that, after the collapse of the Soviet Union, the Defense Department became the largest centrally planned economy in the world, with the intelligence community running a respectable second.

We know what happened to the Soviet Union. Although central planning seemed rational and efficient, it was unable to keep up with the variety and capriciousness of consumer demands. Eventually, the Soviet system was hopelessly outpaced by changes in the Soviet society, not to mention changes in the global economy and advances in technology. Similarly, traditional intelligence planning methods will be unable to keep up with the rapidly changing information technologies and requirements of the future.

This is why, contrary to what most would-be reformers have proposed, intelligence planning needs to become less rigidly centralized, not more. It is not that decentralized planning is always better. Rather, planning decisions should be allowed to gravitate to wherever they can be made most efficiently, and loosening organizational constraints is necessary to allow this to happen. Top intelligence officials can still exert control to make broad decisions on spending levels and goals. But, to take advantage of the new technologies and keep pace with changing requirements and opportunities, they will need more flexible, and often less direct, management methods.

There is no single measure that will impose this kind of market-style approach onto intelligence planning. There are, however, a number of diverse steps that can insure greater flexibility, adaptability, and responsiveness. Most fit into three categories:

- Measures that allow authority to devolve to the most appropriate level and give intelligence users a direct say in planning;
- Measures that allow government organizations to use private-sector expertise and investment more easily and effectively; and
- Measures that create competition and redundancy—in effect, an artificial market—within the government in those cases where only the government can provide a technology or a service.

As will be seen, we already have some experience in using these kinds of mechanisms—often in the intelligence community itself—or at least measures similar to them. Much of the challenge of intelligence reform is understanding how they have worked, and using them more widely.

Devolving the Planning of Intelligence Assets

One way to allow intelligence planning to gravitate to its most efficient level would be to take some of the money currently given to central intelligence planners and give it directly to intelligence users. This could be done either in real money or in the form of vouchers. This approach would enable intelligence consumers to make their own decisions in selecting sensors and platforms, instead of depending on issue coordinators to interpret their priorities accurately and then hoping that the coordinators' recommendations will survive the passage through the bureaucratic labyrinth.

Consider satellite imagery, for example. If an organization had the required cash or a voucher, it might decide to buy its own satellite. Such a satellite would likely be less capable than current NRO satellites, but the organization would enjoy the advantage of having a dedicated system tailored to its specific needs. Many agencies—especially those that believe they do not current receive adequate support—would likely prefer such an arrangement. Alternatively, the organization could return its voucher to the NRO and contribute to the cost of centrally planned, centrally operated systems. Or the organization could buy commercial satellite imagery if it were adequate for its needs. (By the late 1990s, several U.S. companies were planning to operate imaging satellites on a commercial basis, and had signed contracts with NIMA to deliver imagery for government use.)[22]

The director of the NRO might impose standards and collect all data in a common archive to ensure that agencies could exchange data and communicate with each other easily. The NRO might also act as a broker, facilitating, but not forcing, clusters of agencies to work together. For example, suppose two military commanders, one in the Pacific and the other in the Atlantic, each planned to buy a satellite of similar design. The two commanders might have requirements that complemented each other, and since they were on opposite sides of the world, each commander could share the use of both satellites with little interference. If so, the NRO could encourage the two commanders to cooperate, so that one commander might design his satellite for broad-area search, the other might design his for high resolution. They might also share the cost of ground processing systems.

In general, however, the NRO would simply let the "market" work to decide what the overall mix of satellites would look like. No one could predict what the resulting constellation might be or, for that matter, where the decisions would be made—just as no one can predict what the final distribution of goods in a market economy might be. But a constellation designed by such an invisible hand could provide an overall level of capability and reliability better than that of a centrally planned architecture. Such a constellation would almost certainly be better tailored to meet the needs of users than any system designed by a central manager, just as a market economy almost always meets consumer desires better than a centrally planned economy.

The same approach could also be used in other forms of intelligence. For example, intelligence consumers always seem to complain that they "don't get enough HUMINT," or human source intelligence. Intelligence managers always promise to devote more resources, but the requirement regularly seems to fall beween the cracks. One solution would be to transfer some of the funding for HUMINT to intelligence consumers themselves. Presumably one would not want the Agriculture Department recruiting its own agents in Hunan to gather data on the Chinese rice crop. But one could separate operational control from funding decisions. An agency could use its "collection voucher" to sponsor an intelligence officer who would be focused on meeting the agency's specific information needs. So, the CIA might propose a program to send a case officer to China. If there were any takers, the case officer would pack his bags. If not, the station might close, or the CIA could use its own remaining discretionary funds if it thought the station was truly important.

Exploiting the Private Sector

As we have seen, today the private sector is often better than the government at applying information technology and providing information services. The intelligence community would benefit by taking greater advantage of the private sector's size and flexibility. If intelligence consumers had a greater, more direct role in decisions about funding intelligence programs, it is likely that they would automatically look for commercial alternatives to get better service or to save money.

There will always be cases in which the private sector falls short. In other cases we probably would not want to use nongovernment organizations to carry out certain activities simply as a matter of principle. Yet, even in cases in which a purely commercial approach would not work, there are still halfway measures that could enable the intelligence community to take advantage of the private sector's technical expertise, capital, and ability to deliver goods to market quickly. In other cases, the government itself can adopt some of the practices of the private sector. Some examples that have been proposed or that have already been implemented include:

Subsidization and Partial Privatization

When the commercial market is too small to support an information service, the intelligence community might offer subsidies to fill the gap. When a technology is so risky that private companies cannot raise the capital required to develop it, the intelligence community might insure the risk.

We are already seeing examples of how this might work. For instance, intelligence users often need their imagery delivered faster than the typical commercial customer. A typical commercial user of satellite imagery, such as a city official responsible for planning urban infrastructure, needs information within months. The typical military user of satellite imagery, such as a commander developing plans to destroy infrastructure, needs information within hours. It would be hard for a purely commercial satellite imagery company to justify the investment in high-speed data links, extra computer capability, and other equipment needed to reduce processing time. So, in early 1998, NIMA announced a program in which commercial imagery companies and the Defense Department would share the cost of improving the data transmission links that the companies use. By subsidizing the improvements, the government was able to enjoy the benefits of using commercial satellite operators (such as reducing the government's investment in satellites) while also meeting its requirement for timely delivery of imagery.[23]

Flexible Regulation

There are some information technologies and services that the commercial sector could provide, but which might threaten U.S. security if they were freely available to the public. Even so, it should be possible to allow companies to do business—thus providing a source for the intelligence community—while also protecting security. A recent case suggests how.

In mid-1996, Research & Development Laboratories (RDL), a company based in Culver City, California, announced its plans to build a radar imaging satellite with "one-meter resolution." That is, the RDL satellite would have the capability to detect objects on the earth as small as one meter, making it good enough to accurately identify large trucks. U.S. officials have been concerned that commercial radar imagery this good, if freely available, might threaten U.S. security interests. For example, Iraq might try to buy such radar imagery to find tanks hidden under camouflage netting at U.S. bases in Saudi Arabia. As part of the terms and conditions of its license, RDL agreed to sell imagery with resolution no better than five meters (good enough to accurately identify buildings), a level which U.S. officials believe does not present an unacceptable risk. However, RDL did not change the satellite; rather, the company agreed to "fuzz up" its products to five-meter resolution before selling them.[24]

But the episode raised a larger question that went largely unnoticed at the time. If RDL was willing to invest in a radar satellite that had intelligence-grade capabilities, shouldn't the U.S. intelligence community use this as an opportunity to outsource more of its requirements for radar imagery? RDL showed that it was willing to control the types of data it released to different customers. Logically, RDL could sell intelligence-quality products to the U.S. intelligence community, and degrade the products to commercial levels for non-intelligence customers. RDL, rather than the government, would then bear the cost of developing the satellite, and, by spreading the costs over more users, the price for radar imagery would be lower for everyone. With well-designed regulations, firms should be able to operate even the most capable intelligence collection systems on a commercial basis, and control the quality and distribution of data to protect U.S. security.

Intragovernment Competition

One of the advantages of the commercial market is that competition improves the product. If only the government builds a certain kind of system, it needs to ensure competition within the government. This runs counter to many of the efforts to improve the efficiency of intelligence organizations by "streamlining" and "downsizing." Such policies may reduce costs in the short term. In the long term, however, they can lead to what is, in effect, a cartel over a given technology or service. Cartels are usually inefficient.

This is why intelligence officials may need to fund programs which, at first, might seem like unnecessary duplication. Duplication is necessary for competition. In the long term, competition within the government could save money. It is certainly more likely to promote innovation. Just as "Team A/Team B" exercises have improved intelligence analysis, competition could also improve intelligence technology.

One obstacle to such competition, oddly enough, is resistance from government officials. Bureaucratic officials resemble their private sector counterparts in that both like cartels if the cartel is their own. Protected cartels in the government bureaucracy, like their private sector counterparts, offer job security and a respite from the pressures of competition. This is one underlying reason why officials defend their turf. When a competitor emerges (possibly with a better idea), the typical official will complain that the competing agency is "acting outside its assigned mission," that "it lacks the expertise and experience" to carry out the activity, or that its activities "represent needless and wasteful duplication."

The history of U.S. intelligence is replete with cases in which agencies attempted to eliminate a competitor. For example, the CIA and Air Force struggled over which agency would operate both the U-2 and the SR-71 reconnaissance aircraft in the late 1960s.[25] The CIA has continuously resisted the attempts of the military services to maintain their own clandestine HUMINT capability.[26] The most famous of these competitions is probably the thirty-year off-and-on match between the CIA and Air Force over who would control U.S. imaging satellites.[27] Even the reorganization of the NRO in 1992, which essentially gave the mission to the Air Force, apparently did not end the matter. Recently the media reported efforts by the NRO to block the Defense Advanced Research Projects Agency (DARPA) from demonstrating new imaging satellite technologies.[28]

Much evidence suggests that competition has many of the same benefits in the government as in the market. As a case in point, consider the Clementine moon probe.

By the late 1980s, the minimum cost for a NASA space probe of any kind was around $250 million. Most missions cost much more; the Cassini probe to Saturn cost more than $1 billion. Satellites had grown larger over the years, and the cost of a satellite usually rises proportionally with its mass. Also, satellite designers, like the practitioners of any craft, naturally strive for designs that are "best" rather than "good enough." Getting that last 10 or 20 percent in performance can easily double the price of a spacecraft, but as long as there was no one to show how it was possible to do good science at lower cost, NASA had no incentive to look for another approach.

Space probes gradually grew bigger and bigger, and more and more expensive.

Then, in 1992, the Ballistic Missile Defense Organization (BMDO) needed to test some instruments in deep space. But it had a limited budget and could not afford a space probe costing hundreds of millions of dollars. So, instead, it looked outside NASA, and commissioned the Naval Research Laboratory (NRL) to build a low-cost, no-frills spacecraft. NRL had a long history of building satellites and other space hardware but had not built a complete space probe previously.

Free from the constraints of tradition, NRL took a different approach. It used a much smaller staff. Instead of having NRL design a perfect probe that met as many requirements as possible, BMDO set a cost cap for the program and had NRL fit as much capability as possible into the spacecraft within a fixed budget.[29] The resulting probe, dubbed "Clementine," was launched in 1994 and was surprisingly inexpensive for a space mission at the time—just $110 million, including launch. NASA officials privately disparaged Clementine but shortly after the mission, NASA announced its own series of low-cost space probes. (One was the 1997 Mars Pathfinder mission, which became famous for its miniature robotic rover, Sojourner.) Competition worked—NASA Administrator Daniel Goldin's mantra became "smaller, faster, cheaper!"—and NASA and the country were both better off as a result.

The most direct way to create this kind of "market" in an organization is simply to eliminate rules that reserve specific missions to specific agencies. Instead, no agency would have guaranteed turf, and other agencies, if not encouraged, would be at least allowed to compete for any mission.

Planning Personnel in the Information Age

A parallel (but somewhat different) situation applies to intelligence personnel. In the old days, one could hire analysts or technicians, give them civil service tenure, and move them along into progressively more responsible positions within their specializations. The intelligence community had a continuing need for, say, expertise on Soviet conventional forces or expertise on strategic missiles. The topic changed incrementally. Not so today.

Throughout society, the supply and demand for job skills are much more fluid and chaotic than in the past. So, in the late 1990s, while IBM, AT&T, and Sears were releasing thousands of employees they no longer needed, Oracle, MCI WorldCom, and Wal-Mart were hiring thousands of employees to address new markets. In such an economy, many companies have found themselves hiring and firing torrents of people simultaneously in order to retool for changing markets.

The intelligence community needs at least as much flexibility as private corporations. Many of its requirements for specialized information are likely to change quickly. Traditional civil service tenure is probably suited only for employees with the most general, long-term skills. As the skills the intelligence community requires become even more specialized, the intelligence community will need more flexible arrangements for engaging their services.

During the Cold War, intelligence planners often talked about "surge capacity," the ability to mobilize in crises or war. But the skills that would be surged were mainly the same as those in the standing force—the intelligence community simply needed more of the same people. Because most intelligence analysts were specialists on the Soviet threat, most of the extra personnel that would have reported for work during a surge would have also been Soviet specialists. Given the nature of the threat of the time and how the intelligence community would be used during wars and crises, this was what was needed. Some people suggested at the time creating an "intelligence reserve corps," consisting of retired and part-time analysts who could be called when needed.

Not so today. Intelligence organizations still need to be able to "surge" and add additional personnel on short notice, but now the requirement has changed greatly. Today surge capacity is needed not just to add more people with the same skills to handle a greater volume of work, but to find and add people with different skills to meet rapidly changing requirements for analysis. These required analytical skills are likely to vary greatly, and may be difficult to anticipate. Even if these needs could be predicted perfectly, it would be inefficient and unaffordable to keep the required people on staff permanently because requirements are likely to change often.

Thus, the human resource directors throughout the intelligence community have a new challenge. In the Cold War era, the problem for ensuring adequate intelligence expertise was determining how to plan, recruit, and train new staff. This may remain the problem for ensuring expertise in certain exotic technical topics and on denied territories. However, the more likely problem in the post-Cold War era is determining how to ensure that the expertise U.S. intelligence requires is available from the private sector and is readily accessible. Most likely, the intelligence personnel plan of the future will be defined in terms of three types of individuals:

- A limited number of specialized analysts on staff;
- Individuals outside the intelligence community whose expertise is bought "by the pound," but regularly included in the production of intelligence products; and
- Other personnel in the private sector, identified as potential sources of expertise, to be tapped as needed.

In some cases the intelligence community could subsidize commercial and academic sources to ensure specialized or additional expertise for surge situations. The key challenge in these cases is that, although experts in academia and the media are likely to be eager to assist the government, they may be reluctant to have a direct association with intelligence organizations. U.S. intelligence will need mechanisms that keep these experts at arm's length. One alternative could be to work through agencies such as the State Department and the National Security Council, or private organizations such as the National Science Foundation. Moreover, these buffer mechanisms will need to be real, and not just a cover story. A few stories about how such-and-such organization is a "front for U.S. intelligence" will ensure not only that the organization will lose its access to experts, but that the experts themselves will be less likely to offer their services to the government in the future.

Yet, even if the intelligence community could focus on its optimal niche and ensure its ability to draw on the expertise it needs to deal with post-Cold War threats, there is still an additional task: producing the intelligence product. This is the problem we turn to in the next chapter.

THREE
THE INTELLIGENCE PROCESS AND THE INFORMATION REVOLUTION

Often the hardest part of adopting technology is simply understanding the potential opportunities a new technology offers. This is especially true in a bureaucratic culture like the intelligence community. Bureaucracies are almost always inclined to think of a new technology as just another means to improve its existing way of doing business.[1] Often the true impact of a new technology becomes clear only after officials rethink their basic assumptions about what their mission is and how they are supposed to perform it. The inability of too many officials to perform this mental leap is one reason effective intelligence reform has been so slow in coming.

This would not be the first time that conceptual software lagged behind technological hardware. Consider tanks, for example. The British invented the modern tank during World War I. The war on the Western Front had stalled in a lethal stalemate. Neither side was able to break through the other's lines. The British, with a penchant for offbeat secret weapons, developed a tracked, armored vehicle to cross No Man's Land. When British forces tried out their tanks on July 1, 1916, at the Battle of the Somme, they took the Germans by surprise. Unfortunately, British generals, viewing tanks as merely another support vehicle, attached the tanks to infantry units. As a result, the tanks could advance only as fast as a British soldier could walk. The offensive bogged down, and the British lost over nineteen-thousand dead in a single day—the most costly day in the history of the British army. The element of surprise lost, both sides dug in again, and the battle of attrition continued as before.[2]

The British were defeated not by the German army so much as by three thousand years of infantry dogma. From as far back as the ancient Greece phalanx, the accepted wisdom held that armies had to concentrate their mass and advance as a group, so that soldiers could protect each other and concentrate their firepower. Even when infantry traded swords and arrows for muskets and rifles, the concept of how to fight remained the same. Locked into a culture and way of thinking about warfare, the British were unable to take full advantage of the new technology of mechanized armor.[3] Later, during the interwar years, military theorists like J. F. C. Fuller and B. H. Liddell-Hart began to suggest how mechanization would transform warfare. Much to the derision of the army establishment, they argued that tanks would evolve into fast, heavily armed vehicles that could punch through enemy lines, leaving the infantry behind and racing directly to the enemy's vulnerable rear. Most armies treated their ideas as little more than an interesting notion until the *Werhmacht* used tanks with devastating effect in the strategy of "blitzkrieg" in World War II.[4]

Note the more important point: The breakthrough did not occur just by inventing new technology, or even developing new tactics. Rather, the critical step was daring to abandon the traditional rules of doing business. As long as tanks were employed obeying the old concepts that had been designed for infantry—unified formations advancing along a linear front—strategists could not take advantage of their speed and ability to move rapidly while under fire. Jettisoning the old dogma was key. Until military leaders let go of the old ideas, they could not take advantage of the new technology.

The intelligence community faces a similar situation today. As we have seen, societies in the post-Cold War and post-industrial era are in the midst of an Information Revolution. The intelligence community is itself responsible for developing some of the most advanced information technologies. However, our dogma for producing intelligence—how we think intelligence *ought* to work—has changed little. As a result, the intelligence community is not benefiting from the new technology fully and, in many cases, lags behind the rest of society in how it develops information and provides it to its users.

Consider the failure of U.S. intelligence to predict India's testing of nuclear weapons in May 1998. In the investigations and discussions that followed, experts and political officials cited several specific glitches that led to the failure.[5] Some of the problems they identified included:

Faulty Analysis and Failure to Tap Outside Expertise

Many journalists and scholars anticipated that India would resume testing. As Ved Mehta observed, "any casual tourist to India would have known about the aggressive nuclear policy of the Bharatiya Janata Party." In addition, the prime minister of Pakistan, Mohammed Nawaz Sharif, had sent a letter to President Clinton on April 3 warning of a possible Indian test.[6]

Intelligence analysts dismissed these concerns. According to one account, none of the analysts polled by the national intelligence officer for warning in February 1988 believed the BJP would keep its campaign promise. Lacking hard evidence to the contrary, the officer did not dispute the consensus. An official investigation headed by retired Admiral David Jeremiah called this a classic case of "mirror imaging." Our analysts assumed Indian politicians would act like American politicians and, once in office, would back away from their more controversial campaign commitments. The report also suggested U.S. analysts were guilty of "groupthink" or a "herd mentality." No one was willing to break from the consensus and offer the contrarian view that Indian politicians might actually keep their campaign commitments.[7]

Organizational Snafus and Issue Overload

The intelligence community collected imagery of the Indian preparations a week before the tests, but analysts did not examine the pictures until it was too late. The intelligence community routinely collects huge volumes of raw data, and timely processing is always a challenge. But in this case there was also a chain reaction at work. Because political analysts watching India did not think a test was likely, imagery analysts did not go to a high state of alert. In other words, one failure led to another.[8]

At the same time, top officials in the Clinton administration were focused on many other issues in May 1998: NATO expansion, Iraq, tobacco legislation, and the continuing Whitewater and Lewinski scandals. Thus preoccupied, no high administration official "pinged" the intelligence community for information about the Indian nuclear program. No ping, no priority; no priority, no warning. The topic slipped between the cracks.[9]

Inadequate Sources

Some critics who claim the intelligence community lacks sufficient human-source intelligence, or "HUMINT," have often argued that "technical means" (a euphemism for satellite imagery and signals intelligence) cannot detect an adversary's intentions—such as the intent to resume testing. This sweeping assertion is incorrect; an intercepted message can often reveal as much about an adversary's thinking as can an overheard conversation. But the specific criticism might be on target in the particular case of the Indian failure. HUMINT might have filled gaps in our understanding of Indian decision making. Unfortunately, U.S. intelligence was either unable to generate human sources, or failed to assign the requirement sufficient priority. The Jeremiah study found that the CIA had recruited few agents in India.[10] Porter Goss (R-Fla.), chairman of the House Intelligence Committee and himself a former intelligence officer, suggested after the test that the United States was spending too little on HUMINT.[11]

Compromise of Sources and Indian Deception

U.S. intelligence had previously detected India preparing to test in 1995. Our efforts then to dissuade the Indians from testing taught them how to be cagier in the future. According to one report, then-ambassador Frank Wisner confronted Indian officials with U.S. satellite images showing the Pocharan site gearing up for a test. The Indians backed down. But, having learned the capabilities of U.S. imaging satellites, they adjusted their activities in 1998 to evade them. For example, Indian technicians learned when and under what conditions U.S. satellites could view their test site. So they timed their operations to take advantage of cloud cover, and buried telltale cables to avoid tipping off U.S. analysts.[12]

Meanwhile, the Indian government conducted a concerted disinformation campaign at all levels. Indian officials duped their U.S. counterparts into thinking India felt no urgency to test. For example, Bill Richardson, U.S. ambassador to the United Nations, told Indian officials in April 1998 that he hoped they would not follow through on their campaign commitment. American officials met with Indian representatives in the United States to deliver the same message. The Indians delivered a consistent—which, in retrospect, means orchestrated—response: India was conducting a strategy review and would not make a decision on testing until the end of the year. U.S. officials took these assurances at face value.[13]

One can speculate that U.S. officials were confident of their ability to persuade, and perhaps believed they had deterred India, just as they had in 1995. Also, top U.S. officials believed reason and logic were on their side; witness officials such as Secretary of State Madeleine Albright, who later asserted that India was "less safe" by failing to comply with the nonproliferation and test ban treaties.[14] Such a mindset made it made it easier to deceive U.S. leaders.

India also used deception at the tactical level. They stepped up activity at their missile test range to draw the attention of U.S. technical collection systems away from their nuclear test site. This lure was even more effective because it seemed logical. Pakistan had just tested its new Ghauri medium-range ballistic missile on April 6. It seemed reasonable to assume that India might test a ballistic missile in a tit-for-tat response.

The inability to anticipate the Indian test was the most egregious failure of U.S. intelligence since the end of the Cold War. The chairman of the Senate Intelligence Committee called it "the intelligence failure of the decade." Even administration officials such as Phyllis Oakley, director of the State Department's Bureau of Intelligence and Research, admitted, "Look, we were wrong; we were all wrong."[15] Certainly the Indian failure rates with such classics as failing to anticipate the Soviet deployment of missiles in Cuba in 1962 or the fall of the Shah in 1979. Possibly the most troubling fact, though, was that current U.S. intelligence planning (as codified in PDD-35) designates "monitoring proliferation" as a top U.S. intelligence priority. In other words, the intelligence community was giving its best effort, and it still failed.

A closer look suggests that the Indian failure reveals flaws in the basic model on which U.S. intelligence operates. All of the individual criticisms listed above appear to have some validity, but each raises broader questions. For example, if outside analysts anticipated the intent of the new Indian government, why wasn't the intelligence community able to draw on their views? If imagery analysts failed to detect the signs of the Indian test preparations, why wasn't there a backup system that would ensure other analysts double-checked the data? If top U.S. officials shifted their attention to other issues in 1997–1998, why didn't the process allow other lesser officials (or legislators) to keep the issue alive? Had the consumer-analyst exchange continued at some level, the intelligence community would have had an incentive to continue watching India closely. It would also have been able to alert some political figure who could have drawn the issue to the public's attention.

The answer to all of these questions is that the intelligence community was trapped in its traditional model for producing intelligence, and the traditional model is outdated. It is hierarchical, linear, and isolated. This model worked well in the Cold War, when the United States had a single paramount threat—the Soviet Union—that changed incrementally. However, to monitor a world in which threats change and can appear suddenly from unexpected quarters, the intelligence community needs a more flexible system. The organization should be able to reconfigure itself as needs change. It should be able to draw on expertise and information, wherever it may reside, whenever the need arises. It should be able to maintain multiple lines of communication.

Although there have been many efforts at intelligence reform in recent years, we still lack an intelligence community truly suited to the Information Age. Such an organization requires not only new ideas and resources; it requires us to abandon some of the most ingrained ideas about how the intelligence community is supposed to function. In doing so, we will need to question some of our basic assumptions about how to promote efficiency and prevent intelligence failures. We may even need to reconsider how intelligence fits into the process of making policy.

PRODUCING INTELLIGENCE IN THE INFORMATION AGE

Many intelligence officials understand that information technology is developing rapidly and that the intelligence community must take advantage of it. Indeed, the intelligence community has been a leader in adopting much of this technology. For example, the CIA's Directorate of Intelligence (or the "DI," as it is called in intelligence circles) began to automate its data bases and retrieval systems beginning in the 1970s. One system, SAFE (Support for Analysts' File Environment), was originally an electronic card catalogue of the intelligence community's data bases, which CIA librarians used to search for topical documents and materials. In the early days of SAFE, the librarians retrieved the materials and shipped them in hard-copy form to analysts. The CIA gradually upgraded SAFE and its supporting systems, so that by the mid-1980s, DI analysts could both search for data and download many of the materials they needed using terminals at their desks.[16]

Similarly, in the 1980s, the CIA, like much of corporate America, adopted desktop publishing. Typists gradually disappeared. Analysts wrote their own memos and reports on personal computers linked directly to the offices responsible for printing the agency's publications. The DI continued to automate its production through the 1990s, as the CIA became one of the largest users of Lotus Notes "groupware." Lotus Notes enables several contributors on a local area network to collaborate on a single document and is perfect for coordinating multiple drafts of an intelligence report or memorandum.[17]

More recently, the DI (like most U.S. intelligence organizations) plugged itself into Intelink, the intelligence community's intranet. Like other intranets, Intelink is an in-house version of the Internet. Intelink uses the same technology as other intranets, such as distributed servers and Mosaic software, but adds stronger cryptographic systems and stricter operating rules for the sake of security. Using Intelink, the DI and other intelligence organizations can trade publications electronically. So, for example, instead of waiting for a courier, users can use Intelink to call up satellite photos from the NRO, or International Atomic Energy Association inspection reports from the Nonproliferation Center.[18] By 1996, the CIA's deputy director for intelligence anticipated that within a decade, "every DI analyst will be adept in the use of his/her own interactive terminal combining telephone, computer, and television; worldnet will provide instant communications throughout the IC [intelligence community] and consumer world and across the globe; encryption will be unbreakable and fast; all information—for management as well as analysis—will be digitized or digitizable; and a terabyte (1,000,000,000,000 bytes) will be the norm for storage and retrieval of information."[19]

Using technology to pull more sources together more easily, deliver intelligence faster, and tailor reports for individual consumers is a laudable goal. Yet, despite the new technology, there is a key ingredient missing. Even two former high-ranking officials, Joseph Nye and William Owens, have observed that many national security organizations are handicapped by "outmoded thinking" and "a failure to grasp the nature of information."[20] These organizations do not appreciate how the *use* of information is changing—how consumers want to receive information, and how they will integrate it into their own calculations and deliberations. They do not understand the new concepts that are needed to manage the use of the technology effectively. Without such an understanding, even the best information technology will be rendered as ineffective as the British tanks that squandered their opportunity at the Somme.

Consider a recent case. In the summer of 1995, ethnic Muslims, Serbs, and Croatians were fighting for control over Bosnia, one of the states that had seceded from Yugoslavia in 1992. Bosnian Serbs, supported by the government of Serbia, had seized control of much of the country. Several Muslim enclaves were surrounded by Bosnian Serb military forces. The United Nations designated these locations as "safe areas" that it was committed to protect. One safe area was Srebrenica, a town in southern Bosnia. In July, Bosnian Serbs attacked the city. U.N. officials froze, unable to make a decision to defend the city. The Serbs marched in. The massacre of civilians that followed was the largest in Europe since World War II.[21]

U.S. officials needed intelligence to follow the civil war, determine if a major violation of the cease-fire lines had occurred, and, if so, decide what actions to take. Stephen Engelberg and Tim Wiener of the *New York Times* described the intelligence community's response:

On July 13, as the press reported refugees' accounts of mass killings, a U.S. spy satellite passing over Bosnia recorded pictures of two fields in which hundreds of prisoners were guarded by gunmen. One of these was the stony field of the "rabbit hunt," where the 17-year-old Avdic was shot.

But no one saw that picture for three weeks.

Techno-thriller readers think spy satellites make the CIA all-seeing and all-knowing. In fact, U.S. intelligence collects far more data than it can analyze.

One former National Security Agency director said gleaning hard facts from the avalanche of information was like trying to take a drink of water from a fire hose.

An intelligence official familiar with the Bosnia photos said that "if you saw an overhead photograph of all New York City, and there was a bank robbery going on somewhere, and nobody reported it," detectives would have a hard time finding the scene of the crime. Throughout July, he said, the CIA lacked "information regarding specific places and atrocities." . . .

On July 27, two weeks after the first published accounts of mass killings from survivors of the fall of Srebrenica, a U-2 spy plane passed over the sites of the slaughter and recorded images of newly turned earth. That film was shipped to Washington on a regular military flight July 30.

That day, John Shattuck, the assistant secretary of state for human rights, was in Tuzla, interviewing furious and stunned refugees—among others, Avdic, the teen-ager, and Suljic, the invalid carpenter. His reporting helped give the CIA a push.

By Aug. 2, "enough information had come to us that allowed us to hone in" on the killing grounds, an intelligence official said. An analyst with the CIA's Balkans Task Force stayed up all night, looking through thousands of images, until he matched the men in the fields with the corresponding shot of freshly dug graves. The pictures landed at the White House on Aug. 4. They were riveting. Here was evidence, Shattuck said later, of "direct acts of genocide." Madeleine K. Albright, the chief U.S. delegate at the United Nations, successfully argued that they be made public. . . .

On Aug. 8 . . . Ms. Albright stood before a closed session of the Security Council and told the story of Srebrenica. She said the photos and the accounts by witnesses were "compelling evidence that the Bosnian Serbs had systematically executed people who were defenseless"—thousands of them— "with the direct involvement of high-level Bosnia Serb officials."[22]

In other words, when the intelligence community first learned of the assault on Srebrenica and was told that U.S. officials needed to confirm reports of a massacre, it responded in the conventional manner. Collection managers assigned systems to cover the area, and managers in the agencies responsible for analyzing the data assigned the appropriate personnel to the problem. When the analysts responsible for searching for the reported graves found themselves overwhelmed by the amount of imagery they had to review, managers

again responded in the traditional fashion: they assigned more people to the problem and had the analysts work longer hours.

Then there were additional glitches. The analysts requested additional imagery, only to discover that their requests were being
bumped by military targets that enjoyed higher priority.[23] U.S. officials at the United Nations grew impatient. Higher-level intelligence
officials eventually intervened in the collection planning, and the analysts finally got the information they needed.

With all of the technology currently available to collect data and
support analysts, why did the organization take so long to respond?
Would better technologies have solved the problem? Probably not.
As in the case of tank warfare, the problem was not just adopting
new technology. Rather, the problem lay in outmoded concepts of
how an organization is supposed to work. The old concepts do not
allow the intelligence community to take full advantage of the new
technology.

The Traditional Model

Despite popular conceptions, the defining character of the modern
intelligence community is not Nathan Hale or William Donovan or
even James Bond. It is Max Weber, the German sociologist best
known as the inventor of the concept of bureaucracy.[24] The intelligence community is a classic bureaucracy, characterized by centralized planning, routinized operations, and a hierarchical chain of
command. All of these features leave the intelligence organization ill
suited for the Information Age.

Along with the factory system, the concept of bureaucracy was
one of the great organizational ideas of the nineteenth century. Like
assembly lines for paperwork, bureaucracies are efficient in part because they divide work into manageable units. They also eliminate
the need for everyone to be a jack of all trades; by dividing labor, individuals and smaller units within an organization can concentrate
on honing their specialized skills. But most of all, bureaucracies are
efficient because they adopt standard operating procedures. Members of a bureaucracy do not need to determine with each new assignment who reports to whom, or who is responsible for what.
Someone has settled that beforehand. Assuming the rules are prop-

erly designed, everyone knows what to do and nothing slips between the cracks.[25]

In the intelligence community, the bureaucratic model manifests itself in two central concepts. The first concept is that of the "intelligence cycle." This model shares some of the features of the process for planning intelligence, but occurs in a shorter time frame. The intelligence cycle assumes intelligence is produced through the following steps (see Figure 3.1):

- First, intelligence consumers make known their needs for information. These requests go to the organization that assigns priorities to informa-

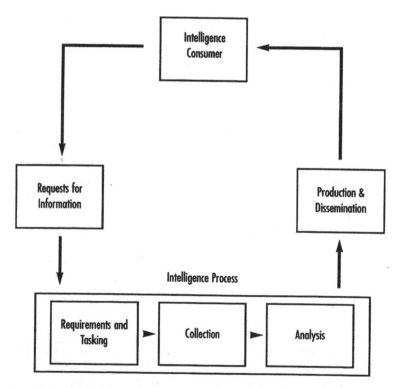

Figure 3.1. Traditional Intelligence Cycle

tion requirements. In the case of national intelligence programs, this is the Community Management Staff (CMS).

- The CMS develops a list of intelligence requirements and priorities. The CMS committees responsible for planning imagery, signals intelligence, and human-source intelligence use these lists "to lay validated requirements" (as the saying goes) on intelligence organizations responsible for collection, such as the NRO, NSA, and the CIA's Directorate of Operations. These organizations then collect the data.
- The collected intelligence information is processed. Analysts, responding to their own list of validated requirements, use the data to prepare reports, studies, briefings, and other products.
- The community is then supposed to coordinate the analysis of various analysts into a product. It notes objections when there is disagreement among agencies within the community (more on this shortly).
- The finished product is delivered to the intelligence consumer, who provides feedback so that the process can be repeated, if necessary.

The intelligence cycle reflects the best thinking of how an information service should work from the late 1940s and 1950s, when people began to write about intelligence policy and develop concepts about how intelligence organizations ought to operate. It has been a durable concept and it pervades our thinking about intelligence. CIA publications and training materials feature it prominently.[26] Even the Aspin-Brown Commission led off its assessment of how the intelligence community works with a description of the intelligence cycle:

The essential role of intelligence is not difficult to understand. It is to provide timely, relevant information to U.S. policymakers, decisionmakers, and warfighters. Accomplishing this mission involves tasking, collecting, processing, analyzing, and disseminating intelligence, commonly referred to as the "intelligence cycle." ... The intelligence cycle drives the day-to-day activities of the Intelligence Community. In the cycle, the consumer of information sets forth a need for information that is relayed to the requirements prioritization committees of the Intelligence Community who then lay the validated requirement on the respective intelligence collection agencies. The collected intelligence information is processed, analyzed, and reported simultaneously to the customer and the Community's all-source analyst who combine it with other intelligence and open-source information to produce a finished intelligence report or assessment of the data. The customer has the option of providing feedback on the degree to which his need has been met and asking for additional analysis or additional collection, if required.... [27]

The second concept the intelligence community borrows from the classical bureaucratic model is the "coordination process;" Figure 3.2 provides an illustration of how an intelligence product might be co-ordinated. Coordination is so ingrained in intelligence that officials even have a formal definition for it; according to the CIA's *Consumer's Guide,* coordination is "the process by which producers gain the views of other producers on the adequacy of a specific draft assessment, estimate, or report; it is intended to increase a product's factual accuracy, clarify its judgments, and resolve or sharpen statements of disagreement on major contentious issues." [28]

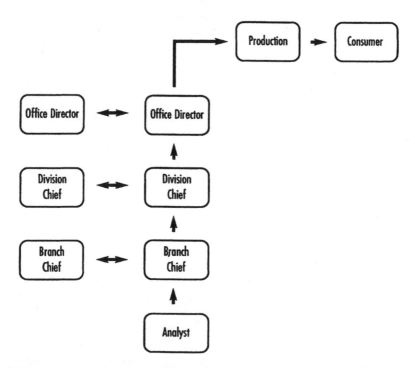

Figure 3.2. Coordination in the Intelligence Community

But intelligence coordination is really just the community's version of how traditional bureaucracies generally work. Bureaucracies are organized vertically, so that lower levels report to higher levels, and horizontally, so each office has responsibility for a different area or issue. This scheme ensures a clearly defined chain of command and delegation of responsibility. To churn out a product, a decision, or an opinion, bureaucracies pass "action items" upward, until they receive a sufficiently authoritative level of approval. At the same time, each unit lets the unit next door have a place in the "chop chain," allowing it the opportunity to add its expertise to the final product. Usually each unit deals with a counterpart unit that is at the same height in the hierarchy. Short-circuiting this process is called making an "end run." Such maneuvers are considered poor form. They can also be career-threatening if a higher-level official finds himself "blind sided." (Bureaucracies often seem to revel in sports metaphors.)

Of course, bureaucracies had been around long before Weber codified their internal rules, just as assembly lines and mass production had been around long before Henry Ford.[29] Even so, Weber's concept of the organization is an essential part of the industrial age. It embodies many of the era's hopes for rational thinking. Just as man established order over nature by the scientific application of physics and chemistry, bureaucracy allowed man to establish order over society and organizations. This may be why so many commissions and committees trying to reform the intelligence community concentrate on fixing its organization. They seem to say that the intelligence community will work if we can just discover the optimal arrangement of boxes on an organization chart, the perfect division of responsibility, and the right rules for who reports to whom. Unfortunately, the problem today for intelligence is not how to find the perfect organization plan. The problem is that our basic notions of organization may be becoming obsolete.

What's Wrong With the Traditional Model

The intelligence process as it is traditionally portrayed resembles an assembly line. One can almost imagine a plant manager overseeing the entire process, making sure the line runs at the optimum speed. Specialization and division of labor improve efficiency. Intelligence products move along a production beltway, where workers insert some collected data or add some analysis. At the end of the line, a quality control inspector tries out the product to see if all of the lights and bells work, an administrative assistant puts a final polish on the cover, and then the report goes out the door.

Admittedly, models of the intelligence cycle and coordination process are idealizations of processes that are more subtle and more complex in practice. But that is exactly the problem. An idealization is supposed to be an aimpoint, or what the process should look like if everything goes as planned.[30] The problem is that today, even if the traditional intelligence process did work as planned, it would often fail to produce the information consumers want. It would also be ineffective in using the technology and vast amounts of data that the Information Revolution has made available. The traditional model suffers from several deficiencies, including:

- It limits interaction between intelligence producers and intelligence consumers. The traditional model assumes that insulation promotes objectivity, and reflects the deference to scholarly authority that prevailed when the intelligence community was established.
- The traditional model assumes a division of responsibility, and also assumes that there is unit somewhere in the intelligence organization that has the expertise to analyze each issue that comes along. This organizational structure may be modified from time to time, but in routine operation it is static.
- The traditional model, as noted, assumes that coordination improves the intelligence product by adding additional information and expertise. This implies two other assumptions: First, the traditional model assumes that coordination will eventually shake out objective truth from conflicting opinion. Second, it assumes that, because analysts are promoted on the basis of their performance and experience, higher levels of review yield products that should command greater authority.
- The traditional model assumes that intelligence provides a comprehensive analysis. Sometimes the model even implies that intelligence subsumes all other information (witness the term "all source intelligence," which includes both classified and publicly available material).

The traditional bureaucratic model, like the traditional factory, may have been good for producing a standard product, using a standard method, under conditions that do not vary significantly. Yet this is exactly why a traditional bureaucratic model like the intelligence cycle is ill suited for today's world, where intelligence users are highly varied and want tailored products, and where conditions are often changing. No static organization and standardized production process can succeed in such a situation.

We should have known that something was wrong with the traditional model. One sign was that, if you read between the lines, even intelligence experts knew the model was a simplification that often—perhaps usually—did not hold in practice. Writers who described the intelligence cycle in recent years almost always added qualifications. They would say something along the lines of, "Although the process is supposed to work this way, it often breaks down in crises or other special situations." Intelligence planners short-circuited the formal process when high-level consumers needed information in a hurry and had the clout to have their way.

A second sign that something was wrong with the traditional model was that intelligence officials would not rely on their standing organizations when a really important issue came along. Instead, they would establish ad hoc "task forces" and "intelligence centers." During the past decade, for example, the intelligence community has created new intelligence centers to cover critical issues such as proliferation, counterterrorism, narcotrafficking, and other special topics. The intelligence centers bring together the specific analysts and collectors needed to address a specific issue. The centers are also intended to connect intelligence consumers directly to intelligence producers.[31] Indeed, establishing new organizations for high priority assignments has become a reflex action: When TWA Flight 800 exploded off Long Island in 1996, the DCI's Counterterrorism Task Force established a team to investigate. In effect, the lean, focused task force designed to escape the encumbrances of the bureaucracy created a new lean, focused team to escape the encumbrances of the task force.[32]

A third sign that something was wrong with the traditional approach was that policymakers began more often to view the value of intelligence differently from those who produced it. Intelligence producers think that their product is special and, perhaps, decisive. Intelligence consumers—especially top-level officials—see intelligence as just one part of a massive amount of information that reaches their desks each day. The higher the pay grade, the more likely an official is to serve as his or her own analyst. In fairness, this is often understandable. The official often has a better understanding of the total context, sometimes has better sources of information, and often has more experience than the analysts who, under the traditional model, are supposedly "bestowing wisdom" upon the consumer.

An Alternative Model

In the post-Cold War, Information Age world, intelligence agencies will need to adapt. An intelligence production process for the Information Age would function according to the following principles:

- Organizations must allow resources to flow freely, so that they can configure themselves into a network of information collectors and analysts suited for the task of the moment, drawing on whoever has the skills for the task at hand, and led by whoever has the best grasp of the problem. Organizational boundaries should not be barriers.

- No central planner can keep up with changing requirements. Therefore, the organization itself must have a mechanism that will automatically allocate the people and information resources needed for an assignment.

- Just as important, it is unlikely that any central planner will be able to predict which combination of analysts and collection assets will prove most successful in dealing with a problem. Therefore, the organization must have a mechanism that will encourage a variety of different approaches.

- The best way to ensure that an intelligence product meets the needs of the consumer is to put the consumer in touch with the analysts preparing the product. Thus, the process should constantly operate so as to minimize the distance between intelligence producers and intelligence consumers, permitting enough interaction so that the product is naturally tailored to the needs of the consumer.

- Bringing together more minds to work on a problem does not necessarily improve the intelligence product. This is especially true when an assessment requires judgment rather than collective knowledge and expertise—as is the case, for example, when the question at hand is more of a "mystery" than a "secret."* When judgments are called for, they should be

---

* In intelligence, it is useful to distinguish among "known facts," "secrets," and "mysteries." *Known facts* can be readily observed, e.g., Britain's policy on adopting the Euro. *Secrets* are facts that actually exist, but which an opponent

made by officials, not analysts. The fact that a judgment is being made should be made explicit, and there should be a process for linking officials to their judgments, such that they cannot hide behind a facade of relying on supposedly "objective intelligence."

In the commercial world, companies are having to deal with challenges similar to those faced by the intelligence community. Some of the concepts they are using may prove useful to intelligence. Consider two recent examples—the "virtual corporation" and "market-based management."

The Virtual Corporation
Companies in the private sector also face a world where requirements are changing more rapidly than ever, and no single organizational structure is suited for all conditions. One response has been to abandon the traditional concept of a static, hierarchical corporation, and adopt a more adaptive, flexible approach.

For example, after a series of mergers and acquisitions in the mid-1990s, Lockheed Martin—already one of the largest defense contractors in the world—ballooned into an empire earning more than $31 billion in annual revenues, with facilities spread across the entire country. The company had experience and expertise in most areas of aerospace. The problem was how to organize this expertise to propose, develop, and deliver products with the speed of a smaller organization—and then reorganize just as quickly as conditions and opportunities changed.

---

is trying hide, e.g., the performance characteristics of a new ballistic missile being developed by Iran or a terrorist group's plan for striking a public transit system. In principle (if not in practice) secrets can be ascertained with enough effort and the right collection resources. *Mysteries* are things that cannot be discovered even in principle, because there are too many variables that may affect future events, or because a decision that will determine a future event has not yet been made. Examples of mysteries include, for example, China's reaction to a unilateral declaration of independence by the ROC government in Taiwan, or whether Japan's economy will return to the growth rates of the 1970s. Known facts and secrets are amenable to analysis. The assessment of mysteries almost always depends on judgment. See Berkowitz and Goodman, *Strategic Intelligence for American National Security* (Princeton, N.J.: Princeton University Press, 1989), pp. 86–106.

Lockheed, like many other companies that have faced a similar situation, adopted a new approach.[33] Under the new system, the company establishes small, ad-hoc groups—virtual corporations—to address opportunities as they come along. The label reflects the fact that these groups are rarely formally chartered and are often physically scattered across a company. Usually the manager who leads the group is the one who identified the opportunity in the first place and sold it to the corporate brass; this encourages entrepreneurship, itself a major challenge in large, mature corporations. Once the project is approved, the manager picks people and offices he needs from throughout the corporation.

For example, when Lockheed decided to compete for the contract to build NASA's X-33 launch vehicle prototype, it drew its team from units scattered across the entire company: the famous Skunk Works prototyping shop, the company's space and missiles division, the information services division, and so on. Lockheed also used outsiders with specialized technology and expertise (such as Rocketdyne, which would build a new type of engine for its proposed vehicle, and Rohr, which had developed a new thermal protection system). Once the virtual corporation was up and running, officials left it alone, so that it had the autonomy it needed to develop the project. If Lockheed won the contract, the virtual corporation would be enlarged to carry out the program. If not, the virtual corporation would disappear. In this case, Lockheed did win the contract, and the virtual corporation became the basis of Venture Star, a new company that would build and operate the vehicle.[34]

True, companies have often created new units to go after new opportunities—just as the intelligence community has created new task forces and centers to address new intelligence requirements. For example, in the early 1980s, IBM created a new subsidiary to design its first personal computer, and Apple established a separate team to design the Macintosh. Similarly, Ford created a new team consisting mainly of executives from its European subsidiary to design the first Taurus.[35]

There are, however, several important features that distinguish the new way of doing business through virtual corporations (or whatever other buzzword one calls them). First, and most important, virtual corporations are not supposed to be special cases. Rather, they are supposed to be a routine part of doing business. When Apple officials created a new team to develop the Macintosh, they understood that they were taking a significant step away from their previous strategy focus to build a new business taking advantage of a new technology. The Macintosh team isolated themselves in a separate building, hoisted a pirate flag outside, and reveled in an "us against them" mindset. Virtual corporations are not supposed to be a challenge to "business as usual." Rather, they are supposed to *be* business as usual.

The second feature that distinguishes this new approach is that recent advances in information technology are essential to the concept. In order for ad-hoc organizations to be routine, they must be easy to assemble. Reshuffling people into new configurations must be affordable. Previously, reorganization usually required physical relocation so that the new team members could work with one another. When New York-based IBM created its new personal computer subsidiary, it moved most of the personnel to a new facility in Boca Raton, Florida. Today, using cheap communications and data processing technology, people can remain where they are; assembling a new team often takes little more than editing a new mail group in one's Internet software.

The third feature that makes virtual corporations special is that they are contrary to the usual rules of structure and hierarchy. In the older approaches, even when one created a new team or task force, the new group fit somewhere into the traditional corporate structure—recall how, for instance, the new Saturn team eventually became just another car division within General Motors. Hierarchies and areas of responsibility are much less important when you know these relationships can change as soon as the next project comes along. In fact, if one insists on maintaining rigid hierarchies and areas of responsibility, networked organizations and virtual corporations will simply not work. It would be the equivalent of requiring tanks to operate in infantry formations.

The intelligence community could use a similar approach, and most of the same principles would apply. Figure 3.3 illustrates schematically how the process might work. To drive the process, intelligence consumers could each have a "principal analyst" responsible for assembling the intelligence product (some thinkers in the intelligence community who have been developing new operating concepts have taken to calling this analyst a "trusted interlocutor"). The principal analyst would deal directly with a consumer so that he or she would know what the intelligence product should cover, how it needs to be delivered, how much time is available, and so on. At the same time, the principal analyst would be responsible for assembling the team necessary to develop the product. As the diagram shows, this team could be drawn from several sources: dedicated or shared information sources; classified or unclassified data; and whatever combination of analysts were needed to develop the particular product in question. The members of the analytical team could work together in subgroups as needed, using local area networks, Internet, telephone, etc.

Notice that an additional benefit of this approach is that there is a built-in incentive for intelligence analysts to use commercial or open sources when they are more effective. Already, as some experts declared to the Aspin-Brown Commission, more than 80 percent of the data used by the intelligence community now comes from open sources. Even during the Cold War, George Kennan reflected recently, the vast majority of information U. S. policymakers required could have been obtained by analysts using such open sources as the nation's libraries, archives, and the media.[36] In a world where information is abundant, the comparative advantage of specialized intelligence collection and analysis will vary from situation to situation, and there needs to be a mechanism built into the intelligence process that automatically steers an analyst to open sources first.

Instead of the assembly-line organization for producing an intelligence product depicted in Figure 3-2, the resulting "virtual team" that tackles an assignment under this kind of approach might look like the organization depicted in Figure 3-4. Each circle represents a participant in the assignment, or a "node" in the ad hoc network. This particular configuration of analysts, collection assets, and communications links might apply only to this particular job and might exist only briefly if the problem is transient. Or, if the problem is recurring or persistent, the team might hang together longer. When the

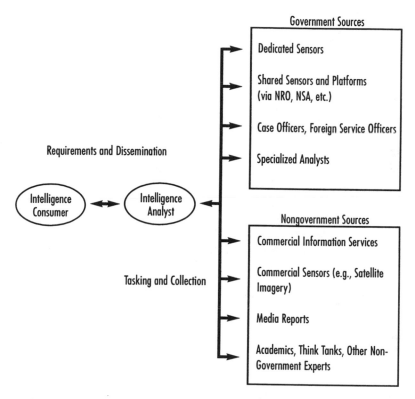

Figure 3.3. Alternative Model for the Relationship among Consumers, Analysts, and Collection Assets

task is completed, though, the participants can reassemble themselves into a new configuration.

Technology makes a virtual organization approach possible, but the most important obstacles have little to do with hardware or software. Rather, the larger issues concern whether intelligence officials can abandon traditional dogma about how intelligence is "supposed to work"—the old rules that say intelligence analysts must deal with their consumers at arm's distance, that coordinated intelligence is

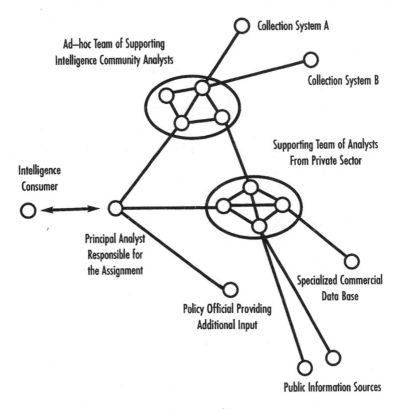

Figure 3.4. An Example of an Intelligence "Virtual Team"

better than an assessment provided by a single trusted analyst, and so on. These dogmas are incompatible with the new approach.

Much of the problem is culture, which discourages both networking and direct contact between analyst and consumers. Officials generally agree that using tailored products and reducing the distance between analysts and users improves intelligence. The problem occurs when years of training and socialization in the intelligence culture defeat the best efforts at reform. The problem is subtle. Intelligence officials revert back to old behavior, instinctively compartmenting information or relying on classified sources when public sources would suffice (and make it easier to write transparent, explicit analysis). Managers continue to insist on "polishing" or "refining" a product, rather than allowing their analysts to give their personal assessments. Managers believe that this is, after all, their responsibility and that it improves the intelligence product.

When the intelligence community has tried to change its ways, the results, alas, have resembled the overage uncle who tries too hard to be current with the latest fads. In the early 1990s, for example, critics argued that the DI was out of touch and that there needed to be more interaction between analysts and policymakers. So analysts began to prepare formal briefings, and traveled from CIA headquarters in suburban Virginia to downtown Washington in order to brief policymakers firsthand. Probably the officials would have preferred simply talking directly to an analyst in a ten-minute telephone call. These days Intelink and classified fax reduce the need to take the bus ride, but even so, the new version of intelligence production is really a speeded-up version of the old one. The basic constraints of the old process remain.

Technology will make some change inevitable. Many intelligence officials understand at least the need for a new operating approach. In the case of the CIA's Directorate of Intelligence, many analysts and even managers expressed enthusiasm about the DI's new strategy when it was announced. Ruth David, the CIA's deputy director for science and technology from 1995 to 1998, has written at some length about how an "agile intelligence enterprise" might work.[37] The CIA has also demonstrated, using a self-contained prototype intranet, how such a virtual team system could work on a small scale for a specified subject. Unfortunately, until the culture of intelligence changes, changes in the day-to-day operation of the intelligence community will be slow and intelligence consumers may never realize how a properly running intelligence organization is supposed to operate and support its users.

Intelligence consumers (or the "principal analysts" working for them) are the best position to tailor the intelligence product and decide how much of the specialized resources of the intelligence community are needed. There is a risk, of course, that such proximity will lead to the politicization of analysis and groupthink, or that policymakers will still be unwilling to rely on the judgment of intelligence officers they do not know. But these types of potential problems are largely solvable. Both analysts and policymakers can be sensitized to the subtle ways in which knowing an intelligence consumer's interests and preferences can adversely influence judgments. Also, officials can be required (either formally or by social norms) to make clear when they are citing "analysis" to describe facts and secrets, and when they are using "judgment" to assess mysteries. Indeed, many other professions face similar dilemmas and have developed methods and canons to promote objectivity.[38] The larger challenge to the future of the intelligence community is whether organizations originally designed to collect and analyze limited amounts of specialized (and usually secret) information can adapt and become flexible information integrators.

Market-Based Management
As we saw in the preceding chapter, the intelligence community's planning of hardware and personnel resembles Soviet-style centralized planning. The day-to-day operations of the community follow the same pattern. Organizations base most of their operations on monthly, quarterly, and annual production plans, leaving some margin for responding to special assignments. Unfortunately, this approach to planning cannot keep up with the requirements of modern intelligence consumers, which routinely change rapidly. Such rigid, centralized planning also defeats much of the purpose of having a network-style organization. In other words, new organizations require new types of management tools.

Think, for example, how could the intelligence community have responded more effectively in the case of the Bosnian graves? Even if the intelligence community had been prepared to configure itself as needed for the task at hand, no traditional management process for allocating resources could have kept up with events. The management problem actually consisted of two parts. The first problem was assigning more resources (analysts, collection efforts, etc.) to the task as the demand for information became more urgent. The second problem was casting a wide enough net so that anyone in the community with a bright idea for finding the graves—rather than just the imagery analysts or the Bosnian Task Force—would have the opportunity to take a crack at the problem.

Intelligence officials might have been better off simply putting the assignment up for bids. An analyst assigned to the U.S. representative to the U.N. could have offered a bounty to whoever found the sites, using whatever means they thought would be effective. Analysts throughout the agency would have thought about the problem at least for a moment. If the analyst wanted more intelligence staffers to work on the problem, or to give it higher priority, he or she could increase the incentive.

If intelligence managers had taken this approach, analysts who did not regularly follow the Bosnian account might have "assigned themselves" to the problem. For instance, analysts familiar with the problem of tracking mobile missile launchers ("strategic relocatable targets," or "SRTs" in intelligence vernacular) might have realized that their skills in trafficability analysis and area delineation could be used to narrow down the most promising areas for the search. Just as there are only so many places one can hide a missile launcher, there are only so many places one can locate a mass grave. But would one really expect the typical intelligence manager to understand the connection between the two problems? One of the great strengths of the market is that it flushes out innovative ideas from even the most unexpected quarters, which is exactly what we need in an era of unconventional, rapidly materializing threats.

For that matter, the intelligence community could have simply made its requirements for information public and offered the bounty to all comers. Although intelligence sources are frequently sensitive, the identities of the targets of U.S. intelligence usually are not. In July 1995 everyone knew that U.S. officials were concerned about the Srebrenica massacre and wanted to find the suspected graves. Intelligence officials could have simply made the requirement public, just as the FBI does with its Ten Most Wanted Fugitives list.* This would

---

* The FBI even posts its Ten Most Wanted list on the World Wide Web. The URL is *http://www.fbi.gov/most want/tenlist.htm*. In 1996, this led a fourteen-year-old boy in Antigua, Guatemala, to realize one of his neighbors was

have had the effect of "tasking" experts in the private sector to work on the problem. Since the commercial information industry is becoming more and more capable, it is important to have this feature built into the intelligence planning process, (Currently intelligence officials talk about open source intelligence and use contractors, but they are considered a special case or an auxiliary to the "real" intelligence community.)

Market-based management has been used in the private sector with considerable success.[39] It is especially useful in organizations that must deal with a variety of changing demands and an unpredictable range of clients—a description that fits the intelligence community. Table 3.1 summarizes the most important differences between the traditional model and such a market-style approach.

One important reason why traditional intelligence organizations have such difficulty dealing with unanticipated threats is that their hard-wired structure and staffing focuses them on specific topics. Traditional bureaucracies, by their nature, not only defend their turf; they also shun assignments that are not germane to their mission. A naval officer who becomes an expert in tank warfare is unlikely to be promoted, and one can imagine the reaction to an air force officer who requests money to study how to design a better guided missile cruiser. Similarly, under the traditional model, an office responsible for analyzing, say, Latin America, will have a hard time securing the funds for collecting data on fundamentalist Hinduism.

In other words, organizations in traditional bureaucracies have an incentive to focus and exclude. Companies in the competitive market, on the other hand, have an incentive to search and expand. They survive only if they detect previously unseen market niches, figure out how to serve them at a profit, and then adapt to address them. As a result, the market is always presenting surprise "solutions" to consumer demands—often demands that no one even knew existed. Was

---

Leslie Isben Rogge, a bank robber who had escaped from jail in Idaho and fled the United States. Fearing that someone might kill him in order to collect the reward, Rogge turned himself in to the U.S. embassy and was shipped back to Miami. See Molly Moore, "You Can Run, But Not Hide, From the Net," *Washington Post,* June 6, 1996.

Table 3.1: Comparison Of Traditional And New Intelligence Analysis Production Processes

	OLD MODEL	NEW MODEL
Role of Analysts	Most full-time staff analysts fit one of two roles: (a) experts in a substantive field who cover a defined "beat"; or (b) managers who come up through the ranks to supervise, assign projects, and review products	Most full-time staff analysts fit one of three roles: (a) analysts attached to users, and generally paid for by users; (b) "super analysts" in the intelligence community (IC) who respond directly to user requests and allocate resources for tasks; or (c) a limited number of highly specialized experts in areas the private sector cannot support and who are in sufficient demand to warrant IC funding
Organizational Structure	Hierarchical and static	Networked and fluid
Quality Control and Review Process	Products are reviewed by successive levels of management in order to ensure quality and make certain that the "organizational viewpoint" is represented	Products are delivered directly to users. Managers monitor products to determine whether disagreement exists within the IC so that users are aware of variations in confidence levels and analysts can consider sources of disagreement
Surge Capacity	Surge capacity is a "special case" to meet crises. Most surge capacity consists of extra people with skills similar to full-time staff	Surge capacity—in the form of "just in time" analytic capability—is the norm, enabling IC to obtain the required skills for a given assignment

Table 3.1: Comparison Of Traditional And New Intelligence Analysis Production Processes (cont.)

	OLD MODEL	NEW MODEL
Role of Non-Full-Time Staff	Contractors and part-time help are used for a limited number of narrow, specialized tasks, and are segregated both organizationally and by security restrictions (e.g., the "NOCONTRACT" classification)	The talent for a task is bought as needed in order to maintain required flexibility and responsiveness for meeting potentially infinite requirements with finite resources. Part-time help and contractors are fully integrated into the team as required
Planning and Recruitment	Managers make a major effort to identify the requirements of key users in order to have the required talent on staff in time to respond to events.	Managers make a major effort to identify future requirements so they know where to find talent when they need it. If necessary, they subsidize areas of the private sector to ensure availability. It is assumed that many requirements will be unanticipated, and that specialized talent will need to be brought in "on the fly"

there ever a central planner, for example, who would have dreamed an urgent need existed for a Starbucks coffee shop on every street corner? Could any central planner have anticipated that the optimal choice for transporting families in suburbia would be the sport utility vehicle?

The intelligence community needs this ability to "detect the unanticipated" to deal with many post-Cold War threats. The characteristic feature of these threats is that we often will not know in advance who will pose them or how they will operate. As a result, intelligence officials cannot know in advance which individuals or organizations in the intelligence community will have the best understanding of such threats or the best methodology for analyzing them.

We can already see examples of how the traditional approach to organizing intelligence is likely to fail when faced with such threats. Consider the case of the Aum Shinrikyo, for instance. For years, the Aum was a little-known cult, led by Shoko Asahara, a mostly blind guru who affected the trappings of a Buddhist cleric (in fact, Asahara's Buddhist grounding was slight). The group seemed to have a small following and the Tokyo city government officially recognized it as a religious organization in August 1989. In March 1994, however, the Aum surprised everyone when it staged a nerve gas attack in the Tokyo subway system, killing twelve people and injuring five thousand.

Japanese authorities later discovered that the surface appearance of the Aum bore little resemblance to the reality. Investigators found that what appeared to be a small religious cult was actually an organization with a following of thousands and a worldwide network of contacts. Some members of the Aum were highly skilled scientists and technicians. Some of these members had tried to acquire materials for a nuclear weapon from the former Soviet Union. Others had searched in Africa and elsewhere for specimens that could be used to develop biological weapons. The investigators reported that the Aum had built a facility capable of producing chemical weapons in bulk, and had begun making plans to strike targets in the United States with nerve gas.[40]

It is impossible to understate the significance of this failure. The Aum was totally off the screen of U.S. intelligence, and, for that matter, all other Western intelligence organizations. Even after the attack, U.S. intelligence was slow in gathering information about the group. Months later, the press and congressional investigators still often had better information than intelligence organizations.

One reason why the Aum went undetected is that it did not fit into the structure of any intelligence organization. No agency had an "Office of Northeast Asian Techno-Terrorist Quasi-Religious Cults." The threat did not match any of the established boxes on the intelligence community's organization chart or production plan for collecting and analyzing information on terrorism, and so it fell through the cracks. This kind of situation is likely to occur more often as a result of the singular and largely predictable Soviet threat having been replaced by numerous, rapidly generated threats, often originating from unusual sources.

The intelligence community needs a more effective mechanism for detecting, assessing, and monitoring these unlikely threats. As in the case of the economy, an "invisible hand" will often be a better cultivator of ideas and allocator of effort. The challenge for intelligence officials in the Information Age is to understand how to integrate these indirect mechanisms into their operations.

The Case of the RSA Key
Many intelligence experts, wedded to the traditional model, question whether market-style approaches will work in practice. They ask, can analysts organize themselves—that is, without managers and formal production plans—to solve a problem? Can they locate the specialized skills and data they need, parcel out work, produce a product, and then disassemble themselves so that they are ready for the next problem that comes along? A recent case suggests that, not only can such market-based management work; it might even succeed when traditional methods fail. The case, in which a makeshift band of cryptography experts organized themselves across national borders to break a long-standing cipher problem, is interesting because of the logistics involved, because of the technology used, and because the puzzle in question resembles many real-life intelligence problems.

Few fields have historically been as critical to intelligence as cryptography, or cipher-breaking. History has sometimes turned on cryptography. The ability of British intelligence to intercept and crack the Zimmermann telegram was critical in the decision of the United States to join the Allies in World War I, which was, in turn, critical to the defeat of Germany.[41] Cipher-breaking was also essential for the Allied victories in World War II, and the onset of the Cold War was brought about, in part, when the United States discovered Soviet espionage through decrypted intercepts.[42] It is little wonder governments keep codes and ciphers, and methods for cracking them, tightly held secrets.

The most important feature of a modern encryption system is the length of its key. Such encryption systems consist of two parts: the algorithm, or logic that scrambles a message; and the key, or the settings that determine how the algorithm will scramble a particular message. All users of a cipher must have a copy of the algorithm, so it is impractical to protect and is a less significant intelligence challenge. The harder target for breaking an encrypted message is the key, which is shared only among the parties who are supposed to have access to a specific message.

Today's keys are usually numbers that are specified as products of prime numbers, so to crack the key one needs to factor a number. Suppose the key is the number 2362634. To figure out how the algorithm turns a plaintext message into a code, one needs to know that the combination of numbers that, when multiplied, yields 2362634 is 2, 3, 3, 7, 13, 37, and 39. The longer the key, the greater the number of potential combinations, and the more difficult the cipher is to break. Security specialists like this kind of cipher because they are easy to maintain and because visitors can use the cipher without having to receive the key in advance.

The ability of a cipher to resist decryption can thus be measured as the number of computer operations that would be necessary to factor the key and try all of the numerical combinations produced by the key and the algorithm. Since we know how many operations per second a computer can calculate, we can extrapolate to determine how long a computer will likely require to break a cipher. Sophisticated ciphers require thousands or even millions of years of computer operations to attempt all of the possible numerical combinations. Experts consider them secure because the would-be codebreaker—and several generations of his progeny—would die of old age before finishing the task.*

---

* The reason for using keys based on long combinations of prime numbers is that factoring a number is a brute-force mathematical operation. To find the prime roots, one basically has to try all of the possible combinations. Although some search strategies are more efficient than others, there is no simplifying algorithm that solves the question. So one can share or even publish such a key freely, knowing that outsiders, who don't know the prime roots, will have difficulty deriving them. When the people who are supposed to

Some officials fear that commercial communications systems might become so secure that even U.S. intelligence and law enforcement agencies, with the most powerful computers in the world, would be unable to crack them. This is why federal authorities have sometimes tried to allow the government to regulate cryptography technology the same way it regulates weapons and munitions. For example, for many years the U.S. government prohibited U.S. companies from exporting encryption systems using keys longer than forty bits (a "bit" is the smallest unit of information in a formula or algorithm).

Software companies have criticized these regulations, arguing that such controls are not only unfair, but ineffective. The mathematical theories that underpin modern ciphers are well known, and high-speed computers are now widely available. As a result, the companies argue, it is impossible to limit the complexity of a cipher so that the government can crack it without leaving the cipher vulnerable to many other parties, too. They claim that no one will buy communications or financial software from U.S. companies if it contains such weaknesses, and warn that Microsoft, Oracle, IBM, Novell, et al., will lose business to unregulated foreign competitors.[43]

Paul Leyland of Oxford University decided to prove the point by showing how so-called "amateurs" could crack even a long key. Leyland contacted Arjen Lenstra of Bellcore Corporation, who had developed a method (called a "siever") that would allow one to parcel out the problem of factoring a large number to many computers. Leyland and Lenstra then selected a target.[44]

RSA Data Security, a leading supplier of cryptographic software to the commercial computer industry, specializes in factor-based keys. To demonstrate the strength of their encryption system, in August 1977 RSA challenged readers of *Scientific American* to factor a 129-digit number, which they dubbed RSA-129. Then, using the number to determine the key to the cipher, the readers were to find a secret message. At the time even the most powerful computer would have required thousands of years to work through all the various possible

---

have access to the code change, one simply chooses a new key. Because the key can be freely published without fear of compromising the encrypted message, these ciphers are called "public key" ciphers.

combinations of prime numbers, so, for all practical purposes, the key was uncrackable. The prize: a hundred dollars (plus bragging rights) for the first correct solution. Lenstra suggested to Leyland that this made RSA-129 a perfect target.

In 1994 they posted their proposed project on Internet bulletin boards, along with the necessary algorithms, and asked for volunteers. (There is an international community of encryption devotees, consisting largely of mathematicians, computer specialists, and assorted people who feel insufficiently challenged by the New York Times crossword puzzle.) Michael Graff, an Iowa State University undergraduate at the time, wrote a program that would allocate work to participants as more and more of the problem was completed. Derek Atkins, an MIT grad student, provided the computer for saving and verifying the partial solutions as they came in. Before the project was done, hundreds of people had taken part, using whatever computing resources they could find. In ten months the team had their answer. The secret message was "THE MAGIC WORDS ARE SQUEAMISH OSSIFRAGE."[45]

A few months later, Leyland and Lenstra demonstrated that not only could they crack a long key by pooling computer capacity, but they could do the operation secretly. This time they factored a shorter number that RSA had published, but handled all of the work themselves, using spare computing capacity in bits and pieces from several facilities. Their point was that a spy agency or even a ragtag nongovernment organization could pool the computers required to crack highly sophisticated ciphers without calling attention to themselves.

Since then, cryptography enthusiasts have turned factoring into an informal international competition. RSA has begun a contest in which it posts complex numbers and keys, and awards prizes to anyone able to factor them. (In one case, a Cal Berkeley graduate student cracked a forty-bit key—the longest allowed at the time under U.S. restrictions on commercial cryptography—three and a half hours after it was posted. The message was, predictably, "THIS IS WHY YOU SHOULD USE A LONGER KEY,")[46]

When these stories were first publicized, most of the media focused on whether the ciphers that U.S. industry currently uses are secure, and whether private citizens should be permitted better ciphers. Few bothered to discuss the *process* behind the rash of key-breaking. Note some key features (so to speak):

- The methods for cracking the codes were developed entirely in the private sector;
- The team members were separated by thousands of miles and—even more important—set up their own ad hoc team to carry out the task (Lenstra described the process as "chaotic," but it worked);
- The team was able to enlist the assist of hundreds of highly skilled specialists in an incredibly esoteric field simply by posting a request on the Internet; and
- The team was able to identify and task the required hardware around the world, and collate the results in a single node using an automated processing system.

In other words, the most significant lesson of the incident was not that the team broke the code, but how they did it. Even complex, esoteric, intelligence-style problems can be tackled with an impromptu network of experts mustered with a minimum of formal organization. Indeed, this account was itself put together by a similar process. We "interviewed" Lenstra, Leyland, and Graff via e-mail, after identifying them through a review of media reports and finding their e-mail addresses via an Internet search engine. We then downloaded technical papers further describing the algorithms and methodologies from various home pages, including RSA's. This is the style of intelligence production that will often be needed to tackle the challenges of the Information Age.

ISSUES RAISED BY THE NEW INTELLIGENCE MODEL

The decentralized, market-based, fluid model for intelligence presented here flouts convention. Indeed, in those cases where it has been used up until now, intelligence traditionalists have already taken issue with some of its features. A few of the concerns include:

- Fluid, decentralized organizations are less efficient than traditional organizations because they are constantly reconfiguring themselves, and because it is harder to pass information efficiently through a changing network structure.

- The new model lacks adequate accountability in the use of intelligence resources.
- The new model lacks adequate accountability in ensuring the quality of intelligence.
- The new model lacks adequate opportunities for gadflies to critique the prevailing wisdom. It offers less protection for critics and Cassandras, and may not take full advantage of graybeards.
- Putting consumers in direct contact with analysts carries the risk of "politicizing" intelligence.

Some of these concerns are banal because they amount to tautologies. For example, critics who claim that fluid, networked organizations are less efficient are really only saying that the Information Revolution has not occurred, at least not within some organizations. Networked organizations have emerged precisely because new information technology has reduced the cost of reorganization, and made communicating through ad hoc networks more efficient. Some organizations may be profoundly unable to take advantage of the new technology, but there is no reason to think that the intelligence community is one of them.

Other criticisms, however, are more significant. The concern that networked, fluid organizations lack accountability reflects deeply ingrained attitudes about how accountability is supposed to work. The new model lacks the usual chain of command and formal procedures that are supposed to ensure order and accountability. The new approach described here reduces the ability of intelligence agencies to develop a corporate point of view. Without such a single point of view, it is harder to hold an intelligence organization or its managers responsible for a product. As Peter Sharfman, a specialist on the impact of the Information Revolution on organizational behavior, has noted, when "a senior policymaker or military commander exchanges E-mail directly with the analyst who is the acknowledged exert on the issue at hand, what is the function of that expert's boss, or of the boss's boss?"[47] Senior analysts will have an increasingly difficult time asserting their primacy in such an environment. Indeed, one of the most revolutionary effects of the Information Revolution is that consumers are valuing age and experience less as a measure of wisdom and judgment.

Yet, in reality, everyone knows that the ability of the intelligence community to exercise an authoritative voice has been declining for more than two decades—just like almost every other institution that provides assessments and analysis. Indeed, the intelligence product itself reflects this. In the early days of the Cold War, National Intelligence Estimates were short and provided summary judgments. This was to protect intelligence sources (even at the expense of consumers being able to assess the quality of the intelligence for themselves), but it also reflected the fact that most information consumers were more willing to accept authority. Since the early 1970s, though, NIEs have become longer, more detailed, and contain more background data. By the early 1980s the real value of coordinated national estimates was less in the product and more in the process. The intelligence community was more willing to be explicit about those matters on which intelligence analysts disagreed, and the estimating process highlighted disagreements. This, in turn, forced participants in the coordination process to make clear exactly why and on what basis they disagreed on a issue, and focused future intelligence efforts on resolving these points of contention by collecting critical data.

Officials and experts often display cognitive dissonance when asked what they think of these trends. They know how they really want intelligence to be provided to them, but they cling to the traditional model about how the intelligence community is supposed to be organized and how its performance is supposed to be evaluated. Even today, as the intelligence community has tried to remove some of the bureaucracy separating analysts and consumers, there is resistance. For example, shortly after being confirmed as DCI, Robert Gates said in an address to DI analysts: "We do produce a corporate product. If the policymaker wants the opinion of a single individual, he or she can (and frequently does) consult any one of a dozen outside experts on a given issue. Your work, on the other hand, counts because it represents the well-considered views of an entire directorate and, in the case of National Estimates, the entire Intelligence Community. . . . Analysts must understand and practice the corporate concept.

They must discard the academic mindset that says their work is their own, and they must take into account the views of others during the coordination process."[48]

The issue of whether the intelligence community should express an "individual view" or a "corporate view" raises the broader issue of whether coordination improves intelligence, and whether organizational consensus is a good indicator of objective truth. The traditional model assumes that coordination improves analysis. It assumes higher levels of authority are more likely to be correct, and that greater participation by more experts and more agencies is more likely to reveal truth. This is why, for example, National Intelligence Estimates (NIEs) hold pride of place in the hierarchy of intelligence publications; why the DIA "validates" threat assessments produced by the individual services; and so on.

In fact, the ability to discover truth through consensus varies greatly from case to case. Historically, intelligence coordination has often led to the rejection of better estimates in favor of estimates that were, in retrospect, further from the truth. This occurred, for example, all through the intelligence community's estimates of Soviet strategic forces during the Cold War. From 1958 through 1961, the coordination process rejected the views of the Army and State Department (who believed the Soviet Union would deploy relatively few, if any, ICBMs) in favor of the CIA's view (which believed the Soviets would deploy about five hundred ICBMs in the next five years). The State Department and Army were later proved correct. From 1962 through 1972, the process of coordinating the national estimate rejected the Air Force's forecast that the Soviet Union would deploy more than twelve hundred ICBMs, and adopted the CIA's view that the Soviets would complete the ICBMs they currently had under construction, and no more. The Air Force estimate proved closer to reality.[49]

Consensus is most helpful in identifying truth when there is really an objective truth to be discovered. In such cases, teamwork helps individuals define the issues and sort through hard evidence. In cases where the problem is more a "mystery" than a "secret," consensus may offer few advantages. The longer-range forecasts of Soviet strategic forces or Soviet activities in the developing world that the intelligence community made during the Cold War were often assessments of policies that probably even the Soviet leadership had not yet completely decided. Free of hard facts (secret or otherwise), the estimate seems merely to have converged to the mean.

Further, there is more than one way to develop and test ideas. The "graybeard" approach of a Board of National Estimates or National Intelligence Council is one way. Subjecting an idea to the marketplace of ideas is another, and it may often be more effective in the Information Age, when expertise is more widespread.

Recall the case in March 1989 when Stanley Pons and Martin Fleischmann, two researchers at the University of Utah, claimed to have discovered a means to produce nuclear fusion under ordinary temperatures and pressures. Pons and Fleischmann bypassed the institutional arbiter of ideas in physics, the scholarly journals—the physics community's functional equivalent of the National Intelligence Council. Although the debate was chaotic at first, it required just five weeks for independent researchers, acting without any central organization, to collect the data and organize the critical experiments to test the cold fusion theory. On May 1st, 1989, three Caltech researchers—Steven Koonin, Nathan Lewis, and Charles Barnes—presented results at a Baltimore meeting of the American Physical Society that proved the theory false (at least for now).[50]

Such market forces can also protect against the possibility that intelligence can become "politicized." Concerns about politicization strike at the heart of intelligence. Politicization carries the threat of bad intelligence, and it raises issues of ethics and professionalism.[51]

The traditional model attempted to curb politicization by separating analysts from consumers, and having experts within the intelligence community reach a consensus. The new model is also concerned with politicization, but takes a different approach to combat it. It forces officials (or their designated representatives) to take responsibility for whichever assessment they adopt and use as the basis for their decision. It also exposes an official's assessment to outside criticism. The odds that a political official could shop around for an estimate and get away with it—one underlying fear of letting individual analysts express their uncoordinated views to consumers—is small if the official's judgment is held out for public and professional scrutiny.

Ironically, some of the features of the traditional model probably have facilitated, not curbed politicization. The assumption that analysts are objective has often provided analysts an opportunity to pass off opinions as facts. This has been especially true when analysts had strong views of their own about U.S. policy, or at least intelligence that might shape U.S. policy. For example, in the case of the estimate of Soviet strategic forces, all analysts were working off of essentially the same data. When there was good data, disagreements were small. The big disagreements were over assessments that depended on incomplete data or judgment. In these cases, disagreements simply reflected that some analysts were hawks and some were doves, and each had a different view of the Soviet Union. Much of the controversy over the Soviet strategic estimate might have been avoided if analysts had not been compelled to compete over what a single, official NIE contained.[52]

In such cases, isolating analysts in the wont of the traditional model merely prevents a wider audience from scrutinizing judgments that may have been politicized. By opening up the system to more points of view and maintaining multiple centers of expertise, the new model accelerates the rate at which the marketplace of ideas can examine the facts and judgments that an official is using. Just as "cold fusion" was debunked relatively quickly by an ad hoc network facilitated by modern communications, this process can also expose faulty assessments adopted mainly to achieve political goals. Moreover, officials who know that their decisions will be subjected to such scrutiny will be less likely to pressure an analyst to mold intelligence to support policy, or to "shop" for an assessment that supports their political leaning.

Possibly most important of all, a networked, decentralized intelligence community is more likely to allow dissenting views to survive. The survivability of such dissent is essential to debunking skewed estimates. Such scrutiny is the ultimate defense against politicization. In a decentralized organization, analysts with judgments that are currently out of political favor can find safe haven, whereas the traditional, centralized organization is more likely to force dissenters into retirement or out onto the street. Once they are out of the official loop, dissenters usually lack the access or the credentials to criticize the official view.

Whether the intelligence community can adopt the new model is probably a question of whether it can change its basic culture. As can be seen, the new model is much more than technology or changing lines on organization charts. It also requires us to reconsider what an intelligence organization is supposed to do and how. Even more fundamentally, it requires us to reconsider some very basic assumptions, such as how intelligence affects policy and who should take responsibility for the intelligence that supports policy. Short of war, economic disaster, or draconian intervention from outside, few organizations are capable of completely changing their culture so radically. Yet, if it is to remain effective, the intelligence community will have to change—so much that, when these changes are completed, it will likely bear little resemblance to the organization created fifty years ago. Those responsible for national security should want nothing less.

FOUR
THE PROBLEM OF ANALYSIS IN THE NEW ERA

Peter Drucker, the guru of the modern corporation, observes that "information is data endowed with relevance and purpose."[1] This observation is worth keeping in mind when designing an intelligence community for the Information Age. Even the best data will not yield effective policies if its analysis does not keep up with the changing needs of intelligence consumers. It will be irrelevant and have no purpose.

While the basic definition of intelligence may not have changed in fifty years, almost everything else about the analyst's job has.[2] Most of the methods used in intelligence analysis today were developed during the Cold War. Some were ingenious. For example, U.S. imagery analysts developed an entire science of recognition, association, and inference to extract intelligence from satellite photography. One famous technique, dubbed "cratology," linked shipping containers of a given size and shape with specific weapons they were known to contain. Using this approach, an analyst could, for example, estimate Soviet military shipments to client states even when there was little data from firsthand sources. Imagery analysts also estimated the production capacity of a factory by measuring its floor space, or its throughput by looking for chokepoints in its layout. In one famous case, analysts determined a military base was Soviet rather than Cuban on the basis of its having a soccer field rather than a baseball diamond.[3]

Of course, U.S. intelligence analysis has not always been successful. Sometimes the method was ingenious, elegant, and, alas, wrong. But the point is clear: Even the best data leads to bad intelligence if the analysis is faulty. This fact remains important because intelligence analysts today face a changed and intellectually challenging environment that has created requirements for new approaches to analysis. Specifically:

■ As we have seen, the subject matter for analysis is different and more varied. This means that a wider variety of analytical methodologies is needed.

Just as important, analysts and consumers are likely to be faced with a greater number of alternative models competing for acceptance.

- Because the actors influencing global politics have become more fluid, and more subject to internal change, it is harder to specify a reliable analytic model or methodology to assess events.

- Standards of proof have changed. Partly this is because intelligence consumers want a greater role in making judgment calls, but it is also because intelligence is more likely to be used in public debates over policy. In the past, intelligence was required to be the best estimate under the circumstances. Today, intelligence reports are likely to be scrutinized like evidence in a legal procedure, because they will frequently be the focus of a political dispute concerning such issues as arms control compliance, the potential use of military force, or the imposition of sanctions.

- In a vast, interconnected world with many centers of decision making and an overload of information, an intelligence estimate may itself shape the phenomena that are being analyzed—a sort of Heisenberg Effect for the policy world. For example, if word gets out that an official U.S. government intelligence estimate concludes that the value of the Indonesian rupiah is shaky, one can almost guarantee that, if it is not, it soon will be.

If one needs proof that analysis has become more challenging, recall again the August 1998 cruise missile strikes the United States launched against the Osama bin Laden terrorist organization. The exile from Saudi Arabia was suspected of directing the bombing of the U.S. embassies in Kenya and Tanzania. The bombings had killed hundreds of people, and U.S. officials ordered two missile strikes in retaliation. One strike was directed at the Zhawar Kili guerrilla camp near Khost, Afghanistan. As we noted in Chapter 1, some critics questioned whether the strike was an effective response. Even so, almost no one questioned whether the base was a legitimate target.[4]

However, the other strike, directed at the same time against the Al Shifa pharmaceutical plant in Khartoum, proved more controversial. U.S. officials claimed the facility produced chemical weapons for the bin Laden network. Sudan protested the attack, claiming that the plant was used only to manufacture medicine. American officials claimed U.S. intelligence had obtained records indicating the facility had been financed in part by bin Laden. The officials also claimed that soil samples collected near the plant contained traces of EMPTA, a suspected precursor chemical for VX, a nerve gas agent. The apparent connection to a known terrorist and the evidence of chemical weapons production, these officials argued, made the plant a legitimate target for a retaliatory strike.[5]

Unfortunately, evidence emerged after the attack suggesting that the plant's terrorist connections were not as clear as U.S. officials claimed. Some critics argued that a more comprehensive reading of the evidence suggested that any role bin Laden played in financing the plant was minor at best. In addition, at least one U.S. national who had worked in Khartoum for many years and who had toured the plant said he saw no evidence of weapons production.[6]

Regardless of the specific merits of the intelligence community's case, the episode illustrates how new intelligence problems make analysis more challenging. During the Cold War, a Defense Intelligence Agency analyst might advise mission planners at the Strategic Air Command to target a nuclear weapon on a building in Prague because emigré reports suggested it might contain machinery useful to Soviet military production. The reliability of the evidence and the analysis was less critical because, short of a third world war, no one would ever know whether the analyst was correct. The only people who needed to be convinced were military planners and defense officials privy to nuclear war planning. As the Sudan episode illustrates, today the same target analyst may find his work subjected to the scrutiny of critics worldwide who will second-guess the evidence and reasoning behind the analysis. Moreover, intelligence no longer simply tells an official where to aim a bomb; it may serve as the key datum that triggers an air strike—a much more demanding role.

ANALYSIS: THE INTELLIGENCE PROBLEM CHANGES

Table 4-1 summarizes some of these changes that have occurred in traditional analytical problems during just the past five or ten years. As can be seen, the new threats often pose problems for intelligence analysts that differ significantly from those they faced during the Cold War. Some of these changes are incremental and would have been expected. For example, analysts must react more quickly and work faster today if they are to keep up with changing events and requirements for information.

Table 4.1: Comparison of Typical Intelligence Analysis Missions in the Cold War and Post-Cold War Periods

	COLD WAR	POST-COLD WAR
Indications and Warning	Intelligence agencies watched for signs that the Soviet Union was executing a plan to mobilize for war. It was expected that this plan was similar to the ones previously observed in Soviet military exercises, so U.S. analysts could anticipate how it would unfold	The ease of acquiring weapons of mass destruction and the potential for information warfare make the "instantly emerging threat" the primary problem. Analysts must think about "imagined potential threats" that will have few or no material signs of warning
Support to Arms Control	Arms control agreements such as SALT and START established specific parameters for compliance, e.g., number and characteristics of weapons. Superpowers were the key (and often only) players. Intelligence analysis focused on monitoring compliance through "national technical means" aimed at "counting and measuring." Uncovering concealment and deception was an important, but secondary mission, because the costs of violating an agreement were assumed to be great	Arms control agreements such as the Nonproliferation Treaty and CW/BW Conventions serve largely as a way to identify cooperative states and to "flush out" noncooperative ones. Compliance is demonstrated through cooperative measures. Would-be violators are likely to use agreements as "cover" or as a vehicle for deception. Intelligence focuses on detecting circumvention and monitoring noncooperative states. Nonstate actors are a major proliferation threat

Political Analysis	Most U.S. adversaries had authoritarian or totalitarian governments. Political analysis focused on succession scenarios, regime stability, and the power of internal security forces	Democratic governments are multiplying. Political analysis must focus on rapidly changing coalitions and popular opinion in friendly, neutral, and hostile states. Civil society institutions may be as important as governments
Economic Analysis	Analysts concentrated on estimating the size of non-market (e.g., Soviet) economies, military industries, and defense production	The new economic analytical challenges include detecting industrial espionage, corrupt or illegal practices in international trade, critical technologies with military applications, and the vulnerability of banks and financial institutions to external shocks

The more interesting development, though, is how many analytical problems require not just a faster methodology, but a different methodology. Different data and different expertise are needed. In many cases; the underlying logic of the problem is different, and, as a result, the nature of the solution is different, too. Consider the following examples.

Providing Indications and Warning

For the U.S. intelligence community, the "I&W" mission is like the first dollar bill a small business might earn and post behind its cash register. Detecting an impending attack by the Soviet Union was the intelligence community's raison d'etre when it was established in the years following World War II. Pearl Harbor was fresh in the minds of U.S. leaders at the time, and the Soviet Union seemed as great a threat as Germany and Japan had just a few years earlier.[7]

Today, however, the indications and warning mission is more complicated and fundamentally different. Detecting an impending military strike remains important, but because we now face a variety of threats, the intelligence community must monitor a variety of plans, strategies, and doctrines. Each must be modeled if U.S. intelligence is to develop a checklist of indicators that will alert us to an attack. The problem is made harder by the fact that many of our current adversaries often lack an explicit military doctrine that can be studied, or formal plans that can be stolen or compromised.

Also, some of the military forces that the United States now faces often break from what we would consider conventional military thinking. This complicates the I&W mission. As a recent director of the Defense Intelligence Agency observed, "Technology, combined with the creative genius of military thinkers around the world, is leading to the development and application of new forms of warfare, and the innovative modification of traditional military practices."[8]

The Yom Kippur War provided a hint of how difficult it can be to warn of an attack when an adversary uses unconventional tactics. U.S. analysts could not understand why Egypt was massing fire fighting equipment along the Suez Canal in the autumn of 1973. They soon had an explanation, when the Egyptian army used the high pressure hoses to breach the sand berms that comprised Israel's Bar-Lev Line. Almost three decades later, many experts agree that U.S. intelligence is still ill-prepared to provide warning of military forces that depart from what we consider "normal" tactics.

As if warning of conventional military attacks and nuclear strikes were not hard enough, today the United States also faces threats such as chemical, biological, and information warfare. Such threats can be developed and deployed very quickly and are easy to hide. As a result, intelligence analysts now find themselves obligated to detect what some have called "imagined potential threats"—a term that might provoke laughter, except that such threats are quite real. Providing this kind of warning has little in common with the traditional task of analyzing a known adversary's military plans, watching its military exercises, and then waiting for the opponent to put the plan into action.

Support to Arms Control
Cold War arms control agreements such as SALT and START were based on measurable parameters—numbers of launchers, the dimen-

sions of missiles, etc. To monitor whether the Soviet Union was complying with the treaty, U.S. intelligence only had to focus on those parameters. For example, SALT 1 limited the number of missile launchers that each side could have. So, the task for the intelligence community was to count Soviet ICBM silos and submarines. Later arms control agreements were more complicated, but the basic problem of monitoring remained the same—counting and measuring.[9] Often arms control agreements simplified the intelligence community's task by restricting weapon deployments to specific geographic zones.

Now arms control has changed. Agreements such as the Nonproliferation Treaty and the Convention on Chemical and Biological Weapons do not limit force levels; rather, they serve as a means to identify cooperative states and to "flush out" noncooperative states. States that agree to these treaties demonstrate compliance through cooperative measures. For example, the International Atomic Energy Commission inspects civilian reactors to make sure fissile material is not being diverted to evade the Nonproliferation Treaty. The main task for intelligence organizations is to monitor "rogue states" that have not accepted controls or that have a reputation for violating agreements.

Alas, rogue states, by definition, do not agree to "play by the rules." As a result, monitoring arms control is harder. The intelligence community cannot simply count weapons in specified geographic zones to verify that a country has complied with a prescribed limit. Rather, intelligence analysts must watch a potentially infinite number of indicators that may appear at an infinite number of locations, often without knowing the specific signal that would warn of a violation. And, to make matters worse, instead of making the monitoring process as transparent as possible, rogue states will use every possible obstacle, subterfuge, diversion, and obfuscation at their disposal. This not only makes data collection harder; it also forces analysts to perform mental acrobatics to sort fact from deception.

Political Analysis

During the Cold War, most U.S. adversaries had authoritarian or totalitarian governments. The intelligence community's political analysts focused mainly on assessing how secure a dictator's hold on power might be, or speculating on succession possibilities and scenarios. Analyzing such a country's foreign policy meant judging how a regime would react to U.S. policies, where "regime" often meant a single person, or at most a small entourage.

There are several authoritarian governments that still concern U.S. leaders (Iraq and North Korea come to mind), but today, policymakers are at least as likely to be interested in free, democratic countries. According to Freedom House's 1996 report, 79 of the world's 191 countries could be classified as "free" (meaning that individuals enjoyed basic civil liberties). This was the highest number since 1972, when the organization began surveying political rights and civil liberties. Freedom House also noted that there were 118 electoral democracies in the world, accounting for 55 percent of the world's population—also a record level.[10]

Freedom and democracy are welcome, of course, but they can complicate life for the intelligence analyst. Political developments in authoritarian states are driven by a relatively small circle of leaders, most of whom usually have similar backgrounds (the oft-cited "operational code" of a Communist Party politburo, for example). Democracies often have more complex internal politics. Even though information is freely available in democracies, their politics can be difficult to follow. Rapidly changing coalitions and shifts in popular opinion can be difficult to predict. Most intelligence analysts—especially those who started their careers during the Cold War—have little experience analyzing democracies. Also, the information sources used to analyze democratic politics (such as public opinion surveys) are quite different from those used to analyze an authoritarian regime (such as emigré reports).

Moreover, free, modern, democratic countries are more likely to have their own peculiar forms of unrest. As states modernize and their people are exposed to new ideas, traditional institutions are apt to break down and new ones emerge. Or, as Vaclav Havel has noted, states undergoing "a mixing and blending of cultures and a plurality or parallelism of intellectual and spiritual worlds" are encountering "periods when all consistent value systems collapse."[11] Such collapse creates the potential for conflict and political instability, but it also creates the potential for new institutions to take root—churches, unions, political action committees, lobbies, trade and professional organizations, and so on. Civil society institutions can be as important as the government. Such institutions can exist in authoritarian regimes and have played an important role as dissenters (for example, the Catholic Church in Poland during the Cold War), but in democracies these institutions emerge freely, and thus enjoy greater legitimacy and influence.

The growing need to monitor democracies raises new issues about the use of traditional intelligence sources and methods. The United States could justify intrusive or clandestine methods to collect information on Cold War dictatorships. The intelligence community often was the only organization with the necessary information and expertise. Also, there was an implicit consensus among U.S. leaders that we could deal differently with officials in dictatorships. To put it bluntly, we were less reluctant to bribe or coerce a generalissimo to recruit him as an intelligence source than we are to bribe or coerce an elected member of parliament. U.S. leaders know that most Americans would view the use of such clandestine methods in a democracy as meddling, a violation of international law, a breaking of trust, impolitic, or just plain dumb.

Indeed, there are risks in even asking intelligence agencies to analyze democracies. No one may be concerned if U.S. officials raise the question of whether Yugoslavia or China will disintegrate. But imagine the reaction if it became known that U.S. officials had asked the CIA to calculate the probability that Quebec would secede from Canada. Imagine further if CIA officers established relationships with the province's separatist leaders, which would be a routine step in monitoring a typical intelligence target. Suppose the CIA officers exchanged information with their Quebecoise counterparts to obtain data. In such an exchange, the CIA might unintentionally provide the separatists with information that could assist them in achieving their objectives. Controversy would be inevitable and understandable.[12] Such risks are especially foolhardy, considering that the benefits of using clandestine intelligence to analyze democracies are slim. There are too many other good sources of information. The exception may be when foreign democratic leaders are themselves engaged in secret activities, such as graft, corruption, or crime.

In addition to fostering an explosion of democracy, the political scene is more fluid in the post-Cold War era. Potential subjects requiring political analysis are growing in number as well as complexity. In the twenty-first century entire countries are likely to arise because of turmoil. Other actors will emerge from long-repressed ethnic and religious strife. Add in extremists, terrorists, organized crime organizations, and private armies, and one is left with a truly complex brew—all of which intelligence analysts must explain and predict, even though most of their education and training was in Cold War-era theories and experiences.

Economic Analysis

Just as democracy is spreading, more and more of the world is operating under free market principles. Kim Holmes and Bryan Johnson of the Heritage Foundation and Melanie Kirkpatrick of the *Wall Street Journal* have compiled an annual index similar to that of Freedom House, but focusing on economic freedom.[13] Their index scores 150 countries in ten areas: trade policy, taxation, government intervention, monetary policy, capital flows and foreign investment, banking policy, wage and price controls, property rights, regulation, and black market activity. Although, according to this index, only about half of all countries (72 of 150) are "mostly free" or "free," the trajectory is clear. The number of countries in these two categories in 1996 was up from 65 the previous year—an increase of 20 percent.

Just as significant, the vast majority of world economic activity takes place in these free market economies. The least productive economies, such as North Korea and most sub-Saharan African countries, tend to be on the bottom part of the list, and the most productive economies, such as those in the Pacific Rim and North America, tend to be on the top. Or, as the familiar Willie Sutton Principle suggests, if you want to analyze world economic activity today, you need to study market economies, because that's where the money is.[14]

Like the growth of democracy, the growth of market economies is a good trend. However, like democracy, market economics presents problems for intelligence. Historical circumstance has made the intelligence community's economic expertise an intellectual oddity, focused largely on issues that are currently unimportant and based on methodologies that are irrelevant or discredited.

Before the collapse of the Soviet Union, the intelligence community's economic analysis concentrated on analyzing non-market economies and their military industries. This was an important problem at the time, because U.S. leaders wanted to know how much of a burden military spending imposed on the Soviet economy, and how much (or whether) the Soviet economy might grow to support the military. Because the Soviet government set prices by fiat, it was difficult to estimate, say, the size of the Soviet Union's gross domestic product or defense budget. Some intelligence analysts devoted their entire careers to developing models for estimating prices in the Soviet economy. The unintended result, though, was that "economic analysis" within the intelligence community mutated into a form that hardly resembled anything one would find in the private sector.[15]

Today almost everyone agrees there are gaps in the U.S. government's ability to track international capital flows and market trends.[16] The question is, do intelligence agencies have any special advantages in providing such information? Even recent DCIs have expressed skepticism about whether the intelligence community needs to get involved in this area. William Webster, for example, believed that the world of international finance and foreign trade was important, but doubted that there was a significant role for the intelligence community to analyze it.[17] There are several indicators that suggest Judge Webster was on the money.

For example, consider whether the intelligence community has the expertise required to analyze international currency markets. George Sorros has earned billions of dollars through his ability to analyze exchange rates a half step ahead of the rest of the world. Do we really expect a civil servant in the bowels of the intelligence bureaucracy to do better, and if so, why is he or she working for the government? Can the U.S. government attract the caliber of analyst that one finds at Goldman Sachs, Credit Suisse/First Boston, Merrill Lynch, or any of the many other investment firms? Can one expect analysts who have spent most of their careers in government to understand the inside workings of large trading companies and financial institutions? The ideal economic intelligence analyst would be someone who has been successful in international finance. Experience is critical. But such experts are unlikely to accept government salaries.

Economic intelligence also poses legal and ethical issues. Many governments have no qualms about collecting information about foreign companies and then providing it to competitors in their own country. Not so the United States. American officials have always shied away from economic espionage against individual firms, foreign or otherwise. The U.S. intelligence community lacks the experience that foreign intelligence services have in economic espionage. But even if the United States were good at collecting such economic intelligence, there would be problems in using it. Suppose intelligence officials decided to collect intelligence to benefit American companies. What constitutes an "American" company? Today even such apparently true-blue U.S. institutions as Brooks Brothers and Dr. Pepper are actually foreign owned (both have British owners). Many others have large foreign stockholders (Space Systems/Loral, one of the largest U.S. satellite manufacturers, for example, has had up to 49 percent of its stock held by European aerospace companies). Is DaimlerChrysler an American company? German? Or is it both? Indeed, in today's era of international stock trading, buyouts, and mergers, the ownership and nationality of a company can change overnight.

Moreover, there is also the problem of figuring out how companies could use secret data without compromising intelligence sources and methods of collection. In many cases, the contribution of intelligence to a new U.S. product would be immediately apparent when it hit the market—especially if competitors recognized company secrets or proprietary information stolen by the intelligence community. (One is reminded of the efforts by Soviet intelligence to steal the designs for the Concorde supersonic transport from Britain and France during the late 1960s. The resulting aircraft, the Tu-144, resembled the original so closely that it came to be called "Concordski." Economic espionage is hard to hide if one plans to sell a product on the open market.)

The fact is, few business leaders use the economic analysis the intelligence community publishes even today. When U.S. firms need information, they do the work in-house, use specialized consultants, or use one of the increasing number of private and corporate intelligence services. That way they can keep the information to themselves. After all, the objective of such intelligence is to gain a competitive edge.

The one area in which intelligence organizations might have a niche is detecting industrial espionage, corrupt or illegal practices in international trade, and critical technologies with military applications. Yet, even these missions require entirely different skills in collection methods and analysis than those the intelligence community has developed over five decades.

New Missions and Requirements for Analysis

In addition to the changes that have taken place in the requirements for analysis in traditional missions, the intelligence community is faced with some requirements for analysis that are almost entirely new. Consider, for example, intelligence analysis related to environmental change.

One new mission PDD-35 identifies for the intelligence community is monitoring environmental developments that might affect political events or the economy.[18] Several developments have drawn the intelligence community into the environmental field. One is the potential for the intelligence community to provide environmental research data that no one else can. For example, if one wants time series data recording snowfall across the Eurasian land mass for the past three decades, the only source may be U.S. satellite imagery of Soviet ICBM silos. The director of central intelligence established a program in 1995 called "MEDEA," under which environmental scientists would have access to this and other intelligence data.[19]

More significantly, though, officials are beginning to appreciate how much environmental developments affect political and economic stability. Haiti is a case in point. After more than a century of environmental mismanagement—bad farming practices, contamination of water sources, and general neglect of conservation—Haiti has reached a state of agricultural failure. It is difficult to grow almost any kind of crop on the Haitian side of Hispaniola. This environmental disaster has had direct political and national security consequences. As Haiti became unable to support its population, thousands of Haitians began to flee the island. The flow of Haitian refugees trying to reach America created a political crisis in the United States. To stop the exodus of boat people, the United States first tried to pressure the military junta responsible for the corruption and mismanagement to step down. When this failed, the United States prepared in October 1994 to invade Haiti. The invasion was averted by last-minute diplomacy by Jimmy Carter, Sam Nunn, and Colin Powell.

The point is, however, that to understand the situation in Haiti fully, an intelligence analyst would have to understand the environmental elements of the equation and make the connection between environmental degradation and political unrest. The same is true in other cases. What appear to be political or military developments often have demographic or social roots. It is impossible, for example, to analyze the political situation in sub-Saharan Africa without understanding the role of AIDS; conflict in the Middle East without understanding the limited sources of fresh water; Russian-Kazakhstan relations without understanding the pollution resulting from space launch activities and nuclear testing; Belarus politics without understanding the impact of Chernobyl; and so on. These issues and the linkages among them will require new analytic methodologies. If the intelligence community does not develop them or is unable to tap them effectively from the outside, it will not be able to respond effectively.

INTELLIGENCE ANALYSIS AND SUPPORT TO MILITARY FORCES

While some critics of U.S. intelligence policy argue that intelligence planning is skewed too much toward supporting military forces, the mission has traditionally been an important one and it has greatly shaped the bureaucratic culture.[20] Many of the CIA's leaders learned the craft of intelligence during their service in the Office of Strategic Services in World War II (including Richard Helms, William Colby, and William Casey).[21] Support to the military has also become more important as military commanders have become more concerned with strategic intelligence (as opposed to tactical intelligence, which has always been a concern).[22] Requirements for providing intelligence support to military forces today have changed greatly. Table

4–2 summarizes some these changes. Some of the more significant trends include:

New Operations and Doctrine

National intelligence support to military forces during most of the Cold War focused primarily on supporting two kinds of operations: nuclear war targeting and conventional forces (the latter mainly in Europe). Today, intelligence organizations must support the U.S. military in a wide variety of scenarios. The information requirements for these new missions and environments are significantly different.

Compare the intelligence required by an armor battalion during the Cold War to the intelligence a special operations team requires today, for instance. The commanders of the armored battalion not only knew where they would be fighting (some designated sector on the Central Front), but often they even knew who the adversary was likely to be (a particular Warsaw Pact unit stationed on the opposite side of the front). Conventional military operations are more predictable, and their forces can be analyzed prior to actual combat.

A Navy SEAL team or Army Ranger unit, on the other hand, can expect to be deployed almost anywhere in the world on short notice. Special operations and low intensity conflict are more varied and more ad hoc. There is a wider variety of potential opponents. Some, such as terrorist groups, can be difficult to analyze, if, in fact, we even know who they are in advance.

Greater Complexity and Variety of Foreign Military Threats

In measuring the capabilities of Cold War era military opponents, intelligence analyses focused on the opponent's "order of battle," or numbers of personnel and weapons. Intelligence analysts can count soldiers, tanks, ships, and aircraft easily, and update their databases incrementally.

Today, the "unit of military capability" varies greatly from case to case, depending on the type of group the United States faces. Compare the Cold War problem of analyzing the Soviet's First Guards Division to the problem of analyzing new threats like the Peruvian *Sendero Luminoso* terrorists, whose organization and capabilities were largely unknown through most of the period when it was active. Not

Table 4.2: Comparison of Cold War and Post-Cold War Requirements For Intelligence Support to Military Forces

	COLD WAR	POST-COLD WAR
Nature of Military Threat	The main component was the Soviet Union, manifested in a nuclear and conventional military threat. Military planners assumed other adversaries were the "lesser included threat"—so if the U.S. could deter the Soviets, it had the capability to deter or defeat most other opponents	The United States potentially faces multiple opponents, employing a variety of strategies over time, including conventional military operations and low intensity threats such as terrorism. Because our adversaries will vary greatly, actions taken to deter one threat may not deter other potential threats. Deterrence may need to be tailored to specific adversaries
Requirements to Support Military Operations	Intelligence organizations planned primarily to provide support to nuclear war targeting and conventional operations in Europe	Intelligence organizations must be prepared to provide support to the U.S. military in a variety of conventional and nonconventional scenarios, including low intensity conflict
Requirements to Estimate the Capabilities of Opponents	Analyses focused on order of battle of conventional forces, which could be readily counted and which changed incrementally	The "unit of capability" varies from case to case and can be difficult to measure, e.g. the capability of one terrorist group versus another

Requirements for Interoperability and Security	Allies were assumed to be members of NATO or other standing organizations, so intelligence planners could confidently plan measures to protect shared intelligence data and ensure the data was compatible with multinational operations	Intelligence planners face difficulty in planning procedures for sharing data because of U.S. forces' need to prepare for varied, unrehearsed scenarios with a fluid set of coalition partners, many of whom will have only transient interests in common with the United States and each other
Requirements for Supporting Data Bases for Weapons Development and Programming	Most opponents employed Soviet weapons, so efforts to analyze signatures could be keyed to a limited set of weapons which evolved incrementally	Opponents are likely to use a variety of weapons, including some homegrown systems and greatly modified Soviet and NATO systems. This greatly increases the difficulty of developing signatures and supporting data bases

only is it easier to analyze conventional military forces; the methodologies used to analyze them are well established, and have been used for many decades. Most methodologies for analyzing unconventional military organizations lack this heritage. As a result, an appropriate measure of capability can be difficult to define, let alone measure.

Greater Variety of Potential Allies

Intelligence planners in the Cold War assumed that if the United States carried out military operations with an ally, the ally would most likely be a member of NATO. At a minimum, it was assumed that U.S. forces would have had experience in working with the ally, most likely as part of a standing organization. This would permit intelligence planners to plan how they would share information necessary for battle, and also how they would protect sensitive sources.

Today, in contrast, intelligence organizations must prepare for a variety of unrehearsed scenarios with a fluid set of coalition partners. U.S. military doctrine currently assumes that U.S. forces will often operate in a changing array of coalitions, with a range of partners varying from situation to situation. So, for instance, now U.S. Army troops may find themselves working with Bangladeshi and Canadian units in a peacekeeping operation in Haiti, while at the same time, U.S. Navy ships could be taking part in a "show of force" in the Persian Gulf with Saudi Arabian units, and U.S. Marines could be working with British and French forces in an evacuation mission in Africa. This greatly complicates the planning process.

Under current plans, the main U.S. contribution to these coalitions could be intelligence. (The "controlling legal authority" is Presidential Decision Directive 25, "U.S. Policy on Reforming Multilateral Peace Operations.")[23] For the intelligence planner, the question is, how do you make sure that the U.S. intelligence systems can "talk" to the Bangladeshi, Canadian, Saudi, British, and French forces? Moreover, how do you determine what information can be shared with the partners; do you give the Bangladeshis the same access to U.S. intelligence as the Canadians? And what about technology? If you tell the French how to interface their weapons systems with U.S. communications links, will they give the information to French electronics manufacturers?

New Requirements for Data Bases

One of the most important trends of the U.S. military in the 1990s is the continuing—indeed, accelerating—growth in the deployment of precision-guided munitions, or smart weapons. Laser-guided bombs were first used by U.S. forces in Vietnam, but only a handful actually made it to the front. Even in Desert Storm, while the public was fascinated with footage of smart bombs falling through the airshafts of Iraqi bunkers, only about 30 percent of all weapons were precision-guided. But just seven years later, in Desert Fox, fully 80 percent of all U.S. weapons used against Iraqi targets were precision-guided munitions.

This trend presents several problems for intelligence. First, of course, the amount of data the intelligence community must collect to support smart munitions increases as the number of weapons increases. In the past, there have often been significant shortfalls and gaps in the data needed to program smart weapons. With the collapse of the Soviet Union and the rise of regional powers, the problem has become even more complicated. Most of the opponents the United States was likely to face during the Cold War used Soviet weapons. Thus, much of the data—especially signatures—that U.S. intelligence collected for Soviet weapons applied to the weapons of other potential opponents, too. Now our likely adversaries use a variety of weapons, including some homegrown systems and some greatly modified Soviet and NATO systems. This greatly increases the difficulty of developing the signatures and other data bases U.S. military forces require.

In addition to collecting signatures, the intelligence community must also now maintain charts and maps to support military missions in a greater variety of regions. And, to make the task even more daunting, all of these data bases need to be updated regularly.

The costs of error can be considerable. Recall, for example, the inadvertent bombing of the Chinese embassy in Belgrade in May 1999 during Operation Allied Force, the intervention by NATO to protect Albanians in Kosovo from Serbian ethnic cleansing. The intelligence community first failed to note that the embassy had moved to a new building, and then mistakenly identified the new embassy building as the Yugoslav Federal Directorate of Supply and Procurement. The bombing resulted in the deaths of three people and created significant complications for the United States and its NATO allies at a sensitive moment. In Germany, Green Party members opposing the operation, using the incident as political fodder, threatened to bring down the coalition government of Gerhard Schröder. The Chinese, meanwhile, used the incident as a pretext to stall U.S. efforts to resolve the crisis through the U.N. Security Council.

Low Intensity Conflict

Low intensity conflict—"LIC"—is defined as operations in which the level of force used lies somewhere between diplomacy and full-scale combat. Examples of LIC include peacekeeping operations, hostage rescue, counterinsurgency operations, counternarcotics operations, and intercepting refugees and other illegal entrants to the United

States. Usually military forces in LIC are tightly integrated with political and intelligence operations.

During the Cold War, the U.S. military and the intelligence community prepared for LIC mainly as part of their preparations for full-scale war with the Soviet Union. The assumption was that LIC was unlikely to occur by itself. More likely it would be part of a larger conflict—for example, managing the flow of refugees headed westward in front of a Soviet attack on Europe. U.S. officials also assumed that LIC was a "lesser included threat," meaning that, if the United States had the capability necessary to deal with the Soviet Union, it would, in the process, acquire the capability to deal with LIC.

In the post-Cold War era, views of LIC have changed. U.S. officials now believe that LIC is much more likely than full-scale war. Often it is a preferred option by both the United States and our adversaries. Thus, in the new view, LIC would most likely occur independently of a conventional military conflict. Moreover, U.S. officials now believe that LIC is qualitatively different from conventional military operations, rather than just a scaled-down version. As a result; LIC presents another set of new problems for intelligence.

For example, consider the problem of civilian casualties. In conventional military operations, civilian casualties are tragic, but they are considered part of the inevitable costs of war. In an LIC operation such as a peacekeeping mission, civilian casualties must be kept to an absolute minimum. Otherwise, the mission would lose the support of the parties to the peacekeeping agreement and the U.S. public. Avoiding civilian casualties increases the burden on intelligence, because military planners need more information about the civilian populations that might be in the line of fire.

The New Analytic Problem

As hard as the traditional military threats were to analyze, the new threats are, step for step, harder. For example, compare the steps in analyzing three different types of threats: a Cold War-style conventional attack on Western Europe; a traditional form of terrorist attack, such as the 1983 bombing of the Marine barracks in Beirut or the attack on the World Trade Center ten years later; and a potential strike today using biological warfare, or "BW." Many experts believe that as medical technology becomes more widely available, even middleweight countries and terrorist groups will be able to mount a significant BW threat.

Traditionally, the process for analyzing a potential strike or an actual attack can be broken down into four generic steps:

- *Detection,* or perceiving the fact that one is under attack. Obviously, if a target does not know it is under attack, it is utterly unable to respond.
- *Localization* is understanding where the attacker is, and where it plans to go; again, before one can respond to an attack, one needs to know where to direct one's forces.
- *Identification* refers to determining who the opponent is, so that one knows how best to respond. Each potential opponent presents its own strengths, weaknesses, and constraints on action. The steps necessary and appropriate for dealing with, say, Libya, would be different than those for dealing with China.
- *Assessment* refers to the steps taken to understand the opponent's strategy, tactics, and vulnerabilities, so that one can counter them most effectively.

Intelligence experts have long understood that usually each of these steps is progressively more difficult. Localization is harder than simple detection, identification of an attack is usually harder than determining where the attacker is, and analyzing the capabilities and vulnerabilities of an attacker is hardest of all. Yet, as Table 4.3 shows, each of these steps is more difficult to perform for new threats than old threats.

In conventional warfare, for example, most of the analytic process is straightforward. The fact that an attack is underway is obvious; look for the smoke and listen for the explosions. Usually the origin and identification of the attacker is apparent, too. Stealth technology and camouflage may make it hard to find the opponent on the battlefield, but it is difficult to conceal who is responsible for a conventional military operation for very long. Moreover, conventional military forces have distinctive insignia and uniforms. Not only do the international rules of war require them; they also usually simplify organization and logistics for conventional forces. Assessing the opponent's strengths and weakness may be difficult, however.

Table 4.3: Comparison of the Analytical Problems for Conventional Warfare, Counterterrorism, and Biological Warfare Threats

	CONVENTIONAL WARFARE	TRADITIONAL TERRORIST STRIKE	BW TERRORIST STRIKE
Detection	NOT HARD	NOT HARD	HARD
Localization	NOT HARD	NOT HARD	HARD
Identification	NOT HARD	HARD	HARD
Analysis	HARD	HARD	HARD

A traditional terrorist threat presents a more difficult challenge for intelligence. Terrorist attacks are easy to detect—again, look for the smoke and fire—but terrorists themselves are not. Terrorists often try to reduce their vulnerability by hiding their identities and their base of operations. In the case of the 1989 bombing of Pan Am Flight 007 over Lockerbie, Scotland, for example, it took more than a year to link the bombing to Libya, and even then the evidence was not airtight. Terrorists may seek publicity when it serves their political objectives, but even in these cases, competing terrorist groups often claim or disavow responsibility for the same strike.

Yet, as difficult as these traditional analytical challenges are, they pale in comparison to the analysis of new threats such as biological warfare. Not only can opponents hide their identity, but they can even hide their actions. Often one of the biggest challenges for analyzing BW is simply understanding there is a threat and that you are under attack. We know from experience that even naturally occurring diseases can be difficult to analyze and trace to a specific cause. It is possible that an adversary would attempt to make a BW attack blend into the background noise, or would use an agent that is especially difficult to diagnose.

Or consider the dynamics of how new-era threats change over time, as illustrated in Table 4.4. One of the difficulties with the emerging international environment is that the characteristics of all threats are inherently harder to detect. The Soviet threat, for example, was paced by a political process—Soviet succession politics, the Five Year Plan, and so on. BW threats, on the other hand, are paced by developments in one of the fastest-changing fields in society—medical research and technology development. Similarly, traditional threats have been, by necessity, organized by large institutions. It may have been hard to penetrate the Soviet political system—especially at the upper echelons—but at least the United States knew it was there. BW can be organized by small groups—a few technically knowledgeable people or even some solitary operators working in a single room. In the process, we lose the traditional intelligence targets—military bases, defense industries, command and control centers—that intelligence has learned to monitor.

Another key difference of BW is that the threat can appear almost instantly. The intelligence community used to learn about the Soviet threat by watching it deploy new forces or carry out military exercises. Conventional war was impossible without an industrial buildup, and mobilization. There was even an annual military parade where

Table 4.4: Comparison of the Potential Rates of Change in Traditional and Biological Warfare Threats

	SOVIET AND MOST OTHER TRADITIONAL THREATS	BIOLOGICAL WARFARE THREATS
Rate of Technology Development and Change	INCREMENTAL—GEARED TO POLITICAL PROCESS	RADICAL—GEARED TO TECHNOLOGICAL INNOVATION
Nature of the Threat Organization	LARGE, INSTITUTIONALIZED	SMALL, AD HOC
Time Required to Generate Threat Force and Plans	DECADES	DAYS
Time Required to Stage Attack	WEEKS	IMMEDIATE

new weapons could be seen and any changes in the political pecking order could be confirmed by photographing who stood next to whom on the reviewing stand. A credible BW capability, on the other hand, can be bought off the shelf from many medical supply houses by an organization whose composition may itself be extremely fluid.

Many of the analytic problems presented by biological warfare also hold for other newly significant threats, such as chemical warfare and information warfare (attacking an opponent's electronic systems, communication, computers, and data bases). As with biological agents, it is possible to manufacture many extremely potent chemical agents in a one-room facility. It is hard to distinguish a chemical weapons plant from facilities used to manufacture pesticides or several other products. In the case of information warfare, the required equipment and techniques are, in fact, identical to those used in business and science. Manufacturing a weapon is simply a matter changing a few lines of code or dialing into a computing center.

A NEW PARADIGM FOR INTELLIGENCE ANALYSIS

The intelligence community thus has to plan now for a future that is hardly self-evident and the contours of which have not yet come into focus. Even the intelligence community's sharpest critics do not doubt that the government will continue to need intelligence. The number and variety of intelligence users have increased as rapidly as the threats to national security. Not only will the intelligence community need regular links to these consumers; the analysis itself will need to be tailored to the requirements of these consumers. This new way of doing business will be hard for intelligence officers without some practical exposure to their new consumers. It would be foolish to think that these new consumers are just like traditional ones. It would be even more foolish to propose that these users become accustomed to intelligence products as they have traditionally been produced. The burden is on the intelligence community to adapt.

A flexible, decentralized intelligence community managed through market-like mechanisms is better suited to the new environment. However, even it will not solve the problem by itself. Intelligence producers will need to become familiar with totally new sources of information—many of which will be unclassified—and will need to develop new ways to determine the validity of such information. In the Cold War, analysts learned how to take the measure of clandestine sources and understand the limitations of technical collection. In the future, analysts will need to understand concepts of scientific validity and the reliability of information from sources such as the Internet, where anyone is free to publish anything.

Doing what is necessary to improve the quality of analysis also poses a new set of challenges for intelligence managers, who will have to encourage analysts to make connections to policymakers and reach judgments based on data sets and sources that are new to intelligence professionals. Today's midlevel managers have no guide to this terrain. Most are probably less able to use and judge the new sources than the analysts they supervise. At present, however, the intelligence culture is inclined to find virtue in sticking to established plans and ways of doing business. Improving analysis will require a major intellectual shift as much as it will require better methods, training, and management.

FIVE
COVERT ACTION IN THE INFORMATION AGE

Nothing brings the intelligence community as close to the making of policy as covert action. The CIA officially defines covert action as "an operation designed to influence governments, events, organizations, or persons in support of foreign policy in a manner that is not necessarily attributable to the sponsoring power." Covert action operations "may include political, economic, propaganda, or paramilitary activities."[1] The use of such operations is an outgrowth of policymakers' need for so-called "quiet" and "middle" options (that is, tools that are more powerful than diplomacy but short of using military forces) to counter dangerous adversaries.

Most intelligence professionals, it seems safe to say, put a higher priority on providing intelligence support than on carrying out covert action, and covert action is actually just a small part of what the CIA does. According to published reports, spending on covert action does not even account for 2–3 percent of the agency's total budget. In fact, when the U.S. intelligence community was established in the early years of the Cold War, most intelligence officials did not even want responsibility for covert action. Roscoe Hillenkoetter, a navy admiral who served as one of the early directors of central intelligence, tried his best to keep the CIA from getting stuck with the covert action portfolio.[2] Lawrence Houston, the CIA's general counsel, told Hillenkoetter that the laws establishing the CIA did not give the agency authority to conduct covert action. Richard Helms, a long-time OSS and CIA official who eventually rose to head the agency, thought covert action actually got in the way of espionage.[3]

It was to no avail. No other agency seemed suited to the task. President Truman did not want covert operations hobbled by the cumbersome (and highly public) budget procedures that most government departments must follow. Secretary of State George Marshall did not want the State Department involved in covert operations that might reflect badly on the country's public diplomatic activities. Military leaders, traditionally wary of unconventional operations of any kind, argued that the armed services were ill suited to carry out covert action.[4]

Meanwhile, the CIA, which was exempt from many budget procedures and already had a network of undercover case officers operating abroad, seemed like an organization that could also conduct covert operations. It also seemed to have a legal basis for doing so. The National Security Act of 1947, which established the CIA, authorized its head, the director of central intelligence, "to perform such other functions and duties related to intelligence affecting the national security as the President or the National Security Council may direct."[5] The fit between the CIA and covert operations was irresistible. So the CIA got the job, and ever since it has been hard to talk about intelligence policy and intelligence reform without including a discussion of covert action.

There are other reasons to discuss covert action and intelligence in tandem. Covert action has historically had an influence on the intelligence community's culture far beyond what mere budget and staffing levels might suggest. Furthermore, the congressional committees responsible for overseeing the intelligence community are also responsible for overseeing covert action, and this further reinforces the connection. And covert action has often been controversial. Operations gone awry like the Bay of Pigs and Iran-Contra have had ripple effects far beyond the intelligence community. Covert action has had an outsized influence on U.S. policy toward certain countries (Cuba, for example) and even entire regions (such as the Levant). All of this makes covert action impossible to ignore in a study of the future of U.S. intelligence.

Like intelligence collection and analysis, covert action at the end of the twentieth century faces a fundamentally new set of conditions. Many of these conditions are a result of the Information Revolution. Even so, most discussions of U.S. policy for covert action are stuck in Cold War language. Covert action must change for the Information Age if the United States is to keep the covert action option.

WHAT IS COVERT ACTION?

U.S. foreign policy officials such as Marshall and George Kennan argued in favor of covert action in the early years of the Cold War because they wanted a "middle option." Relying only on diplomatic pressure against an uncooperative, hostile power like the Soviet Union seemed ineffective. On the other hand, military action seemed too risky, especially when the Soviets had overwhelming forces in Europe and, after 1949, the atomic bomb. Covert action seemed like a prudent alternative.[6] The thinking of U.S. leaders was also shaped by their experience in World War II. The CIA's predecessor, the OSS, ran commando raids and psychological operations during the war. There were skeptics, but many U.S. leaders thought the OSS had been effective.[7] After the war, moreover, the Soviet Union began its own covert operations. A Soviet-sponsored coup overthrew the democratic government of Czechoslovakia, and it was clear that communist parties in Central European countries were receiving covert assistance from the Soviet government. If the Soviets were doing this, some officials believed, the United States needed similar capabilities to counter them.

Unfortunately, the term "covert action" has become synonymous with the operations that have been carried out covertly. As a result, many public officials and people who write about covert action—even those who argue most passionately in support of retaining the option—do not seem to understand what covert action really is and what makes it unique.[8] This is why so many policy debates about covert action often miss the most important issues.

Simply put, covert operations are *activities in which the United States conceals its responsibility*. Because so many officials, pundits, and scholars miss this point, they never address the single most important issue that follows from this definition: When should an action be conducted covertly? That is, *when should the United States hide its responsibility?* Some people who think that the United States must be able to carry out paramilitary operations, propaganda, political action, and similar activities argue that we need covert action. What they really mean is that the United States simply needs the capability to carry out paramilitary operations, propaganda, political action, and similar activities. It is true that these kinds of operations have been carried out as covert action in the past. However, these operations do not define covert action because such activities do not necessarily need to be covert. Indeed, almost all activities that have been carried out as covert action in the past have also been carried out overtly in other situations. Consider a few examples.[9]

Paramilitary Operations
In the early 1960s, the CIA supported the anticommunist Hmong resistance against the procommunist Pathet Lao regime in Laos. The CIA did not acknowledge its role because the United States and the Soviet Union had agreed to allow Laos to remain neutral (the Soviets violated Laotian neutrality, too).[10] In contrast, in the 1980s the United States provided off-and-on overt support to the Nicaraguan contras.[11] Also, CIA assistance to the Afghanistan *mujahideen* during the 1980s, although formally covert, was actually an open secret.[12]

Propaganda
In the early years of the Cold War, Radio Free Europe and Radio Liberty broadcast news, entertainment, and propaganda to stir dissent in Eastern Europe.[13] Both were operated covertly by the CIA. During the same period, Voice of America—openly sponsored by the U.S. government—also broadcast a pro-American message to foreign audiences.

Political and Economic Influence Operations
The CIA provided covert financial assistance to the Christian Democratic Party in the 1948 Italian national election to help it defeat the Communist Party. In the 1970s, the CIA covertly subsidized Chilean labor unions as part of its effort to undermine the Marxist regime of Salvador Allende.[14] On the other hand, in the 1980s, the U.S. government openly encouraged U.S. labor unions and other nonprofit organizations to support the anticommunist Solidarity labor union in Poland. The National Endowment for Democracy, which is funded by the U.S. government, continues today to provide assistance to prodemocracy organizations abroad.

Assassination
The United States has carried out several operations in peacetime which, if successful, would have resulted in the death of a hostile foreign leader. Some were covert, as when the CIA tried to kill Fidel

Castro in the 1960s, using Mafia figures to provide a cutout.[15] Other operations were overt. In 1963, there was little that was either secret or deniable about the role of the CIA in Vietnam and in supporting the coup leaders and their plan to assassinate Ngo Dinh Diem.[16] In 1986, the United States carried out an air strike against Libya in retaliation for a terrorist attack the Libyan government had sponsored against U.S. military personnel in Germany. The aircraft specifically targeted the tent in which Muammar Quaddafi was known to sleep. The F-111s that targeted the tent carried the insignia of the U.S. Air Force, and the United States made sure that the operation—and U.S. responsibility—received as much attention as possible.

Coups

In 1954, the CIA covertly supported a coup against the government of Guatemala, which U.S. leaders feared might offer the Soviet Union influence in Central America.[17] In 1953, the CIA covertly fomented public demonstrations against the Mosadeq regime in Iran to assist the Shah to reclaim his throne.[18] On the other hand, in 1986 the United States openly supported Corazon Aquino's "People Power" demonstrations against the regime of Ferdinand Marcos. U.S. military aircraft based at nearby Clark Field flew over the demonstrations to deter Marcos from using military forces to quash the demonstrations.

In each instance, the United States carried out a similar kind of operation. Sometimes the government acted covertly. Sometimes it acted overtly. Many people might question whether the United States should support coups, meddle in foreign elections, or kill foreign leaders. Others might argue in favor of one or more of these actions, depending on the situation. (The classic example: "Should we have tried to assassinate Castro? How about Pol Pot? Hitler?") However, the nature of these activities is a separate issue from whether or not the United States should carry them out covertly.

Deniability raises at least three issues. First, when is deniability essential for the success of an operation? Second, when is deniability plausible and effective? Third, what are the implications of deniable policies for a democratic government?

Why Deniability?

Why does an operation need to be deniable? Officials—including many we interviewed for this book who were skeptical about the effectiveness or morality of covert action—find covertness attractive in direct proportion to the level of difficulty and controversy of the problem at hand. Covert action allows officials to avoid having to explain the policy to the general public. It requires less time convincing allies to support U.S. policy. And covert action requires less review by Congress. During the early 1980s, William Casey had exactly this rationale in mind when he called covert action the "cornerstone" of a proactive U.S. policy to line up governments in the developing world to support U.S. policies and interests.[19]

In reality, running an operation covertly may offer flexibility, but it also adds complexity, costs, and risks. If a covert operation is exposed, there is always a cost when other governments, Congress, and the public find out they were left out of the loop. They may say they approve of the operation after the fact, but anyone who was misled or not informed—whether they admit it or not—will trust the United States less. Sometimes the benefits of a covert operation outweigh this loss of trust. No one, however, should fool themselves into thinking that this cost is zero. It never is.

There are also other costs. As we have seen, intelligence operations in the Information Age should benefit more from the ability to use fluid, networked organizations. Networks allow people to exchange ideas and information more easily. This increases creativity and improves the opportunity for innovation. The new organizations are better at drawing on new talent as needed, too. But planning an operation so that it is covert has the opposite effect. By its very nature, covert action limits the number of people and organizations who are able to know that it is being planned and participate in a sanity check.

There are two legitimate reasons for carrying out an operation covertly rather than overtly. One is when open knowledge of U.S. responsibility would make an operation infeasible. For example, if Italian voters knew that the CIA was financing the Christian Democratic Party in 1948, the Communists would have painted the Christian Democrats as U.S. lackeys. U.S. support would have backfired. Indeed, even many years later, the operation created a major flap in Italy when U.S. officials disclosed it. Similarly, the CIA has sometimes paid foreign government officials to act in way that would benefit American interests. If their governments knew this, the officials would be fired, imprisoned, or executed. Foreign leaders known to receive money from the United States are frequently the targets of coup attempts as well as popular revolts.

The other reason for carrying out an operation covertly is implicit, but just as important: to avoid retaliation or control escalation. In some cases covertness is no more than a fig leaf, but a useful fig leaf. In the late 1940s, for example, the Soviet government knew the CIA was supporting resistance fighters in the Ukraine. Soviet intelligence had penetrated most of the groups. Similarly, the Soviet leadership knew that the United States was supporting the Afghan *mujahideen* in the 1980s. If U.S. leaders had admitted responsibility, Soviet leaders would have been compelled to retaliate, perhaps with military action. Also, the Soviet Union could have created complications for the United States. In the case of the CIA program in Afghanistan, Pakistan provided a base for the operation and Arab countries such as Egypt and Saudi Arabia assisted in the supply of arms and materiel. All of these countries wanted to avoid a direct confrontation with the Soviet Union.

Because the United States did not openly admit responsibility, Soviet leaders had breathing space, or at least thought they did. In the case of the Ukrainian operation, the Soviets worked steadily to roll up the resistance groups. They eventually succeeded. Soviet leaders believed that they would similarly succeed in defeating the Afghan *mujahideen.* In that case, of course, the Soviets were wrong. In both cases, though, official deniability by the United States averted Soviet retaliation, which could have been catastrophic.

The goal of averting retaliation is an important point to keep in mind when deciding whether or not to carry out a covert action. If covertness will not avert retaliation, much of the rationale for covertness disappears.

Deniability and Accountability

The most important problems that covert action presents have to do with accountability and participation. How can one carry out covert action and still ensure that officials will be held responsible for their decisions? Similarly, how does one include an adequate number of officials in decisions to carry out covert action and still maintain deniability? It is true that some activities undertaken as "covert action" have been highly controversial: assassination attempts, attempts to influence democratic elections abroad, and support of corrupt dictators come to mind. However, most of these would be controversial even if they were carried out overtly. In other words, it was not the covertness of covert action that was the problem; it was the action.

In the early days of the Cold War, "plausible deniability" of the U.S. role in covert action meant exactly that. The whole idea was to avoid linking the president, top leaders, and the U.S. government to an operation. However, when some of the CIA's covert operations became known in the mid-1970s, critics of the intelligence community were concerned that obscuring these links often made it difficult to hold U.S. leaders responsible for their decisions. Some of these critics also believed that plausible deniability encouraged CIA officers to think they could do what they wanted, entirely independently of American values and overt foreign policy.[20]

Such critics, especially in Congress, began to insist on control measures. First, they wanted the president to accept formal (albeit secret) responsibility for any activity that the United States would publicly disavow. Second, they wanted the president to inform Congress that he had authorized such an operation.

Congress imposed these requirements in the 1974 Hughes-Ryan Amendment. Hughes-Ryan required the president to affirm that a covert action was required in a specific situation through a formal, documented "finding." These provisions were later incorporated into the Intelligence Oversight Act of 1980, and then the Intelligence Oversight Act of 1991, the current statute under which Congress monitors the intelligence community. The 1980 act reduced the number of legislators the president was required to notify to just the members of the House Permanent Select Committee on Intelligence and the Senate Select Committee on Intelligence. The committees cannot veto a covert action, but they can vote to withhold funding.[21]

Many hard-line critics of the CIA and covert action claim these procedures inevitably short-circuit or shortchange the democratic process.[22] Yet limiting covert action oversight to a select group of officials really is not that different from many other government procedures. The fact is, there are numerous features in the U.S. political process that limit the number of people who can take part in a decision, know about an activity, or both.[23]

Consider all of the restrictions that limit political participation in the American democratic system. The most restrictive, of course, is simply the institution of representative government. In the American system, elected legislators, rather than individuals, pass most laws. The power of political parties and the primary system restrict participation in elections. In the legislative bodies themselves there are further restrictions. In the House of Representatives, for example, the Rules Committee can prohibit amendments on a bill going to the floor for debate, so that only the members of the committee reporting a bill have the opportunity to modify it. This particular restriction is not much different from the exclusive jurisdiction members of the intelligence committees have in passing the authorization for covert action. The process fails only when those responsible for reviewing covert action do not take the time to study the issues involved and ask hard questions when a proposed operation would put the national interest is put at risk or seriously conflict with American values and laws.

Similarly, the U.S. political process, allows for many restrictions on the release of information to the general public. For example, there are shield laws that protect the identities of certain witnesses or defendants in court proceedings. For that matter, all of the proceedings of grand juries are supposed to be secret. Government agencies are required to protect proprietary information when they review contract proposals. And, although the entire Congress votes on defense authorization and appropriation bills, usually only the committee members responsible for overseeing the Defense Department have complete access to detailed information about classified weapons systems. In some case, opportunities to participate in the democratic process of making decisions is restricted in order to prevent it from becoming unwieldy. In other cases, information is withheld in order to protect individual rights, commerce, or national security. Most people are willing to accept some compromises in democracy in order to make the system work.

There is a fine line between practicality and principle. One cannot limit participation so much that the government does not respond to

public opinion, and secrecy should not allow officials to duck responsibility for their decisions. The more important point to understand,
however, is that the issues involved in balancing the need for secrecy
with democratic governance are not unique to covert action. Rather,
they are all part of a general problem that often arises in democratic
governments. Any solution is a compromise. The main issues in rec-
onciling covert action, public deniability, and democracy seem to be:

- Whether officials are, at some point, held accountable for their decisions—
  if not for specific actions, then for general policy;
- Whether the limited group of officials who oversee covert action is representative of the general public;
- Whether there is sufficient rotation among these officials (in both the
  Congress and the executive branch) such that covert action policies are
  not, in effect, decided by static, elite group; and
- Whether the process ensures accountability in time for extreme abuses or
  foolish policies to be reexamined before something really bad happens.

Although the general public often seems unaware of how much
opportunity Congress has to review covert action, the current oversight process seems to meet these "best practices" of democratic governance—at least, it does on paper. Currently the legal underpinnings
for oversight have some deep flaws, and Congress itself must accept
much of the blame. It botched the issue in the Iran-Contra affair and
never completely recovered.[24]

Most Americans recall the basics of the Iran-Contra fiasco and the
controversy that followed: In late 1985, Director of Central Intelligence
William Casey and other CIA and National Security Council officials
developed a plan to trade weapons for U.S. hostages held by Iranian-
backed terrorists in Lebanon. President Reagan and his advisors decided not to tell Congress about the plan, arguing that the operation
was too sensitive to share. Critics later claimed that the officials knew
that Congress and the American public would object to what was, in
effect, paying ransom to Iran, and did not want to face the criticism.
In either case, no one informed Congress about the plan.

The operation careened along until November 1986, when a Beirut
newspaper disclosed the arms-for-hostages plan. Members of Con-

gress realized they had not been told about an operation involving the CIA. The result was predictable. The House and Senate intelligence oversight committees organized hearings. Members of Congress were already wary because they did not believe Casey kept them adequately informed. Then White House officials discovered documents suggesting that National Security Council staffers planned to use some of the receipts from the Iranian arms sale to buy weapons for the Contras, the U.S.-backed guerrillas fighting the leftist Sandinista regime in Nicaragua. (CIA support to the Contras had been a controversial issue throughout the Reagan administration, and Congress had periodically imposed various bans on U.S. assistance.) Attorney General Edwin Meese requested the appointment of an independent counsel to look into whether anyone had violated the law. The resulting investigation went on for almost seven years.[25]

Meanwhile, the House and Senate appointed a joint committee to investigate. But instead of exposing the project as the harebrained lunacy it was, the proceedings had exactly the opposite effect. The hearings were televised. Marine Lieutenant Colonel Oliver North, the NSC staffer most identified with the operation, successfully portrayed himself as a take-charge leader, unfairly prosecuted by powerful members of Congress who had no business inquiring into covert activities. Most observers agreed that the hearings were a public relations disaster for Congress. Even worse, the convictions of North and others for having misled Congress were later overturned, after the courts ruled that the joint committee had violated North's civil rights when it compelled him to testify.

After the joint committee finished its hearings, the House Permanent Select Committee on Intelligence and the Senate Select Committee on Intelligence tried to draft new legislation that would prevent future administrations from hiding covert action from Congress. Unfortunately, the committees allowed themselves to get sidetracked. The key issue was whether the president needed to notify Congress, and whom in Congress he needed to notify. Instead, the committees became preoccupied with a secondary and spurious issue: how long and under what conditions could the president delay notification?

When administration officials had decided not to notify Congress about the arms-for-hostages deal, Casey had asked the CIA's general counsel, Stanley Sporkin (today a federal judge), to provide a rationale. Sporkin dug up a provision in the Intelligence Oversight Act that said the president could defer notification when there was not enough time to consult with Congress. The provision was originally intended to allow the president to act in fast-breaking, urgent situations. It was never intended to be used as a means to protect especially sensitive operations. This was clear because the Intelligence Oversight Act had a specific mechanism for dealing with such situations. It allowed the president to limit notification to just eight legislators when he believed an operation was so delicate that informing the thirty-odd members of the two oversight committees was too risky. The so-called "Gang of Eight" consisted of the party leaders of each house and the chairmen and vice-chairmen of the committees.

Until Iran-Contra, no one had ever presumed that the president could delay notifying Congress because a covert action was too sensitive. The House and Senate committees should have simply told the administration that its loophole was bogus. Instead, they bought Sporkin's basic argument, and began bargaining with the White House over the details. Most of the resulting arcane argument—by this time the public had lost interest—dwelt on exactly how long the president could defer notification, or whether Congress could even pin him to a specific deadline. The committees included a forty-eight-hour limit on defering notification in the 1991 intelligence authorization bill.[26] The new administration—George Bush entered office in 1989—vetoed the bill. Congress backed down. It settled for an informal assurance in which the president promised to notify Congress of covert actions in advance in all but the most extraordinary cases, and never more than two days after the operation. The net result was that Congress conceded that the president was not obliged to use the "Gang of Eight" mechanism and also failed to get the president to agree that there was a statutory limit to the amount of time he could defer notification.

The Iran-Contra affair, in effect, gutted the legal basis for an effective oversight process. As long as Congress and the intelligence community remain on good terms and agree on most policy issues, this may not be an issue. The train wreck will occur when the executive and the legislative branches are at odds with each other—exactly the kind of situation laws are needed to resolve.*

Covert Action and Strategy

Despite the preoccupation with prior notification and countdown clocks arising in the wake of the Iran-Contra affair, the most significant problem in recent covert action failures has not been accountability and control. A greater problem has been bad strategic thinking.

There is a memorable *New Yorker* cartoon in which two scientists are standing in front of a blackboard. The left third of the blackboard is covered with complicated equations and formulas. The right third is filled with similar hieroglyphics. The middle third of the blackboard contains a giant arrow running left to right, explaining the process with the annotation, "THEN A MIRACLE OCCURS." One scientist is saying to the other, "I have some reservations about your methodology." Some recent covert operations suggest, unfortunately, that U.S. officials have been using a similar methodology to plan covert action. They seem to see covert action as a quick fix that magically solves problems when all else fails. In reality, covert action works like other foreign policy activities. Poorly conceived covert operations usually fail. Few covert operations have succeeded that were not based on a clear set of objectives, an accurate understanding of

---

* It is interesting to note that, although the Iran-Contra controversy focused on when and how Congress should be informed about covert action, the arms-for-hostages deal was itself not a covert operation at all. There was no deniability of the U.S. role. The Iranians knew that they were negotiating with the United States, and the Americans participating in the operation did not try to conceal the fact that they were U.S. officials. The operation was really a secret diplomatic initiative, which does not require Congressional notification. The main legal reason Congress should have been notified about the Iranian side of the operation was that the CIA used some of its personnel, aircraft, and communications systems to support the activity.

The diverting of money from the weapons sales to Iran—there was always some question about how much actually made it to the Contras—was likely a violation of law. But even this was more a question of whether someone had circumvented Congressional restrictions on foreign assistance than whether they had failed to provide timely notification of a covert operation.

the prevailing conditions, and sound logic on how the proposed operation was supposed to obtain its goals.

For example, consider the CIA's covert operations in Iraq from 1992 to 1996.[27] The objective was to eliminate Iraq's Saddam Hussein as a threat to the United States and our allies. The operations were to accomplish this either by encouraging a military coup or by reducing Saddam's power by supporting a separetist movement of Kurds living in northern Iraq.

There are about twenty-six million Kurds. Most live in 230,000-square-mile region that overlaps Turkey, Iraq, Iran, and small parts of Syria and Armenia—a population about equal to that of Canada, living in an area about equal to that of France. Until World War I, the Kurds were one of the many peoples who lived under the Ottoman Empire.[28] After the war, the Allies split up the empires controlled by Russia, Germany, Turkey, and Austria-Hungary. In the Middle East, the peace agreements drew national boundaries that divided some ethnic groups. The Kurds were left as minorities distributed among several countries. Even so, the Kurds have kept their own language and culture, and many Kurdish leaders still seek nationhood. Naturally, Turkey, Iraq, and Iran have all resisted. An independent Kurdistan would come at the cost of their territorial integrity, and might even threaten the viability of their own countries. Half of all Turks are Kurds; one quarter of Iraq's population are Kurds.

As a result, since World War II, Kurds have often been caught in the crossfire of great power politics and regional rivalries. In the early 1970s, the long-simmering rivalry between Iran and Iraq was heating up. Some Iraqi Kurd resistance groups allied themselves with Iran (then ruled by the Shah) and the United States, hoping to carve out a territory for themselves. Unfortunately for the Kurds, Iran and Iraq agreed in 1973 to bury their conflict in a peace treaty. Iran and the United States abandoned the Iraqi Kurds, who were promptly crushed by Saddam. Ten years later, the Kurds lost out again. When Iraq invaded Iran in 1982, many Kurds supported the new Islamic government in Iran. (Although the Iranian fundamentalists are Shiite Muslims, Kurdish Muslims are almost all Sunnis; this was an alliance of convenience.) Iraq responded by attacking Kurdish towns with poison gas.

Then, at the end of Desert Storm in January 1991, the Iraqi Kurds tried again. With most of Iraq's armies defeated and in disarray, Saddam's hold on power seemed to be weakening. Kurds revolted and tried to establish a separate state in northern Iraq. The Iraqi army was not completely destroyed, however, and the remaining forces quashed the rebellion. Kurds fled their cities for the mountains. When the media began to report a potential refugee disaster, the United Nations reacted by imposing a "no fly zone" in the northern third of Iraq and provided food and supplies to the Kurds. As a result, the Kurds enjoyed increasing autonomy from 1992 to 1995.

This is when the United States began its covert effort to eliminate Saddam. The initial program began under the Bush administration. At the time, U.S. officials did not have a sense of urgency because they believed Saddam was weak and that his opponents would succeed in removing him. Press reports suggest that this plan was gradually expanded after Bill Clinton took office. The strategy was to create an environment in which Saddam would be isolated, marginalized, and weakened by increasing the autonomy the Kurds exercised in the U.N.-protected areas. According to CIA officers quoted in the press, the operation changed during the 1995–1996 period. These sources claimed that President Clinton signed an order in early 1996 to provide arms and other assistance to Iraqi groups seeking to overthrow Saddam. Other sources report that some members of Congress also wanted the CIA to take stronger action to remove Saddam.[29]

The anti-Saddam alliance that reportedly received CIA support in the mid-1990s was characterized as a "patchwork" of various anti-Saddam groups, including Iraqi political and military officials living in exile, separatist movements, and members of the Iraqi military opposed to Saddam (or at least willing to plot against him).[30] Two rival Kurdish nationalist groups were also members: the Kurdistan Democratic Party (KDP) and the Patriotic Union of Kurdistan (PUK).[31] The plan began to unravel in June 1996, when Saddam moved against the military officials plotting against him. The cabal had been penetrated early on, and was quickly rolled up. Then in August, Masoud Barzani, the leader of the KDP, turned against the PUK. In effect, he dumped his partners and made an alliance with Saddam. Barzani invited the Iraqi government to send its forces into the Kurdish region.

The CIA operation was routed. Iraqi authorities captured agents who had been working for the CIA, as well as computers and communications equipment that the United States had supplied them.

Most Americans did not pay close attention to the operation or its collapse. The failure was mainly drowned out in the press by the 1996 presidential elections. Few Americans were directly involved, and there was little television footage available, so most of the media quickly moved on to new topics. But make no mistake—the Iraq operation was a disaster. More than one hundred Iraqi dissidents and military officers cooperating with the United States were executed when the Iraqi forces rolled up the operation.[32] Saddam also gained information on U.S. intelligence tradecraft and the organization of his opposition. U.S. credibility with our coalition partners, necessary for containing Saddam, suffered. Most importantly, the Iraq operation suggests how poorly U.S. officials appear to understand the problems entailed in covert action and how to use covert action effectively. The U.S. covert program in Kurdistan, especially in its latter stages, was a classic example of bad strategy and bad policy. In fact, it is hard to think of how a program could have been conceived more poorly. It failed on at least three different counts.

Failure #1: Poor Strategic Concept

The ostensible objective of the program was to remove Saddam or, as one former CIA official described it, reduce him to "the mayor of Baghdad." Iraq seemed weak following its defeat in Desert Storm. Its military was crippled. It was occupied by U.N. forces assigned to monitor the dismantlement of its weapons of mass destruction. No-fly zones prevented the Iraqi Air Force from operating in much of the air space of its own country. Kurdish nationalism was strong. Yet despite all of this, in reality the dynamics of the situation favored Saddam.

The United States was inherently limited in the amount of support it could provide the Kurds. There are few locales more distant from the United States. Kurdistan itself is mainly surrounded by Iran and Iraq—sworn enemies of the United States. The only direct access is through Turkey, which, as we shall see momentarily, presents its own problems. The coalition that had liberated Kuwait five years earlier had frayed badly. It had been difficult even to maintain support for continuing U.N. economic sanctions against Iraq.

Meanwhile, the Kurds were known to be badly split. The alliance between the KDP and PUK had always been a marriage of convenience (or, according to some, a shotgun wedding engineered by the United States). It was only a matter of time before they would be at odds with each other over one issue or another. What is more, because the two Kurdish factions were rivals, each was susceptible to an offer that would allow it to prevail over its ostensible partner. The only question was, when would the opportunity appear, and what would be the price.

These facts ensured that Iraq would have the dominant position as events unfolded. As each opportunity presented itself, Iraq could ratchet the two factions apart. Critics claim that the United States, with just a little more money—some said $2 million—could have held the Kurdish resistance together in the summer of 1996.[33] Maybe; maybe not. But even if the CIA had forestalled this split, Saddam could have waited for another opportunity to peel off one of the factions, which undoubtedly would have arisen.

Failure #2: Geopolitical Simplemindedness

Never mind that the Iraq program was bound to fail. Even if it had succeeded, it would have been counter to U.S. interests in the region.

The plan to increase the autonomy of the Kurds, leading to a de facto Kurdish state, was inconsistent with broader, overt U.S. policy. One of our most important allies in the region is Turkey. Despite many disagreements over human rights and control of Cyprus, every post-World War II U.S. administration has tried to maintain good relations with Turkey because of its strategic importance. Though it has a mainly Muslim population, Turkey has supported secular government since the time of Attaturk. Turkey also borders Europe, and controls the passage between the Black Sea and the Mediterranean. Turkey would never agree to an independent Kurdish state along its borders—formal or informal. So it was not tenable for the United States to support a separate Kurdistan. If the program had reached its goals, the split between covert and overt policy would have become more and more apparent.

Moreover, if the covert operation had succeeded, its net result would have been a weak Iraq. Most experts agree that Iran, not Iraq, is the more significant potential threat in the region. One reason the objectives of Desert Storm were limited to liberating Kuwait was that U.S. leaders believed we needed a viable Iraq to counterbalance Iran. If we had turned Saddam into the "mayor of Baghdad," we would have created a power vacuum in the region. Dealing with Iran would have been more difficult than ever.

How weak might have Iraq become following a successful covert operation to destabilize Saddam's hold on power? Recall Afghanistan, where the CIA supported the *mujahideen* for almost a decade. Witness the moonscape that currently passes for Kabul, and you will see that even "successful" covert actions of this magnitude are impossible to plan with precision, and often end as horrible, bloody affairs.

The goal of the Afghan operation was, implicitly, to bleed the Soviets, and it worked. One might argue that the operation was worthwhile, however tragic for the Afghans, because it contributed to the end of the Cold War. Not so in Iraq, where chaos would have only created an opportunity for a more aggressive Iran. The Afghan experience is an important lesson for anyone who thinks that covert action had a chance to "liberate" Iraq, or replace a repressive government with a better one.

Failure #3: Deniability Never Made Sense
The United States was never able to keep the Iraq operation deniable. The program was thoroughly compromised early on. Kurdish leaders talked freely to the press.

Indeed, it is not even clear why deniability was necessary. The objective of the Iraq operation was to eliminate Saddam. U.S. officials acknowledged that there was a good probability that Saddam would be killed.[34] The United States had strong grounds for such an operation. Iraq reportedly had tried to assassinate former president George Bush when he visited Kuwait in 1993. Iraq has also continued to develop weapons of mass destruction and supported terrorism. The United States had at least as much justification for taking overt action against Saddam Hussein as it had for taking action against Muammar Quaddafi in 1986.

In the case of programs such as the assistance to the *mujahideen* in Afghanistan, the United States kept its role covert to avoid alienating some of our allies in the region and to avoid providing the Soviet Union a pretext for taking action against us and our partners. (As it was, the Soviets did react to the Afghan program by trying to destabilize U.S. allies such as Pakistan, which was assisting us in the operation.) Also, if U.S. support of the Afghan resistance had been overt, the Soviets would have had justification for diplomatic retaliation, such as refusing to cooperate on arms control.

In the case of the Iraq operation, deniability was not effective in precluding retaliation because Saddam was determined to take action against the United States in any event. The Iraqi government was inevitably going to carry out terrorism, develop weapons of mass destruction, and try to intimidate its neighbors in the region. It did not matter whether Iraq had firm evidence of U.S. involvement in a coup. So why did the operation against Saddam need to be deniable?

For that matter, why was such a poorly conceived plan able to proceed? Some critics of the policy claim that politics played a part; they say administration officials wanted to get rid of Saddam before the 1996 presidential election. These claims are difficult to prove. However, one thing seems clear: There was no one in the chain of approving the operation—especially in 1995–1996—who had the experience, stature, or inclination to recognize a misguided policy, alert colleagues, and kill the program.

It is ironic. Iran-Contra was a half-baked scheme that captured America's attention for almost a year and dominated discussions of U.S. intelligence policy for several years after that. Yet it ultimately had little effect on U.S.-Iranian relations, the balance of power in the Persian Gulf, or, for that matter, the outcome of events in Nicaragua. In contrast, the program to support the Kurds resulted in a hundred or more deaths, undercut U.S. credibility in a critical region, and cost over $100 million. Yet, apparently, no one responsible for the program has ever had to account for the consequences of this ill-conceived plan.*

---

* There was an odd and disconcerting epilogue to the Kurdish operation. Some of the Kurds evacuated by the United States when the operation collapsed were later alleged to be national security risks by the Immigration and

COVERT ACTION IN THE INFORMATION AGE

The recent lapses in U.S. covert action are even more troubling because covert action is in the process of becoming even more complex than before. Just as many experts are beginning to agree that old-style covert activities are no longer effective, a new form of covert action has emerged and needs to be addressed.

During the mid-1990s a new buzzword entered national security conversations: "information warfare." Information warfare, or, in the inevitable abbreviation of the national community, "IW," refers to attacks on an adversary's information systems or the use of information as a weapon.

Governments and their armies have always tried to use information to their advantage. Almost as soon as someone learned how to send messages by smoke signals, his opponent probably began to send bogus signals from a nearby hill to mislead him. The difference today is that the Information Revolution has made such measures much more important. Now it is often more effective to attack an opponent's sensors, communications links, computers, and data bases than it is to destroy its tanks, aircraft, and naval vessels.

Also, the dependence of modern societies on information systems has given a new twist to both strategic warfare and limited war. Often the best way to defeat an opponent is to attack its civilian information infrastructure—that is, its telephone system, television and radio stations, financial data systems, and the control centers that operate transportation systems and utilities. These civilian systems are likely to be protected less effectively than military systems, making them more vulnerable to attack.

Defense and intelligence specialists are concerned about the possibility that our adversaries may use IW against the United States, and they use a succinct topology to describe the potential threats: denial,

---

Naturalization Service. The INS wanted to return the Kurds to Iraq. This, of course, was the equivalent of a death sentence. U.S. intelligence was apparently unable or unwilling to extricate the Kurds from their legal morass. The Kurds could not hire legal counsel because the INS claimed there were no lawyers cleared to know about the operation and the intelligence information related to it. Eventually James Woolsey, former director of central intelligence and a lawyer, offered to represent the Kurds. See R. James Woolsey, "Iraqi Dissidents Railroaded—by U.S." *Wall Street Journal,* June 10, 1998.

deception, destruction, and exploitation. Our adversaries could find it easier, less expensive, and less risky to attack information systems within the United States rather than, say, to try to carry out sabotage, assassination, hijacking, or hostage-taking. This could make IW their strategy of choice. In effect, the IW threat is really the dark side of the Information Age. The vulnerability of the United States to an IW attack is a direct result of our leadership in the application of information technology.

IW may be as much an opportunity as it is a threat. Because information technology is a U.S. strong suit, the United States could use its know-how to improve its national security options, perhaps dramatically. It might be possible for the United States to deter all kinds of opponents more effectively if it were clear that the United States could retaliate through information warfare. If deterrence failed, and U.S. forces were required to fight, IW could make it possible to win more quickly, more decisively, and with fewer casualties. Most interesting of all, IW could open new options that would allow the United States to take action without resorting to military force. If this sounds familiar, it is because IW is a lineal descendent of traditional forms of covert action.[36]

U.S. officials are understandably reluctant to discuss U.S. policy and planning for offensive information warfare (although they often discuss the IW threat presented by our opponents, and the press has occasionally reported the use of sophisticated offensive IW measures by the United States).[37] It is a sensitive subject. Naturally, there is the problem of protecting U.S. capabilities. The effectiveness of IW measures can depend simply on whether or not the opponent knows about them. If opponents are aware that the United States can jam, spoof, or exploit an information system, they will stop relying on it. Thus, one thing is clear: if the United States decides to make use of information warfare, much of it will be covert. Information warfare is most effective when the target does not know the identify of the attacker. Indeed, in a well-designed IW operation, the target often does not even know that it is a target. People are so accustomed to glitches and failures in information systems that it may take them a while to realize that someone is systematically causing problems.

So, just as many of the traditional forms of covert action have passed from the scene, there may be a significant role for a new form of covert action in the era ahead. It would be tragic, however, if the United States were to use this weapon in the Information Age and repeat the mistakes in oversight and accountability that have made it consistently controversial.

THE FUTURE OF COVERT ACTION

When we began this book, we debated at some length whether even to include a chapter on covert action. This aspect of intelligence seemed so rooted in a past era that we nearly convinced ourselves that the topic could be laid to rest. As we proceeded, recent events and our discussions with people inside and outside the government convinced us otherwise.

The magic of covert action still appeals, as does the illusion that both secrecy and deniability are cost-free. The appeal of covert action will actually increase, not only because of its potential in information warfare, but also because of the need for flexibility in dealing with an environment composed of multiple threats from a bewildering array of sources.

Yet, if U.S. leaders have proved inept at the old covert options, how reasonable is it to expect them to understand the potential and the limitations of the new ones? This is why the reluctance of U.S. officials to reform intelligence operations or discuss the potential and also the limits of covert action is worrisome. Without public debate, we cannot develop a national consensus or policy on such issues as:

- What are the capabilities U.S. military forces and intelligence organizations must develop to use covert action effectively? What are the strengths and weaknesses of these capabilities? Can they reduce the need for conventional military forces and military operations? Under what conditions?
- Can we develop these capabilities without exposing the United States and our allies to the threat of retaliation?
- Which potential targets, if any, should be off-limits?
- How can we develop the laws, expertise, and institutions necessary to oversee this new potential form of covert action?

This discussion needs to be carried out in public. Although we need to protect the details of our plans and capabilities, we can nevertheless discuss general principles. If we do not, we are bound to repeat the mistakes in oversight, accountability, and effectiveness that have plagued covert action in the past.

SIX
THE INTELLIGENCE CULTURE AND THE FUTURE

In the late 1970s, social scientists, journalists, and other analysts made a remarkable discovery: *culture matters*. This may seem obvious today, but for years the use of culture as a concept for explaining events had been declining. Social scientists and pundits alike thought it was a backward, outmoded idea. After a few years of ethnically driven civil wars, failed economic plans, and catastrophic "scientific management" strategies, though, people began to rethink their conclusions. The success of nations, businesses, and even government organizations is indeed shaped by their cultures.[1]

But what is culture? The concept covers many things. One basic feature of a culture is that it distinguishes insiders from outsiders, and friend from foe. To wit:

The Gileadites captured the fords of the Jordan leading to Ephraim, and whenever a survivor of Ephraim said, "Let me cross over," the men of Gilead asked him, "Are you an Ephraimite?" If he replied, "No," they said, "All right, say 'Shibboleth.' " If he said, "Sibboleth," because he could not pronounce the word correctly, they seized him and killed him at the fords of the Jordan. And there fell at that time of the Ephraimites forty and two thousand.[2]

Another feature is that members of a culture share values, practices, and beliefs, in addition to a common set of assumptions about how the world works. This encourages predictability and stability. But an ingrained culture can also be a headache for anyone interested in reforming an organization—which is to say, anyone trying to overcome predictability and stability. As Franklin Roosevelt recalled his own experience with the culture of the U.S. Navy in 1940:

"The Treasury is so large and far-flung and ingrained in its practices that I find it almost impossible to get the actions and results I want—even with Henry [Morgenthau] there. But the Treasury is not to be compared with the

State Department. You should go through the experience of trying to get any changes in the thinking, policy, and action of career diplomats and then you'd know what a real problem was. But the Treasury and the State Department put together are nothing compared to the Na-avy [*sic*]. The admirals are really something to deal with, and I should know. To change anything in the Na-avy is like punching a feather bed. You punch it with your right hand, and you punch it with your left until you are finally exhausted, and then you will find the damn bed just as it was before you started punching."[3]

This is why culture can be a force for both good and bad. Cultures can lead individuals to "do the right thing" even when greed or sloth might lead them to do otherwise, or when they simply cannot figure out what the right thing is. Alternatively, culture can prevent an organization from keeping up with changing times, or replacing practices that are inefficient, out of date, or simply wrong.

We note all of this to return to the issues we raised at the beginning of this book: How can the intelligence community avoid the failings of the past? How can it prepare for the future? What is the future of the intelligence community, anyway? How the intelligence community will deal with these questions depends, as much as anything, on whether its culture can adapt.

All cultures have core concepts or principles that members believe. The traditional culture of U.S. intelligence, it seems fair to say, includes at least two such beliefs:

- Intelligence usually involves secrecy; and
- The intelligence community can provide "wisdom," or judgments on international events that are better than those one would find elsewhere.

One problem is that these key features of the intelligence culture—secrecy and wisdom—collide with the Information Age. The intelligence community's culture may thus prevent it from making the most of new technology. It may prevent the community from adapting to how its customers want to use information.

Also, culture is a two-way street. Culture not only defines how a group sees itself; it also shapes how others see the group. Intelligence consumers today also believe that intelligence entails secrecy and provides wisdom. This affects their own expectations for how intelligence is supposed to work, and that can lead to trouble, too.

THE CULTURE OF SECRECY

Secrecy may be the single most important trait that has defined the intelligence culture.[4] This is understandable. Many organizations do the kinds of things that the intelligence community does. Universities and think tanks study problems and publish papers. Journalists collect first-hand information. Many laboratories develop advanced technology for collecting and processing information. The difference that has distinguished the intelligence community, however, is that it has usually done these things secretly.

Is this secrecy necessary? In an op-ed article in the *New York Times,* George Kennan, the doyen of American cold warriors, wrote that, "The need by our government for secret intelligence about affairs elsewhere in the world has been vastly overrated. I would say that something upward of 95 percent of what we need to know could be very well obtained by the careful and competent study of perfectly legitimate sources of information open and available to us in the rich library and archival holdings of this country. Much of the remainder, if it could not be found here ... could easily be non-secretively elicited from similar sources abroad."[5]

It is easy to dismiss Kennan as a man from another era. Probably no one in the CIA reading the newspaper that morning took Kennan's column seriously. But Kennan was stating a basic fact that is at the cutting edge of the Information Age: Information is more abundant, and it is increasingly possible to use nonsecret methods to obtain it. The burden is on the intelligence community to justify why it needs secrecy, secret sources, and secret operations.

It is not an easy case to make. First, it is hard to base the operation of any organization on secrecy because secrets can be hard to keep. To quote Poor Richard, "Three may keep a secret if two of them are dead." Two centuries later, modern communications and the media make secrecy harder than ever. Large government organizations in democratic societies have a special disadvantage in keeping secrets. Such organizations are subject to public accountability, and frequent turnovers of both leaders and staff. This helps explain why the recipe for Coca-Cola and the identity of Deep Throat remain secret, while the name, function, and location of the National Reconnaissance Office was widely cited in the press years before the government officially acknowledged its existence.[6] There are many things that the intelligence community has been able to keep secret, but blanket secrecy over big organizations is difficult and expensive to maintain today.

Just as important, Americans have generally been skeptical of secrecy. Throughout history, Americans have never felt comfortable with the idea that the government or some powerful organization knows something that they do not. We take this for granted, but it is an especially American trait. Even a country such as Great Britain, which enjoys a sterling tradition for democracy, has an Official Secrets Act. Not so the United States. The exceptions usually occurred when the country was at war. As early as 1775, for instance, the Continental Congress established its Committee on Secret Correspondence. The purpose of the committee was to influence foreign governments to sympathize with the American Revolution. Once the war was over, however, Congress abolished the committee. In later wars, the United States followed the same pattern.

It is difficult for an outsider to appreciate just how thoroughly secrecy shapes the intelligence culture. For example, in the military, the first experience a new Marine recruit enjoys is learning how to take orders, usually through the gentle prodding of a drill sergeant. In contrast, the first experience a person has in an intelligence career is filling out a form for a security clearance—that is, the process by which the intelligence community decides whether it will share secrets with him or her. The clearance process is an experience all intelligence professionals share, just as all Marines share the experience of boot camp. Once on the job, one of the first appointments a newly minted intelligence officer has on his or her schedule is to attend a briefing on security procedures—that is, to learn how to handle secrets. At each step in a career, moving to a new assignment usually means being "read into" a program, or learning new secrets.

Also, like the Gileadites and most other cultures, the intelligence community's culture serves to distinguish members from outsiders. For the intelligence community, the borderline is defined in terms of secrecy. Security clearances, classification systems, and compartmentation separate members of the community from what intelligence specialists themselves often call the "outside world." The borderline also works in reverse; outsiders refer to intelligence professionals as "spooks" and an intelligence organization such as NSA as "The Puzzle Palace."

The result is almost subliminal, and we don't mean to sound sinister or conspiratorial in saying that the intelligence community has a "culture of secrecy." But this culture defines an essential part of both how intelligence specialists see themselves and how the rest of society sees the intelligence community. Secrecy is necessary for some operations. Most Americans agree that the government needs to keep some activities secret. The problem for the intelligence community culture, however, is that it too often makes secrecy the default option.

A culture that assumes facts are secret until determined otherwise can have all kinds of pernicious effects. An organization based on such a culture can lose touch with the larger society, and thus become insensitive to its concerns and attitudes. The society itself may feel that it has lost control of the organization. If the organization makes mistakes, the public reaction will be magnified because the public will feel that it was left out of the loop. And the public will have unreasonable expectations for the organization because they do not understand its limitations and constraints.

Moreover, secrecy can have unintended side effects. Secrecy runs counter to the essence of the Information Revolution, where the free flow of information drives productivity and creativity. The procedures and technologies of the Information Revolution—open architectures, public data bases, and the ability to form networks with almost anyone, anywhere—are all defeated by secrecy. It is odd that the intelligence community, which pioneered so many of the technologies that made the Information Revolution possible, is now so far out of step with the revolution that it is unable to enjoy many of its benefits. One never knows where the next great idea will come from, or who may have a new twist on an old idea. Organizations in the Information Age take advantage of such ideas by operating as open, fluid networks. Secrecy and compartmentation prevent networks from working. In other words, a foolish preoccupation with secrecy could be the hobgoblin that isolates the intelligence community from the Information Revolution.

Secrecy and Security

A culture of secrecy can, oddly enough, make it harder to protect those things that really do need to be kept secret. Take the case of Aldrich Ames.[7] As anyone who has read this far undoubtedly knows, Ames was a career officer in the CIA's Directorate of Operations, or, as it is known in the intelligence community, the "DO." Ames volunteered to work for Soviet intelligence in 1984. He was motivated partly by money, and partly because he seems to have lacked loyalty to the CIA or, for that matter, much of anything. Ames exposed as many agents working for U.S. intelligence as he could, and was paid about four million dollars for his efforts. The Soviets executed ten of the agents he betrayed. Ames was not caught until 1994.

Criticism of U.S. intelligence grew in the late 1990s, partly as a result of a string of intelligence failures: missing the Indian nuclear tests, not anticipating North Korea's testing of long-range missiles, miscues in identifying targets during Operation Allied Force in Yugoslavia, and so on. But it seems fair to say that the Ames affair was the key event raising concerns and shaping perceptions about U.S. intelligence in the 1990s, just as Iran-Contra was in the 1980s, the reports of covert action abuse were in the 1970s, and the Bay of Pigs was in the 1960s. Certainly no episode was more damaging to the reputation of the CIA and the intelligence community. U.S. intelligence became the target of official criticism and—possibly more telling—the butt of jokes in editorials, cartoons, and late-night television monologues. People wondered how the country's leading intelligence experts could be so bumbling as to miss a spy right in their own organization for almost a decade.

The CIA conducted at least three investigations of the Ames affair (one to learn what went wrong, one to assess the damage, and one as part of a general review of security). The Senate and House intelligence committees also conducted their own investigations. However, all of the investigations took the same basic approach. They focused on what the Senate committee called "the greatest managerial breakdown in the CIA's history." The investigators looked at the effectiveness of formal procedures and the culpability of individual managers.[8]

The investigators asked why, for example, the DO had promoted Ames, who was supposedly a mediocre case officer. They questioned why the CIA would assign such an employee to especially sensitive positions, such as the staff for counterintelligence. The investigators also asked how the CIA's system of background checks and polygraph exams let Ames slip through. They asked why CIA officials were not more alarmed when the Soviets rolled up the agency's operations in Moscow, and why the agency did not consult with the FBI more quickly.

Each investigation proposed measures to ensure such a failure did not happen again. The Senate report, for example, listed twenty-three specific actions for the CIA to consider for adoption. To make sure the agency got the message, the committee made a point of saying that it would make "the CIA's response to this report an area of 'special oversight interest' in the years ahead."[9] In other words, the investigators made a procedural and policy response to what they perceived to be a failure of procedures and policies.

No one, it seems, asked the larger question: Did the CIA's culture make a failure of this kind more likely, or even inevitable? For example, if there were so many warning signs that Ames was a mole, why weren't officials more inquisitive? They were, after all, *intelligence* officials. They are supposed to be people whose business is to ask questions and analyze events. The staff of the DO itself—the people Ames worked with, side by side, day in and day out—consists of experienced professionals who are supposed to be experts in observing people and deducing their motivations. Clearly there must have been powerful, though subtle forces at work that curbed these instincts.

That force was culture. Intelligence officers are trained (or, to put it more precisely, socialized) not to ask too many questions about their colleagues. It runs counter to the formal rules of "need to know" and compartmentation. More important, it runs counter to the social norms that accompany these rules. There were also specific disincentives to deter the would-be questioner. During the period he spied for Moscow, Ames passed two polygraph tests. The polygraph is the gold standard of security in the CIA. In a culture of secrecy and discretion, this was enough to deter most of those with suspicions from questioning Ames further.

Investigations of the Ames case noted that the polygraphers examining Ames in 1991 were unaware that the Office of Security (OS) had raised questions about Ames' finances. The investigating committees called this an organizational failure or a management oversight. But that begs the question: Why didn't the polygraphers simply get on the phone, tell their OS colleagues that they were examining Ames, and ask if anything unusual had turned up in his background investigation? The answer is that such a call would have run counter to years of training and socialization. The polygraphers were following good discipline by respecting compartmentation—that is, if they thought about it at all.

Secrecy and the Intelligence Consumer

The culture of secrecy was also responsible for a second, related scandal that rippled from the Ames affair. When the agents Ames exposed started to disappear, CIA officials could not be sure when and how the compromise had occurred. Thus, the information the agents provided had to be considered suspect. The agents may have been "under control" during part of the time they reported. The Soviets might have used them as channels for deceptive information. In addition, once Ames let the Soviets know how the CIA penetrated their intelligence and defense organizations, the Soviets might have set up bogus agents to spread additional disinformation.

Yet, even after the CIA realized it had a problem, the reports officers at headquarters did not inform the U.S. officials who received the intelligence. (Reports officers are responsible for summarizing and disseminating HUMINT information from the field.) Administration officials and members of Congress demanded an investigation. The CIA inspector general later reported to the Senate Intelligence Committee:

> The officer who served as chief of CE [Central Europe] Division reports and requirements for 11 years, and who was the division's principal liaison with Department of Defense consumers of sensitive reporting, told us that he had never explicitly informed Department of Defense consumers that sen-

sitive sources of reporting were known or suspected to be controlled. He recalled telling consumers to exercise caution in using reporting from new or
invalidated sources or to look closely at certain reporting and get back to
him on whether it was consistent with existing knowledge of the subject.

He acknowledged, however, that *this was not a departure from the routine interaction he had with intelligence consumers throughout his tenure as chief of reports and requirements. In fact, he said that he would not have informed consumers
about indications that sources were controlled because this might have caused consumers to disregard the "valid" and "authentic" information those sources were providing* [emphasis added].

In summary, documentary material determined to be authentic was
treated as able to "stand on its own" notwithstanding the fact that the material was known to have been provided by a controlled source. Those involved
in the dissemination of reporting from controlled sources appear to have had
great confidence in their ability to determine the genuineness of documentary material supplied by those sources.[10]

In other words, the CIA reports officer disseminated what could
well have been fiction because he judged it consistent with what he
believed was true. Moreover, he did not tell intelligence consumers
that the information came from sources that might have been compromised because he thought this would dilute important information that he judged to be valid.

When these facts became public, the reaction was predictable.
The media asked, how could the reports officer have been so care-
less—or arrogant? Defense Department officials and members of
Congress started to worry, for example, that the Pentagon had based
its plans for new weapons on tainted information.[11]

Yet one needs to read between the lines to see the more interesting fact. According to the inspector general's assessment, the reports
officer said his actions were "not a departure from the routine interaction he had with intelligence consumers." The reports officer was
right. It is a tradition in the intelligence culture to keep analysts at
arm's length from sources and consumers at arm's length from analysts. This is all part of compartmentation, protecting sources and
methods—in other words, secrecy. Indeed, there is a long tradition of
phonying up the description of sources in the intelligence culture.
During World War II, for example, the British often disguised intel-

ligence from decrypted German communications—the famous "Ultra" intercepts—as intelligence from human sources before sending the material to consumers. Often the source for intelligence data is simply labeled as, to use the cliché, "a source with access who has reported reliably in the past." That is what the reports officers were talking about when they said that they "had great confidence in their ability to determine the genuineness of documentary material supplied by those sources." Because analysts and consumers rarely see the raw data that an agent provides, assessing the reliability of the material is part of a reports officer's job.

No one worries that consumers were misled in cases where intelligence operations are successful, as was the case in the Ultra operation. After the dust clears, the intelligence officials tell the historians in a serious tone, "Of course, we couldn't tell them just how we knew what we knew. Security, you know." The consumers might not even care that they were duped. The problem occurs when operations fail or go awry, as in the Ames case. Even if some of the information provided by the agents Ames betrayed was bogus, some—perhaps most— was probably genuine. The agents might have sneaked valid information past the Soviet authorities who were monitoring them. Or the Soviet authorities might have intentionally allowed the agents to pass along valid information so that U.S. intelligence officials would not suspect that a mole had penetrated the CIA. In either case, someone needed to sort through the agents' information to decide which was accurate and which had been designed to mislead. In the traditional model of intelligence, that was the responsibility of the reports officer.

The reports officers reprimanded in the Ames case might have made errors in judgment. But it is important to realize that what they were doing—assessing the quality of raw intelligence without informing the analysts or consumers who used it—was entirely consistent with the traditional model of how intelligence is supposed to work. Critics suggested that the reports officers should have withheld the material from the agents Ames betrayed. Yet in other instances the same reports officers were criticized for *not* passing along intelligence data when they doubted its quality.[12] Clearly, the larger problem is that the compartmentation and central control of information—that is, the secrecy—built into the traditional model of intelligence is simply inconsistent with how people expect to use information today.*

Secrecy and Controversial Sources

Consider another case. In the early 1990s, Congress began to raise questions about whether Guatemalan military officers that the CIA paid as informants were guilty of human rights abuses. Legislators became especially concerned when they learned that the CIA had been using Julio Roberto, a Guatemalan army officer who had been implicated in the murders of Michael DeVine, an American innkeeper, and Efrain Bamaca Velasquez, a rebel leader. Velasquez was married to Jennifer Harbury, a U.S. citizen who took her case to the media.

The intelligence oversight committees had passed a requirement requiring the CIA to report on human rights abuses by its agents in

---

*The CIA's investigation of the Ames affair itself provides insight into the intelligence community culture. For example, the CIA inspector general's report conceded that, although Ames was a mediocre officer in the field, he performed well when stationed at headquarters and when he handled assets in the United States. However, the inspector general discounted this part of Ames's career, since it was not overseas. He suggested that CIA officials had erred when they rewarded Ames with greater responsibilities for his work while posted in the United States. Real CIA officers, the inspector general seemed to say, work abroad.

This is after-the-fact reasoning. One of the assets Ames handled in the United States was Arkady Shevchenko, a high-ranking Soviet diplomat appointed to the United Nations. Shevchenko was one of the most valuable Soviet agents working for the CIA at the time. Moreover, the Shevchenko case had an extremely high profile within the agency. Those who worked on it gained stature, and were bound to go on to better things. After Ames's success with Shevchenko, the logical response would have been to overlook his earlier failings. "Maybe Rick has finally turned a corner," was the reasonable conclusion. "Looks like the old boy has found his niche and is going to work out."

One irony of the Ames-Shevchenko relationship is that Shevchenko was successful in the Soviet Foreign Ministry largely because he, like Ames, was a good writer. In other words, it was a meeting of the memo drafters. Of course, another irony is that, no matter what his job performance evaluations said, it seems that Ames—unfortunately—really was good at espionage, after all.

Guatemala. When the media reports appeared, the committees began asking questions. In the spring of 1995, President Clinton responded to Congress's demands for action by directing the Intelligence Oversight Board (IOB) to look into the matter. The report of the IOB is telling. It stated:

We found no evidence that Guatemala station was a "rogue" station operating independently of control by its headquarters; it generally kept the DO headquarters well-informed of developments, negative or otherwise, including allegations implicating CIA assets as each allegation surfaced. DO headquarters officials, generally on an ad hoc basis, provided guidance to Guatemala station in the late 1980's and early 1990's advising it to avoid assets against whom human rights violations had been alleged, but the number of such assets retained or recruited without any evident deliberation suggests that this guidance was neither strictly enforced by headquarters nor observed by the station. DO managers rarely focused on specific allegations and did not systematically review assets in Guatemala for allegations of human rights abuse until the September 1994 review. Moreover, the balancing of allegations against contributions, on those occasions it was done, was conducted exclusively by division-level managers and chiefs of station, whose performance and rewards systems were principally based on establishing and maintaining relationships with productive assets and who had little incentive to give great weight to allegations of abuse.[13]

In other words, the CIA officers and the Guatemalan station followed the formal rules to the letter. But that clearly was not enough. Why didn't the officers think about how the public might react if it learned the CIA was dealing with possible (and, in some case, probable) human rights abusers? If nothing else, they should have been thinking about how the operation would reflect on the CIA itself. In addition to the disincentives the IOB cited, one likely reason the officers did not act more aggressively in checking out their assets and voicing any concerns they might have had was the culture of secrecy.

Indeed, the oversight committees rejected the IOB's conclusions. John Deutch, who had assumed office a few months earlier, decided that a new investigation was needed. This investigation, carried out under the DCI's executive director, concluded that formal compliance was not good enough. On the basis of the new investigation,

Deutch fired two DO officials and issued official reprimands to eight others.[14]

Today there is little that is still secret about what CIA case officers do. The agency selects people who are skilled in understanding human motivations and able to adapt to foreign situations. Case officers cultivate relationships with foreign nationals who can provide information. The case officer develops a plan to recruit these "assets," "sources," and "agents", bearing in mind both the kind of information that the United States needs and the motivation of the source. In the course of carrying out these plans, U.S. intelligence agents may often need to deal with some especially evil characters. What makes sources valuable, however, is not their character, but their information. This is why intelligence officers will sometimes have to maintain relationships with truly loathsome characters over a long period of time. The objective is to get information. The classic example is gathering intelligence on terrorists. The CIA may persuade or coerce a member of a terrorist group to become an asset. However, to preserve the agent's access to information, the CIA may allow him to remain a member of the group, where he may continue to participate in terrorist activities.

The point is not that the CIA should not recruit the agent; in many cases, it probably should. The agent may take part in terrorist attacks while he is, as it will later be reported, "on the payroll of the U.S. government," but his information may enable the United States to eliminate the terrorist organization permanently. The issue is accountability. Responsible officials need to be fully aware of what is going on. Congress and even critics of the intelligence community will accept tough decisions like these if they are made deliberately, at a high enough level, and if an official takes responsibility.

Again, the problem is really one of culture. FBI special agents, for example, often face similar issues when they deal with members of organized crime to obtain information or testimony. These criminals are often just as loathsome as the terrorists or human rights abusers with whom the CIA must deal. But FBI special agents appear to have a better appreciation of the need to keep their superiors informed and when they need to get approval. Case officers, as the IOB study noted, are rewarded for the number and quality of sources they recruit. This may encourage them to give a productive source the benefit of the doubt when, for example, circumstances suggest that human rights violations may be part of a source's job. At a minimum, at least some case officers have not been eager to ask tough questions about their sources' ancilliary activities. The culture of secrecy reinforces these leanings. Secrecy isolates intelligence officers. Secrecy prevents intelligence officers from scrutinizing one another's judgment and blurs what the intelligence organization believes is acceptable and expected behavior.

The intelligence community will always need to deal with some secrets. But secrecy should be a tool used in the job, not an all-pervasive trait of the culture. Consider this analogy: Police officers carry firearms and can resort to force. Yet firearms and force are not the defining elements of the police profession. To the contrary, police officers are taught from the beginning of their training to use "command presence" and the "aura of authority" to do their job, leaving force as a less-preferred alternative.

Similarly, intelligence personnel should be experts in the management of information from all sources, secret and public. Case officers and analysts should be trained to consider secrecy the same kind of tool as a police officer's service revolver: a useful tool when necessary, but one that imposes costs and that should be used only when it is really necessary.

THE CULTURE OF WISDOM

Intelligence professionals would probably never use the term, but they often perceive their role as developing "wisdom." It is as almost much a part of the intelligence culture as is secrecy. As with most cultural traits, outsiders often reinforce this trait by having the same perception. The public expects that the intelligence community can provide judgments that are, at least on some subjects, better than those they can find elsewhere. This cultural trait is related to secrecy. Access to secrets, people seem to believe, leads to better knowledge, and that can be interpreted as wisdom.

How did the intelligence community assume this role? Part of it goes back to how people viewed authority when the intelligence community was created. In the 1940s, people were more inclined to defer to the man in the lab coat or the Ivy League professor. Like the culture of secrecy, it is hard to convey the full flavor of this kind of thinking. For a taste of the times, though, consider a paper written in 1945 by Henry de Wolfe Smyth, a scientist who participated in the Manhattan Project. Smyth's paper was the government's first official explanation of the project and the workings of the atomic bomb. The "Smyth Report" began:

> The ultimate responsibility for our nation's policy rests on its citizens and they can discharge such responsibilities wisely only if they are informed. The average citizen cannot be expected to understand clearly how an atomic bomb is constructed or how it works but there is in this country a substantial group of engineers and scientists who can understand such things and who can explain the potentialities of atomic bombs to their fellow citizens. The present report is written for this professional group.[15]

Smyth may seem condescending today, but his report did reflect how people viewed expertise and intellectual authority at the time. The founders of the intelligence community (many of whom were themselves members of the era's eastern, white, male social elite) shared these attitudes. Today, however, the notion that a single organization can serve as the repository for wisdom over all issues is a quaint, outdated idea. Even if the old deference to authority had survived, no organization could maintain the diverse expertise that is now required. The threats and issues that the United States faces are too varied, too numerous, and change too quickly. Even if such an organization were the best source of analysis today, it probably would not be the best source tomorrow.

The signs are already there that the intelligence community is showing the strain. The House Permanent Select Committee on Intelligence reported, for example, that CIA analysts are often "a largely inexperienced work force" lacking "the analytic depth, breadth and expertise to monitor political, military and economic developments worldwide." According to the committee, agency analysts often find themselves working on unfamiliar countries. The committee also found that these analysts are served by collection organizations with "uncertain commitment and capability to collect 'human intelligence' on a worldwide basis through espionage."[16]

There is another, more serious problem. In the Information Age, the old approach of "turning the problem over to a panel of experts" no longer works. Today, especially on controversial issues, there are too many experts, not too few. "Truth," such as it is, emerges from a messy, competitive process that is bounded by objective facts, but also shaped by opinion, politics, and personal judgments. When the intelligence community attempts to offer summary judgements, it will inevitably encounter problems, especially when controversial policies are at stake.

A recent case illustrates the problem. There are few national security issues as contentious as ballistic missile defense (BMD). Officials and pundits on both the left and right ends of the political spectrum consider it a litmus test. For the left, the U.S.-Soviet Anti-Ballistic Missile Treaty of 1971 is the cornerstone of arms control. They oppose the development of BMD with almost religious fervor. The right views BMD as the legacy of Ronald Reagan, Edward Teller, and the Strategic Defense Initiative. They consider the ABM Treaty an obsolete agreement between the United States and a country that no longer exists.

This explains the controversy over an estimate the National Intelligence Council (NIC) published in 1995, *Emerging Missile Threats to North America During the Next 15 Years.* The flap started when Bill Clinton vetoed the annual defense authorization bill passed by Congress. The bill required the Defense Department to accelerate development of BMD. Clinton objected, and, in justifying his veto, used the National Intelligence Estimate as justification. He cited the estimate's judgments that there was a low probability for additional countries to acquire long-range missiles. BMD supporters turned their aim from the veto to the NIE, claiming that the results had been "politicized."[17] Congress directed the director of central intelligence, John Deutch, to appoint a panel to review the NIE's conclusions. Robert Gates, himself a former director of central intelligence, headed the board. Gates presented the findings of the board at a hearing of the Senate Intelligence Committee.[18] Gates said the NIE had not been politicized, although he did give a laundry list of technical problems with its analysis. The NIC also offered a statement, as did Congress's General Accounting Office, which had been critical of the estimate. But the testimony of James Woolsey—another former DCI—was the most interesting.

Woolsey was a BMD supporter. Yet he did not take issue with the analysis of the NIE. He disputed its assumptions. The estimate assumed that international controls would prevent rogue nations from acquiring missile technology. Woolsey warned that controls would be ineffective in precisely those cases where they were most needed. The estimate assumed that any country that developed missiles would use traditional technologies. Woolsey argued that new missile powers were more likely to explore nontraditional technologies, which could lead to a breakthrough, and would be difficult to predict.

It is easy to say that Woolsey was simply out of step with the conventional wisdom. The NIE's assumptions reflected the beliefs of most intelligence community analysts. But remember that the Air Force was similarly out of step in the 1960s, when it argued that the Soviet Union would not follow U.S. concepts in deciding how large a strategic nuclear force to deploy. Air Force intelligence officials warned that the Soviets would not follow American notions about the desirability of "mutual assured destruction" and a balance of nuclear forces. They assumed the Soviets would have their own political goals and military strategy, and this would lead them to build more missiles. The Air Force position proved correct. Similarly, there were good examples supporting Woolsey's concern that rogue states might use different missile technology that the United States might overlook. Iraq, for example, had used uranium enrichment methods discredited in the West in trying to build an atomic bomb in the late 1980s, and U.S. intelligence missed the Iraqi nuclear weapons program. And, in fact, by late 1998, Woolsey was proved to have been on the mark. North Korea surprised U.S. intelligence with its test of a three-stage missile that seemed to have the potential to reach Alaska or Hawaii.[19]

It is impossible to say whose assumptions are correct in this kind of case without a crystal ball, and the estimate's conclusions depended entirely on such assumptions. But why did the NIC try to make such summary judgments? One important reason is that this has been the accepted practice for decades. Providing wisdom—crisp, unambiguous, to-the-point judgments—is part of the culture.

The earliest NIEs were, to use Henry Kissinger's characterization, "Talmudic" summaries providing the consensus of the graybeards. Estimates have evolved since then, so that they present to the reader much more supporting data backing up the conclusions. Also, current NIEs do a more complete job of describing disagreements within the intelligence community. Even so, today's National Intelligence Estimates, like most finished intelligence products, are a poor fit with how people use information in the real world. No corporate CEO would simply accept a summary market forecast at face value. He would insist on interrogating his analysts about the assumptions underlying their forecasts. Most likely, he would decide for himself how to fill in the areas of uncertainty, and then ask that the analysis be built around his assumptions. The CEO would also take responsibility for the assumptions and the resulting forecast.

A more useful NIE on the foreign missile threat would have framed its conclusions by stating, "*if* technology controls are effective, and *if* there are no unexpected breakthroughs that will simplify missile development, and *if* other countries make the political calculations we have assumed, *then* the facts suggest no additional countries will develop long-range missiles during the next fifteen years." The political debate would then have focused on these assumptions. Such assumptions are a matter of judgment and intuition. The intelligence community is not equipped to settle such matters. They are political questions best left to politicians who have to answer to their constituencies.

In fairness to the NIC, however, Clinton administration officials made the problem worse by blithely using the conclusions of the NIE to support their policy. It is the job of intelligence specialists to define facts, gaps in facts, and the logical conclusion of facts. It is the job of public officials to make judgments about risk and articulate their judgments to the public. Expecting the intelligence community to provide summary judgments on unknowable events is a throwback to an older style of using information. In the Information Age, consumers interact with providers. They probe to find out what is fact and what is judgment. They then make the judgments themselves, or turn to someone they trust.

INTELLIGENCE AND CULTURE

Many of the ideas we have presented here are, in fact, being tried in the intelligence community. Whether the intelligence community will adapt to the Information Age depends much on whether its culture can adapt. The record of bureaucracies adapting to changing conditions is not encouraging. Bureaucracies are insulated from most of the forces that make other organizations adapt. Companies in the private sector can go out of business if they fail to meet their customers' needs or become inefficient. Political parties and legislators can be voted out of office. Not so bureaucracies.

Bureaucratic organizations like the intelligence community have only loose connections to their customers and constituencies. Bureaucracies also have built-in inertia that keeps them on their current course. The problem of adapting to change is even more difficult for the intelligence community because, beyond the usual factors that insulate bureaucratic organizations, the intelligence community has the additional protection of secrecy. This limits the number of officials, legislators, journalists, and even customers who can point out its failings and propose alternatives.

History suggests that the risk for the intelligence community is that, if it does not reform, it will meet one of two fates. One is that it will gradually drift into irrelevance, perhaps with the exception of a few functions that are so important that no one will dare to let them fail. Critics would say not only that the intelligence community is following this course, but that it is, intentionally or not, official policy. These critics would cite as proof PDD 35, the directive that focuses the intelligence community's efforts on a limited number of high-priority missions, and implicitly performs triage on the remainder.

The other fate that can befall a bureaucracy that does not keep up is to muddle along until a catastrophe exposes the organization's unseen weaknesses. One can imagine how such a catastrophe might occur for the intelligence community today. It would likely be a threat that is totally off the radar screen now, but which—as was the case with the Iranian Revolution—results in large costs that directly affect the American public. Or it might be a covert action that is so ill-conceived that it becomes a metaphor for disaster; that is, another Bay of Pigs. The failure by the intelligence community to warn U.S. officials of the resumption of nuclear tests by India (and the unveiling of the up-to-then secret nuclear arsenal that Pakistan had developed) came close to being such a catastrophe; it was not only because, while a tremendous intelligence failure, it lacked immediate impact for the average American citizen.[20]

The formula for avoiding "reform by catastrophe" requires two ingredients. One is that someone in the bureaucracy must have a vision of how the organization should reshape itself. Often this means abandoning orthodoxy. For the intelligence community, it means rethinking some of our basic notions about how intelligence operates and what its functions should be in the current era. Such ideas rarely come out of commissions. More often, an individual will float what may seem to be an outlandish idea at first. But, if it is useful, it will be adopted by an wider and wider group of followers. Military reform worked this way in the 1970s and 1980s, as did reform in the American corporation. As we have seen, there are already thinkers who are developing these new ideas. Some of them are in the intelligence community itself.

The other important ingredient is that there needs to be someone with the ability, stature, and willingness to light the fuse. Someone needs to take decisive action to shake up an organization whose natural inclination is to remain as it is. This could be a high-profile individual working from the inside, such as Curtis LeMay, who transformed the Strategic Air Command in the early 1950s. Alternatively, it could be a small group of individuals with the clout, canniness, and vision to force change from the outside. Senator Sam Nunn's efforts on military reform with other members of Congress come to mind.

Keep in mind that the intelligence community has already experienced significant failures during the past decade—problems in the Gulf War, the Ames affair, the covert action in Iraq, the Indian nuclear tests. Yet it has stubbornly resisted reform. This shows just how resilient the intelligence community is to change. If those responsible for American national security in the Information Age wait for a catastrophic failure to propel change, they are taking a risk that even the best truth will not eliminate.

NOTES

ONE The Problem: Providing Intelligence in a Changing World

1 Sherman Kent, *Strategic Intelligence for American World Policy* (Princeton, N.J.: Princeton University Press, 1949), p. vii.

2 The phrase is taken from the first official history of the CIA, which was written by the agency's first historian, Arthur Darling. Thinking of intelligence as an instrument of foreign policy is central to understanding the role that the collection of information from secret sources and its analysis by specially trained experts plays in democratic systems. As the founders of the U. S. intelligence community took pains to point out, the CIA was created to centralize the processing of information that was destined to serve policy rather than to make it. See Arthur B. Darling, *The Central Intelligence Agency: An Instrument of Government, to 1950* (University Park: Pennsylvania State University Press, 1990).

3 For a brief review of the kind of intelligence reports these types of problems now merit, see Steven Greenhouse, "The Greening of U.S. Diplomacy: Focus on Ecology," *New York Times*, October 9, 1995.

4 In addition, there has been considerable discussion about "non-threat threats," or threats that are not the intended result of a specific actor. These include, for example, environmental degradation, global warming, the spread of disease, and other "green threats." We consider these threats to be the result—intended or not—of nations and other global actors. See, for example, Geoffrey D. Dabelko and P. J. Simmons, "Environment and Security: Core Ideas and US Government Initiatives," *SAIS Review* 17, no. 1 (Winter/Spring 1997), 127–146. Also see Nazli Chourci, ed., *Global Accord: Environmental Challenges and International Responses* (Cambridge: MIT Press, 1993); and Greenhouse, "The Greening of American Diplomacy."

5 See, of course, X [George Kennan], "The Sources of Soviet Conduct," *Foreign Affairs* 25, no. 4 (July 1947), 566–582.

6 For a representative collection of estimates declassified and published under the auspices of the CIA, see Scott A. Koch, *Selected Estimates on the Soviet Union, 1950–1959* (Washington, D.C.: CIA History Staff/Center for the Study of Intelligence, 1993); and Donald P. Steury, *Intentions and Capabilities: Estimates on Soviet Strategic Forces* (Washington, D.C.: CIA History Staff/Center for the Study of Intelligence, 1996).

7 Samuel P. Huntington, "The Clash of Civilizations?" *Foreign Affairs* 72 (Summer 1993), 22–49. Also see Huntington's *The Clash of Civilizations and the Remaking of World Order* (New York: Simon and Schuster, 1996);

Michael E. Brown, *Ethnic Conflict and International Security*, (Princeton, N.J.: Princeton University Press, 1993); and Michael E. Brown, *The International Dimensions of Internal Conflict*, (Cambridge: MIT Press, 1996).

8 For example, see Steven Emerson, "Diplomacy That Can Stop Terrorism," *Wall Street Journal*, July 22, 1994. Also see James Phillips, "The Changing Face Of Middle Eastern Terrorism," The Heritage Foundation, Backgrounder #1005 (October 6, 1994). For a critique of Emerson's position, see Robert Friedman, "One Man's Jihad," *The Nation*, May 15, 1995. Mark Juergensmeyer, a professor of religion at the University of Hawaii, has provided a thorough analysis of the idea of a religion-based threat, although he rejects it himself; see his *The New Cold War? Religious Nationalism Confronts the Secular State* (Berkeley: University of California Press, 1993). More recently, Ibrahim A. Karawoon notes that although there is significantly more Islamic awareness in much of the world, this has not necessarily translated into greater political influence by Islamic groups, largely because of a lack of cohesiveness. See his *The Islamic Impasse*, Adelphi Paper No. 314 (London: International Institute for Strategic Studies, 1997). For a background of the Fulan Gong sect and its surprise 1999 march on Tiananmmen Square, see Seth Faison, "10,000 Protestors in Beijing Urge Cult's Recognition," *New York Times*, April 26, 1999.

9 See John Mueller, *Retreat from Doomsday: The Obsolescence of Major War* (New York: Basic, 1989); Francis Fukuyama, "The End of History," *The National Interest* (Summer 1989); pp. 3-28; and Fukuyama, *The End of History and the Last Man* (New York: Free Press, 1992).

10 See, for example, Edward N. Luttwak, *The Endangered American Dream*, (New York: Simon and Schuster, 1993); and Pat Choate, *Agents of Influence: How Japan's Lobbyists in the United States Manipulate America's Political and Economic System*, (New York: Knopf, 1990). James Fallows, *Looking at the Sun: The Rise of the New East Asian Economic and Political System* (New York: Pantheon, 1994) also looks at the issue, albeit from a less alarmist perspective.

For the Japanese perspective, see Shintaro Ishihara, *The Japan That Can Say No*, (New York: Simon and Schuster, 1991). This English translation deleted some of the more inflammatory passages from the original; for a section-by-section summary of the original, see Andrew Goble and James C. Carlson, "Japan's America Bashers," *Orbis* (Winter 1990), 83-102.

11 Stansfield Turner, "Intelligence For A New World Order," *Foreign Affairs* 70, no. 4, (Fall 1991), 150-166. For a more recent discussion of the threat, see the statement by FBI Director Louis J. Freeh at a hearing on economic espionage, Select Committee on Intelligence and Committee on the Judiciary, U.S. Senate (February 28, 1996).

12 John J. Mearshiemer, "Why We Will Soon Miss The Cold War," *Atlantic Monthly* (August 1990). Mearshiemer is part of the decades-long debate among political scientists about whether war is more likely when there are a few dominant countries (a "bipolar" world, in the case of two superpowers), or many equal countries (a "multipolar" world). Social science

aficionados determined to follow the argument can refer to Karl Deutsch and J. David Singer, "Multipolar Power Systems and International Stability," *World Politics,* 16, no. 3 (April 1964), 390–406; Kenneth Waltz, "The Stability of a Bipolar World," *Daedalus 93,* no. 3 (Summer 1964), 881–909; Bruce Bueno de Mesquita, "Measuring Systemic Polarity," *Journal of Conflict Resolution* (June 1975), 187–216; and Bueno de Mesquita, "Systemic Polarization and the Occurrence and Duration of War," *Journal of Conflict Resolution* (June 1978), 241–267. See also Kenneth Waltz, *Man, the State, and War: A Theoretical Analysis* (New York: Columbia University Press, 1959); and Waltz, "The Emerging Structure of International Politics," *International Security* (Fall 1993).

13 Cf. World Bank, *World Development Report* (Washington D.C., 1997), pp. 236–237. Also see the tables provided in *Fortune,* August 5, 1996, pp. F1–F2.

14 See, for example, Robert O. Keohane and Joseph S. Nye, *Power and Interdependence* (Boston: Little Brown, 1973); Robert O. Keohane, *After Hegemony: Cooperation and Discord in the World Political Economy* (Princeton, N.J.: Princeton University Press, 1984).

15 See Walter B. Wriston, *The Twilight of Sovereignty: How the Information Revolution Is Transforming Our World* (New York: Scribners, 1992); and Walter Laqueur, "Postmodern Terrorism," *Foreign Affairs* (September-October 1996), pp. 24–37.

16 Thomas L. Friedman, "Iraq of Ages," *New York Times,* February 28, 1998.

17 For a discussion of the Zapatistas' tactics and of the general problem, see John Arquilla and David Ronfeldt, *The Advent of Netwar* (Santa Monica, Calif.: National Defense Research Institute, RAND, 1996), pp. 72–73.

18 Chris Hedges, "Serbian Response to Tyranny: Take the Movement to the Web," *New York Times,* December 8, 1996.

19 Tom Vogel, Matt Moffett, and Jed Sandberg, "Radical Groups Spread the Word On-Line," *Wall Street Journal,* January 6, 1997.

20 Richard Rosecrance, "The Rise of the Virtual State," *Foreign Affairs* (July-August 1996), 45–61.

21 Jessica T. Matthews, "Power Shift," *Foreign Affairs* (January-February 1997), 50–66.

22 See Tim Weiner, "Afghan Camps, Hidden in Hills, Stymied Soviet Attacks for Years," *New York Times,* August 24, 1998.

23 See Kenichi Ohmae, *The End of the Nation State: The Role of Regional Economies,* (New York: Free Press, 1995). Also see Douglas Hurd, *The Search for Peace,* (London: Little Brown, 1997). As Hurd observed: "The world is run on a paradox. On the one hand, the essential focus of loyalty remains the nation state, and there are nearly two hundred of these. On the other hand, no nation state, not even the single superpower, the United States of America, is capable of delivering to its citizens single-handed the security, the prosperity of the decent environment which the citizens demand."

24 Indeed, when William Riker carried out a survey of federations, he found that the one trait that all successful federations shared when they were formed was the existence of a foreign threat. See William H. Riker, *Federalism: Origin, Operation, Significance* (Boston: Little, Brown, 1964). There are many accounts of how the ethnic problems of the Balkans became driving forces in the breakup of Yugoslavia. See, for example, Susan L. Woodward, *Balkan Tragedy: Chaos and Dissolution After the Cold War,* (Washington, D.C.: Brookings Institution, 1995).

25 Quoted in "Iraq Is One of Many Holders of Doomsday Weaponry," *Wall Street Journal,* February 18, 1997.

26 For a discussion of both the Aum and of the potential development of CW and BW weapons, see the collected witness statements, "Global Proliferation of Weapons of Mass Destruction," presented at the Hearings by the Permanent Subcommittee on Investigations, of the Committee on Government Operations, U.S. Senate (November 1, 1995). Also see floor speech by Sen. Sam Nunn, *Congressional Record* (October 3, 1996), pp. S12284-S12285; and Edward J. Lacey, "Tackling the Biological Weapons Threat: The Next Proliferation Challenge," *Washington Quarterly* (Autumn 1994), 53-65.

27 The estimate of Kalashnikov rifles is cited in Ian V. Hoggs and John Weeks, *Military Small Arms of the Twentieth Century* (London: Arms and Armed Press, 1981). Sam Cummings, owner of Interarms, was quoted by the Associated Press (February 22, 1996) as estimating that 25 million Kalashnikovs are in storage in various locations in Russia. The Mozambique estimate is provided by Terry Gander, editor of *Jane's Infantry Weapons.* Gander also reports that the number of companies manufacturing small arms has increased by 25 percent during the past decade. See *Jane's Infantry Weapons 1996-97* (Alexandria, Va.: Jane's Information Services, 1996). Also see Michael T. Klare, "Stemming the Lethal Trade in Small Arms and Light Weapons," *Issues in Science and Technology* (Fall 1995), 52-58.

28 See Gordon E. Moore, "Cramming More Components Onto Integrated Circuits," *Electronics* (April 19, 1965), pp. 114-117. For a recent assessment, see Peter Leyden, "Moore's Law Repealed, Sort Of," *Wired,* May 1997. For an analysis and history, see Bob Schaller, "Moore's Law: The Benchmark of Progress in Semiconductor Electronics" (September 26, 1996), monograph available at http://mason.gmu.edu/∞rschalle/moore law.html

29 "Network Solutions Announces Millionth Domain Registrant" Network Solutions press release, March 11, 1997.

30 See George Gilder, "Metcalfe's Law and Legacy," *Forbes* (ASAP Supplement), September 13, 1993, pp. 158-166. Also see N. Economides, "The Economics of Networks," *International Journal of Industrial Organization* 16, no. 4 (1996), 673-699.

31 See Bruce D. Berkowitz, "Technology and Intelligence Reform," *Orbis* (Winter 1996-97), 107-119.

32 No official figure has been released for the cost of current intelligence satellites. One example of the typical figure cited by the industry press is provided by Craig Covault in "Advanced KH-11 Broadens U.S. Recon Capabilities," *Aviation Week and Space Technology,* January 6, 1997, p. 24; Covault estimates that an imaging satellite costs $750 million to $1 billion, with the launch costing $200–300 million.

33 See Kenneth W. Dam and Herbert S. Lin, eds., *Cryptography's Role in Securing the Information Society.* (Washington, D.C.: National Academy Press, 1996).

34 See Stacey Evers, "ARPA Pursues Pocket-Sized Pilotless Vehicles," *Jane's Defence Weekly,* March 20, 1996, p. 3; Michael A. Dornheim, "Tiny Drones May Be Soldier's New Tool," *Aviation Week and Space Technology,* June 8, 1998, pp. 42–48.

35 For an analysis of how decision making will be affected by the onset of the Information Revolution see Nicholas Negroponte, *Being Digital,* (New York: Alfred A. Knopf, 1995), pp. 163 ff. Also see Jack Davis, *The Challenge of Managing "Uncertainty": Paul Wolfowitz on Intelligence-Policy Relations,* (Washington D.C.: Product Evaluation Staff, Central Intelligence Agency, March 1995); James A. Barry, Jack Davis, David D. Gries, and Joseph Sullivan, "Bridging the Intelligence-Policy Divide," *Studies in Intelligence* (October 1994), 1–8; and Jack Davis, "A Policymaker's Perspective on Intelligence Analysis," *Studies in Intelligence* (October 1995), 8–15.

36 See R. Jeffrey Smith, "High-Tech Unit Kept Watch Over U.S. Monitors In Bosnia; Intelligence Team Is Honored For Giving Diplomats Swift Access To Top-Secret Data," *Washington Post,* December 9, 1997.

37 Hans Binnendijlk, "Tin Cup Diplomacy," *The National Interest,* no. 49 (Fall 1997), 88–91. See also Casimir Yost and Mary Locke, *U.S. Foreign Affairs Resources: Budget Cuts and Consequences,* (Washington D.C.: Institute for the Study of Diplomacy, Georgetown University, 1996).

38 For a discussion of trends in the U.S. intelligence budget and its linkage to defense spending, see Bruce D. Berkowitz and Allan E. Goodman, *Strategic Intelligence for American National Security* (Princeton, N.J.: Princeton University Press, 1989), pp. 143–148.

39 The intelligence community revealed this figure in 1997 in response to a suit by the Federation of American Scientists. Total funding for FY 1997 was $26.6 billion. See "Statement of the Director of Central Intelligence Regarding the Disclosure of the Aggregate Intelligence Budget for Fiscal Year 1997," Press Release No. 13-97 (Washington, D.C.: Central Intelligence Agency, October 15, 1997). A few months later the intelligence community also revealed total spending for FY 1998, which was $26.7 billion. At the time, the intelligence community stated that, in disclosing spending for FY 1998, it was not making a decision to disclose annual intelligence spending on routine basis. See "CIA Releases Intelligence Budget," *Washington Post,* March 21, 1998.

The following year the intelligence community rejected a FOIA request to disclose the administration's budget request for FY 1999. At the same time, it restated its position that it would decide on a case-by-case basis whether to disclose the amount actually appropriated. See Vernon

Loeb, "CIA Won't Disclose Total Intelligence Appropriation for Fiscal Year," *Washington Post,* December 25, 1998.

40 See Berkowitz and Goodman, *Strategic Intelligence for American National Security,* pp. 143–148.

41 See Commission on Roles and Capabilities of the United States Intelligence Community, *Preparing for the 21st Century: An Appraisal of U.S. Intelligence* (Washington, D.C.: U.S. Government Printing Office, 1996). The commission's report included a graph (p. 132) that depicted the budget and personnel levels of each agency within the national intelligence community—including the Intelligence Community Management Staff and Defense Mapping Agency, whose budgets and personnel levels are unclassified. By extrapolating (i.e., using their rulers), reporters claimed to estimate the spending and personnel levels of the CIA, NRO, National Security Agency, and national intelligence programs within the Defense Department. The report also included a graph (p. 131) comparing annual changes in total U.S. intelligence spending with changes in U.S. defense spending. Since defense spending is unclassified, the press reported that it was possible to estimate trends in intelligence spending as well. Also see R. Jeffrey Smith, "Making Connections with Dots to Decipher U.S. Spy Spending," *Washington Post,* March 12, 1996.

42 Art Pine, "Film Launches Call to Open Secret J.F.K. Files," *Los Angeles Times,* February 12, 1992, the article cites a *Time*–CNN poll taken December 17–22, 1991.

43 The various recent cases appear to fit into the following categories:

■ *Cases in which intelligence officials circumvented legislative or executive branch controls and oversight.* Most of these cases involved a failure to notify Congress (or at least notify Congress adequately) of a covert operation. One example was the CIA mining of Nicaraguan harbors in 1983. See Allan E. Goodman and Bruce D. Berkowitz, *The Need to Know: The Report of the Twentieth Century Fund Task Force on Covert Action and American Democracy* (New York: The Twentieth Century Fund, 1992) chap. 7.

■ *Failures of analysis or warning.* Classic cases include overestimates and underestimates of Soviet strategic forces and the Soviet economy throughout the Cold War, and the failure to anticipate the fall of the Shah. A more recent example was the intelligence community's misidentification of targets during the 1999 NATO intervention in Yugoslavia. See Eric Schmitt, "Aim, Not Arms, at the Root of Mistaken Strike on Embassy," *New York Times,* May 10, 1999; and Eric Schmitt, "Mapping Unit Failures Laid to Reorganization," *New York Times,* May 12, 1999.

■ *Administrative or professional failures by intelligence officials.* The most significant example was probably the Aldrich Ames affair, where CIA managers failed to respond to warning signs that a CIA officer was secretly working for Soviet intelligence. See Frederick P. Hitz, *Unclassified Abstract of the CIA Inspector General's Report on the Aldrich H. Ames Case* (October 21, 1994); and "Statement of Frederick P. Hitz, Inspector General, Central Intelligence Agency," before the Select Committee on Intelligence, United States Senate (November 9, 1995).

- *Intelligence operations contrary to American law or values.* For example, in 1996 some journalists reported that the CIA was involved in a conspiracy to sell illegal drugs to minority communities in the United States. The press report primarily responsible for triggering the controversy was a three-part series by Gary Webb in the *San Jose Mercury News* (August 18–20, 1996). For a follow-up on the investigations that rebutted the story, see Jim Newton and Victor Merina, "L.A. County Probe Finds No CIA Drug Link," *Washington Post,* December 12, 1996.

TWO   Planning Intelligence Resources in the Information Age

1 The best-known was the President's Commission on the Roles and Capabilities of the U.S. Intelligence Community, also known as the Aspin-Brown Commission, after its first chairman, former defense secretary Les Aspin, and former defense secretary Harold Brown, who assumed the chair when Aspin died. The Aspin-Brown Commission issued its report in 1996. In addition, all of the recent directors of central intelligence, upon entering office, have conducted their own extensive in-house reviews of intelligence policies and programs. Congress has sponsored its own studies, the most comprehensive of which was the "IC21" report by the House Permanent Select Committee on Intelligence, also in 1996. In addition, private organizations including the Council on Foreign Relations, the Twentieth Century Fund, the Cato Institute, and the Heritage Foundation have all published reports recommending reforms.

See Commission on the Roles and Capabilities of the United States Intelligence Community, *Preparing for the 21st Century: An Appraisal of U.S. Intelligence* (Washington, D.C.: U.S. Government Printing Office, 1996); Permanent Select Committee on Intelligence, U.S. House of Representatives, *IC21: Intelligence Community in the 21st Century* (Washington, D.C.: U.S. Government Printing Office, 1996); Richard Haass, *Making Intelligence Smarter: The Future of U.S. Intelligence; Report of an Independent Task Force.* (New York: Council on Foreign Relations, 1996); and Allan E. Goodman, Gregory F. Treverton, and Philip Zelikow, *In From the Cold: The Report of the Twentieth Century Fund Task Force on the Future of U.S. Intelligence* (New York: Twentieth Century Fund Press, 1996).

2 See *National Performance Review* (Washington, D.C.: U.S. Government Printing Office, September 7, 1993); and *National Performance Review Phase II Initiatives: Intelligence Community Report* (Washington, D.C.: U.S. Government Printing Office, September 1995).

3 See Richard A. Best, Jr., and Herbert Andrew Boerstling, *Proposals for Intelligence Reorganization, 1949–1996* (Washington, D.C.: Congressional Research Service, 1996); and Ronald C. Moe, *Reorganizing the Executive Branch in the Twentieth Century: Landmark Commissions* (Washington, D.C.: Congressional Research Service, 1992).

The National Performance Review drew from a public administration concept popular at the time: the idea of "entrepreneurial government" proposed by David Osborne and Ted Gaebler. See their *Reinventing Government: How the Entrepreneurial Spirit Is Transforming the Public Sector* (Boston: Addison-Wesley, 1992).

4 See Best and Boerstling, *Intelligence Reorganization* pp. 4–5. They note that the intelligence community was established on July 26, 1947, with the signing of the National Security Act (P.L. 80–253), while the first Hoover Commission, whose Task Force on National Security Organization studied the intelligence community, was authorized under P.L. 80–162 on July 27, 1947.

5 See Craig Covault, "U.S. Intelligence Ops Gear for Iraqi Strike," *Aviation Week and Space Technology,* February 9, 1998, p. 26; Covault compares the NRO's operations preparing for a possible strike against Iraq in early 1998 with the agency's performance in Desert Storm, and notes that many steps had been taken to link the NRO more closely to the operating forces requiring its products.

6 For the official announcement and description of functions, see Press Release by the Assistant Secretary of Defense for Public Affairs, "National Imagery And Mapping Agency Established," Ref. No. 563-96 (October 1, 1996).

7 There are many studies of the intelligence failure at Pearl Harbor. The best known is probably Roberta Wohlstetter, *Pearl Harbor: Warning and Decision* (Stanford, Calif.: Stanford University Press, 1962). Also see Gordon W. Prange, *At Dawn We Slept* (New York: McGraw-Hill, 1981); Gordon W. Prange, *Pearl Harbor: The Verdict of History* (New York: McGraw-Hill, 1986); Lyman B. Kirkpatrick, Jr., *Captains Without Eyes: Intelligence Failures in World War II* (London: Macmillan, 1969); William R. Corson, *The Armies of Ignorance: The Rise of the American Intelligence Empire* (New York: Dial, 1977); and Edwin T. Layton, *"And I Was There": Pearl Harbor and Midway–Breaking the Secrets.* (New York: Morrow, 1985).

8 "Remarks by The President to Staff of the CIA and Intelligence Community," Speech delivered by President Bill Clinton at the Central Intelligence Agency, July 14, 1995.

9 See Press Briefing by Mike McCurry, The White House, Washington, D.C. (March 10, 1995). The relevant parts of the briefing, according to the published transcript, were as follows:

> (T)he President has approved, as I think it was reported in the Post today, that he has signed a presidential directive on intelligence priorities. But the purpose of it is to give some clearer signals to the intelligence community about what the chief customers of intelligence analysis—the President and senior foreign policymakers of the government—what they need to have as we look out into this new world that we live in and assess all those things necessary to protect the national security interests of Americans. It's important in a time of limited resources for the President and his policymakers to give clear priorities to the intelligence com-

munity so that they can gather the type of information that will help them make the right decisions protecting Americans interests around the world.

And that's, broadly defined, exactly what this presidential directive does. It sets up a procedure by which, from time to time, we can review the work of the intelligence community, see that it's addressing exactly those concerns that we have in providing to the President and other principal policymakers and foreign policy the kind of information they need and want so that they can make the right types of decisions. . . .

It reflects, in some ways, the very hopeful nature of the post-Cold War era. There are certain types of threats that are now reduced, specifically the nuclear threat; we don't have Russian strategic intercontinental missiles aimed at the United States anymore. So we have a range of security threats that are different in this world. . . . Quite frankly, proliferation remains a concern. Terrorism remains a concern, International crime remains a concern. And how you structure the priorities of the intelligence community to reflect the new threats that are more urgent in the post-Cold War world is part of what this review and this directive are all about.

10 Quoted by Elaine Sciolino, "In North Korea the Threat is Total Collapse," *New York Times,* February 18, 1996. Such concerns were also paramount in the study of the future of U.S. intelligence by a Twentieth Century Fund commission consisting of former congressional and State Department officials. See Allan E. Goodman, Gregory F. Treverton, and Philip Zelikow, *In From the Cold: The Twentieth Century Fund Task Force Report on the Future of U.S. Intelligence* (New York: The Twentieth Century Fund, 1996).

11 James Risen, "U.S. Cutting Spy Satellite Armada by Half, Ex-Chief of CIA Testifies," *Los Angeles Times,* May 23, 1995. Risen reported: "R. James Woolsey, who stepped down as CIA director in January, also told Congress that several CIA field stations, which house the spy agency's covert operations staff, are being shuttered because of new budget pressures. Other sources said that the CIA offices targeted for closure include several in Africa. Those closures more than offset the opening of new CIA field offices in some of the former Soviet republics, officials said."

12 For an analysis of the year's reform efforts, see Richard A. Best, Jr., *Intelligence Reorganization in the 104th Congress: Prospects for a More Corporate Community* (Washington, D.C.: Congressional Research Service, September 13, 1996); and Best, *Intelligence Issues and the 104th Congress,* CRS Issue Brief (Washington, D.C.: Congressional Research Service, September 26, 1996).

13 See Senate Bill S. 1718 (April 30, 1996), Section 707.

14 See House Bill H.R. 32737 (June 13, 1996).

15 Walter Pincus, "Congress Debates Adding Smaller Spy Satellites to NRO's Menu," *Washington Post,* October 5, 1995.

16 See Bill Gates, *The Road Ahead* (New York: Viking, 1995), for his own account of these developments.

17 See James Wallace, *Overdrive: Bill Gates and the Race to Control Cyberspace* (New York: John Wiley, 1997); Leslie Helm, "Microsoft Outlines Plans to

Make Inroads on Internet," *Los Angeles Times,* December 8, 1995; and Martha Groves and Leslie Helm, "Microsoft to Buy Internet Firm WebTV," *Los Angeles Times,* April 7, 1997. In addition to Vermeer and WebTV, Microsoft also acquired Internet communications technology companies such as HotMail and VXtreme, and Java developers such as Coopers & Peters, Dimension X, and Interse. Microsoft also made significant investments in a speech recognition software manufacturer, Lernout & Hauspie; a video streaming company, VDONet; and a cable TV operator, Comcast. Most important of all, Microsoft licensed browser technology from Spyglass, jump-starting its effort to develop the first version of Explorer. The investment by Microsoft in these deals totaled more than $2 billion.

For an analysis of these investments, see "Why Mess With a Good Thing," *Business Week,* April 20, 1998, p. 116. For a history and summary of Microsoft's Internet strategy, see Steve Lohr with John Markoff, "Why Microsoft Takes Hard Line With Government, *New York Times,* January 12, 1998.

18 As noted previously, public reports estimate the CIA budget at $3.1 billion and staff at seventeen thousand people, although the government has not officially confirmed these figures; see the report of the Commission on Roles and Capabilities of the United States Intelligence Community, and R. Jeffrey Smith's analysis in "Making Connections with Dots to Decipher U.S. Spy Spending," *Washington Post,* March 12, 1996.

19 There is, of course, a large body of literature on the relationship of the public and private sectors in the development of technology and its application. Much of this literature deals with the proper roles of the two sectors in an effective "technology policy." For the historical context, see, for example, James R. Killian, Jr., *Sputnik, Scientists, and Eisenhower* (Cambridge: MIT Press, 1977); and Bruce L. R. Smith, *American Science Policy Since World War II* (Washington, D.C.: Brookings Institution, 1989).

20 Seymour Goodman, *Building on the Basics: An Examination of High-Performance Computing Export Control Policy in the 1990s.* (Stanford, Calif: The Center for International Security and Arms, Stanford University, 1995).

21 House Committee, *Intelligence Community,* p. 88

22 For a comprehensive summary of commercial remote sensing satellites, see William Stoney, *Land Satellite Information in the Next Decade* (McLean, Va: Mitretek, 1996). Also see Vipin Gupta, *New Satellite Images for Sale: The Opportunities and Risks Ahead* (Livermore, Calif.: Center for Security and Technology Studies, Lawrence Livermore National Laboratory, 1994); Bureau of Intelligence, Verification, and Information Management; Intelligence, Technology, and Analysis Division, *High-Resolution Commercial Imagery and Open-Source Information: Implications for Arms Control* (Washington, D.C.: Arms Control and Disarmament Agency, May 13, 1996); Anne M. Florini 1988. "The Opening Skies: Third-Party Imaging Satellites and US Security," *International Security* (Fall 1988), 91-123; and

Michael Krepon, Peter Zimmerman, Leonard Spector, and Mary Umberger, eds., *Commercial Observation Satellites and International Security* (New York: St. Martin's, 1990).

23 Warren Ferster, "NIMA Funds Bolster Private Imagery Firms," *Space News* March 23–29, 1998, p. 4. For the official announcement of the program, see "Commercial Imagery Initiative," Broad Agency Announcement, *Commerce Business Daily,* March 6, 1998.

24 Warren Ferster, "RDL Nabs First License for U.S. Radar Satellite," *Space News,* June 22–28, 1998, p. 1. The authority to regulate commercial imaging satellites is established in 15 USC 82, *Land Remote Sensing Policy Act of 1992,* Subchapter 2, "Licensing of Private Remote Sensing Space Systems." The terms and conditions of the license allow RDL to sell a better-resolution, "unfuzzed" product if a foreign competitor offer a comparable product.

25 Victor Marchetti and John D. Marks, *The CIA and the Cult of Intelligence* (New York, Alfred A. Knopf, 1974), p. 77.

26 Jeffrey T. Richelson, "From MONARCH EAGLE to MODERN AGE: The Centralization of Defense HUMINT." *International Journal of Intelligence and Counterintelligence* (Summer 1997), pp. 131–164.

27 Albert D. Wheelon, "Lifting the Veil on CORONA," *Space Policy* (November 1995), 249–260; Albert D. Wheelon, "CORONA: The First Reconnaissance Satellites," *Physics Today* (February 1997), 24–30; and Jeffrey T. Richelson, *America's Secret Eyes in Space: The U.S. Keyhole Spy Satellite Program* (New York: Harper and Row, 1990), chap. 3.

28 David A. Fughum and Joseph C. Anselmo, "DARPA Pitches Small Sats for Tactical Reconnaissance," *Aviation Week and Space Technology,* June 9, 1997, pp. 29–30; and D. A. Fughum, "Small Recon Satellites Win 1999 Budget Funding," *Aviation Week and Space Technology,* February 9, 1998, p. 28.

29 Donald M. Horan and Bruce D. Berkowitz, "The Clementine Lunar Mission," in James Wertz and Wiley J. Larson, eds., *Reducing Space Mission Cost* (Torrance, Calif.: Space Technology Library, 1996); and Bruce D. Berkowitz, "The Clementine Mission," *Technology Review* (April 1995), 24–31. BMDO also turned to an unconventional source for the probe's sensors–Lawrence Livermore National Laboratory, which had built sensors for satellites that watch for nuclear explosions, but which had never built imaging sensors for a space probe.

THREE The Intelligence Process and the Information Revolution

1 See, for example, Herbert Simon, *Administrative Behavior* (New York: Macmillan, 1975); Frederick Dyer, *Bureaucracy vs. Creativity* (Coral Gables Fla: University of Miami Press, 1965); and Joseph H. Reitz, *Behavior in Organizations* (Homewood Ill.: R.D. Irwin, 1987).

2 For an account of the Battle of the Somme, see John Keegan, *The Face of Battle* (New York: Vintage, 1977).

3 For a discussion of military formations and strategy, see Carl von Clausewitz, *On War* (1820), trans. Michael Howard and Peter Paret (Princeton, N.J.: Princeton University Press, 1976); and James Burke, *Connections* (Boston: Little, Brown, 1978).

4 See B. H. Liddell-Hart, *The Tanks* (London: Cassell, 1959); A. M. Low, *Tanks* (London: Hutchinson & Company, 1941).

5 See "Spies Need a Shake-Up," *Los Angeles Times,* June 5, 1998.

6 Ved Mehta, "India's Combustible Mixture," *New York Times,* May 16, 1998; and Rowland Evans and Robert D. Novak, "What Punishment for India's Audacity," *Washington Post,* May 18, 1998.

7 James Risen, "India's A-Tests Prompt CIA to Review Its Warning Systems," *New York Times,* July 4, 1998.

8 R. Jeffrey Smith, "CIA Missed Signs of India's Tests, U.S. Officials Say," *Washington Post,* May 13, 1998.

9 According to one report, the CIA did try to warn the White House about the impending test in daily briefings, but was "simply ignored." So the snafu may have occurred within the political chain of command, rather than within the intelligence community itself. See "They Knew All Along," *American Spectator,* July 1998, p. 15.

10 Tim Weiner, "Report Finds Basic Flaws in U.S. Intelligence Operations," *New York Times,* June 3, 1998.

11 Interview by Tony Snow, *Fox News Sunday,* August 23, 1998.

12 Tim Weiner and James Risen, "Policy Makers, Diplomats, Intelligence Officers All Missed India's Intentions," *New York Times,* May 25, 1998.

13 Robin Wright, "U.S. Intelligence Failed to Warn of India's Atom Tests," *Los Angeles Times,* May 13, 1998.

14 Madeleine K. Albright, "Remarks to Stimson Center," (Washington, D.C., June 10, 1998), as released by the Office of the Spokesman, U.S. Department of State. On the other hand, for the Indian point of view, see Jaswant Singh, "Against Nuclear Apartheid," *Foreign Affairs* (September-October 1998), 41–52.

15 Weiner and Risen, "India's Intentions."

16 See the reference to the evolution of Directorate of Intelligence communications in the strategic plan of the Directorate of Intelligence, *Analysis: Directorate of Intelligence in the 21st Century* (Washington, D.C.: Central Intelligence Agency, 1996), pp. 1–2.

17 Bart Ziegler, "Internet Software Poses Threat To Notes But Cheaper Programs Are Not As Secure," *Wall Street Journal,* November 7, 1995.

18 For an extensive description of Intelink and its use see Fredrick Thomas Martin, *Top Secret Intranet* (New York: Prentice Hall, 1998). Also see Vernon Loeb, "Weaving A Web of Secrets; Intranet Transforms Intelligence Sharing," *Washington Post,* December 1, 1998. The Mitre Corporation, "Intelink," *Annual Report, 1995* (electronic version); and the news release by Computer Sciences Corporation, "Changing the Way the Intelligence Community Uses Cyberspace" (October 24, 1996).

19 See Directorate of Intelligence, *Analysis* pp. 1–2.

20 See Joseph S. Nye, Jr., and William A. Owens, "America's Information

Edge," *Foreign Affairs* (March-April 1996), 20–36. Nye is a former chairman of the National Intelligence Council and former assistant secretary of defense. Owens retired as vice-chairman of the Joint Chiefs of Staff.

21 For accounts of the events at Srebrenica, see Michael Dobbs and Christine Spolar, "Anybody Who Moved Or Screamed Was Killed; Thousands Massacred On Bosnia Trek In July," *Washington Post,* October 26, 1995. Christine Spolar, "Survivor Tells His Tale Of Horrors; Muslim Farmer Who Survived Tells Of Horrors," *Washington Post,* October 26, 1995; John Pomfret, "Serbs Accused Of Killing Scores of Civilians," *Washington Post,* October 20, 1995.

22 Stephen Engelberg and Tim Weiner, with Raymond Bonner and Jane Perlez, "Srebrenica," *New York Times,* September 29, 1995.

23 See Michael Dobbs and R. Jeffrey Smith, "Proof Offered of Serb Atrocities: U.S. Analysts Identify Sites," *Washington Post,* October 29, 1995.

24 See Max Weber, "Bureaucracy," in *From Max Weber: Essays in Sociology,* trans. H. H. Gerth and C. Wright Mills (New York, Oxford University Press, 1962), pp. 196–244.

25 The literature on bureaucracies is, of course, large. Some of the more fundamental works that discuss hierarchies, division of labor and specialization, and behavior within such organizations include Gerald Garvey, *Facing the Bureaucracy* (New York: Jossey-Bass, 1923); Chester I. Barnard, *The Functions of the Executive* (Cambridge: Harvard University Press, 1938); Herbert A. Simon, *Administrative Behavior: A Study of Decision-Making Processes in Administrative Organization* (New York: Free Press, 1945); James G. March and Herbert A. Simon, *Organizations* (New York: John Wiley, 1958); Anthony Downs, *Inside Bureaucracy* (Boston: Little, Brown, 1967); Charles T. Goodsell, *The Case for Bureaucracy* (Chatham, N.J.: Chatham House Publishers, 1994); and James Q. Wilson, *Bureaucracy: What Government Agencies Do and Why They Do It* (New York: Basic, 1989).

26 For two examples, see Office of Public Affairs, *Factbook on Intelligence* (Washington, D.C.: Central Intelligence Agency, 1997), pp. 12–14; and Office of Public Affairs, *A Consumer's Guide to Intelligence* (Washington, D.C.: Central Intelligence Agency, 1994).

27 Commission on the Roles and Capabilities of the United States Intelligence Community *Preparing for the 21st Century: An Appraisal of U.S. Intelligence* (Washington, D.C.: U.S. Government Printing Office, 1996) p. B-1. For a similar depiction, see Office of Public Affairs, *Factbook on Intelligence* (Washington, D.C.: Central Intelligence Agency, 1998), pp. 12–14.

28 Central Intelligence Agency, *A Consumer's Guide,* p. 38.

29 In the 1800s, the production line and the use of standardized parts was known as the "American System," because it was so closely identified with U.S. industry. Popular legend attributes the American System to Eli Whitney, who used it in manufacturing rifles for the army. In reality, the approach was in use several decades earlier, in both the United States and Europe. See Merritt Roe Smith, *Harper's Ferry Armory and the New Technology* (Ithaca, N.Y.: Cornell University Press, 1977).

30 See Bruce D. Berkowitz and Allan E. Goodman, *Strategic Intelligence for American National Security* (Princeton, N.J.: Princeton University Press, 1989), p. 31. In our study, we used the intelligence cycle as a baseline to show how intelligence failures occur when one step or another goes awry.

31 For a summary of the use of intelligence centers and ad hoc task forces, see Permanent Select Committee on Intelligence, U.S. House of Rep *IC21: Intelligence Community in the 21st Century,* (Washington, D.C.: U.S. Government Printing Office, 1996) pp. 256-271.

32 Alan C. Miller and Robin Wright, "Jet's Downing Sets Off Probe Around World," *Los Angeles Times,* July 27, 1996.

33 See William H. Davidow and Michael S. Malone, *The Virtual Corporation* (New York: HarperCollins, 1992); Peter F. Drucker, "The Coming of the New Organization," *Harvard Business Review* (January-February, 1988), 45-53; and Morton Scott, ed., *The Corporation of the 1990s: Information Technology and Organizational Transformation* (New York: Oxford University Press, 1991).

34 Anthony L. Velocci, Jr., "Virtual Enterprises: A Plus for Lockheed Martin," *Aviation Week and Space Technology,* February 10, 1997, pp. 86-87. Also see Bruce D. Berkowitz, "NASA's X-33," *Air&Space/Smithsonian* (October-November 1996), pp. 32-37. Lockheed later acquired Rockwell's aerospace divisions when Rockwell decided to concentrate on electronics and information systems.

35 See Eric Taub, *Taurus: The Making of the Car that Saved Ford* (New York: Dutton, 1991); and Robert X. Cringley, *Accidental Empires: How the Boys of Silicon Valley Make Their Millions, Battle Foreign Competition, and Still Can't Get a Date* (New York: HarperBusiness, 1996).

36 George F. Kennan "Spy and Counterspy," *New York Times,* May 18, 1997.

37 Ruth A. David, "The Agile Intelligence Enterprise: Enhancing Speed, Flexibility, and Capacity Through Collaborative Operations," Draft Memo, Directorate for Science and Technology, Central Intelligence Agency (Summer 1997).

38 See, for example, Nicos Stavropoulos, *Objectivity in Law* (New York: Clarendon, 1996); M. D. Faber, *Objectivity and Human Perception: Revisions and Crossroads in Psychoanalysis and Philosophy,* Edmonton: University of Alberta Press, 1985); and Gunnar Myrdal, *Objectivity in Social Research* (New York: Pantheon, 1969).

39 For a summary of market-based approaches, see Wayne Gable and Jerry Ellig, *Introduction to Market-Based Management* (Fairfax, Va.: Center for Market Processes, 1993). For examples of research that led to the concept, see Herbert Simon, "What Is Industrial Democracy?" *Challenge* (January-February 1983), 30-39; and Ricardo Semler, "Managing Without Managers," *Harvard Business Review* (September-October 1989), 76-84.

40 See John F. Sopko and Alan Edelman, *A Case Study on the Aum Shinrikyo,* Staff Statement, U.S. Senate Permanent Subcommittee on Investigations, Hearings on Global Proliferation of Weapons of Mass Destruction (October 31, 1995). Also see Davis E. Kaplan and Andrew Marshall, *The Cult at the End of the World* (New York: Crown, 1996); Nicholas D. Kristof,

"Japanese Cult Said to Have Planned Nerve-Gas Attacks in U.S., *New York Times,* March 23, 1997; and William J. Broad, "When a Cult Turns to Germ Warfare," *New York Times,* May 26, 1998.

41 The Zimmermann telegram was a message transmitted from the German Foreign Ministry to its embassy in Mexico in 1917. It contained a secret proposal in which Germany offered to return to Mexico the land it lost to the United States in the 1800s if it would enter the war on its side. British intelligence intercepted the message and disclosed it. American popular opinion, which had been divided, shifted in favor of entering the war against Germany. See Barbara W. Tuchman, *The Zimmermann Telegram* (New York: Macmillan, 1958). Also see Herbert O. Yardley, *The American Black Chamber* (Indianapolis: Bobbs-Merrill, 1931); and David Kahn, *The Codebreakers* (New York: Macmillan, 1967), chap. 12.

42 See F. W. Winterbotham, *The Ultra Secret* (London: Weidenfeld & Nicholson, 1974); Bradley F. Smith, *The Ultra-Magic Deals and the Most Secret Special Relationship, 1940–1946* (Novato, Calif.: Presidio, 1993); Ronald Lewin, *American Magic* (New York: Farrar Straus, 1982); Ronald Lewin, *Ultra Goes to War* (New York: Farrar Straus, 1978); Robert Louis Benson and Michael Warner, eds., *Venona: Soviet Espionage and the American Response 1939–1957* (Washington, D.C.: National Security Agency and Central Intelligence Agency, 1996).

43 For a thorough analysis of the issue and summaries of the positions taken by various parties in the debate, see Computer Science and Telecommunications Board, National Research Council, *Cryptography's Role in Securing the Information Society* (Washington, D.C.: National Academy Press, 1996). Also see Office of Technology Assessment, *Information Security and Privacy in Network Environments* (Washington, D.C.: U.S. Government Printing Office, 1994); and Susan Landau et al., *Codes, Keys and Conflicts: Issues in U.S. Crypto Policy* (New York: Association for Computing Machinery, 1994).

44 The following account is based on communications with Arjen K. Lenstra, Paul Leyland, and Michael Graff, February 3–6, 1997. Also see P. Fahn and M. J. B. Robshaw, *Results from the RSA Factoring Challenge,* Technical Report TR-501, version 1.3, RSA Laboratories (January 1995); and A. K. Lenstra and M. S. Manasse, "Factoring by Electronic Mail," *Advances in Cryptology,* Eurocrypt '89 Lecture Notes in Computer Science, vol. 434 (Springer-Verlag, 1990) pp. 355–371.

45 See D. Atkins, M. Graff, A. K. Lenstra and P. C. Leyland, "The Magic Words Are Squeamish Ossifrage" *Advances in Cryptology,* Asiacrypt '94 (Springer-Verlag, 1995) pp. 263–277. Also see the account of the factoring scene by Richard E. Crandall, "The Challenge of Large Numbers," *Scientific American,* February 1997, and the relationship of factoring to cryptology in G. Brassard, *Modern Cryptology,* Lecture Notes in Computer Science, vol. 325 (Springer-Verlag, 1988).

46 Associated Press, "Student Breaks Highest-Level Encryption Code U.S. Allows," cited in the *Wall Street Journal Interactive Edition,* January 30, 1997.

47 Peter Sharfman, "Intelligence Analysis in an Age of Electronic Dissemination," Paper Prepared for Delivery at the Conference on Intelligence Analysis and Assessment, Canadian Association for Security and Intelligence Studies, Ottawa, October 27–29, 1994, pp. 16–17.

48 Robert M. Gates, Address in the CIA Auditorium (March 16, 1992), reprinted as "Guarding Against Politicization," *Studies in Intelligence* 36, no. 5 (1992), 5–15.

49 Berkowitz and Goodman, *Strategic Intelligence,* pp. 117–136; and Bruce D. Berkowitz, "Intelligence in the Organizational Context," *Orbis* (Fall 1985), 571–596.

50 For an account of this episode, see the monograph by David L. Goodstein, *Whatever Happened to Cold Fusion?* (April 5, 1994). Goodstein is Professor of Physics and Vice Provost at the California Institute of Technology; the monograph is available at >http://www.hss.caltech.edu/∞ses/Goodstein-DavidL.html<. Although the scientific community has been unable to replicate the initial findings by Pons and Fleischmann, research continues in the field. See Eugene Mallove, *Fire From Ice: Searching for the Truth Behind the Cold Fusion Furor* (New York: John Wiley & Sons, 1991); and "*Fusion Energy,* Hearing before the Subcommittee on Energy of the Committee on Science, Space and Technology, U.S. House of Representatives (Washington, D.C.: U.S. Government Printing Office, May 5, 1993). Also see J. R. Huizenga, *Cold Fusion: The Scientific Fiasco of the Century* (New York: Oxford University Press, 1993).

51 For a critique of politicization in the intelligence community during the Casey years, see Melvin A. Goodman, "Ending the CIA's Cold War Legacy," *Foreign Policy* (Spring, 1997) 128–143. During the 1992 nomination hearings of Robert Gates, Goodman and two other CIA analysts alleged that U.S. intelligence had been politicized during William Casey's tenure as director of central intelligence. See *Nomination of Robert M. Gates, Hearings Before the Select Committee on Intelligence of the United States Senate* (Washington, D.C.: Government Printing Office, 1992). Gates responded to these allegations in the hearings. His address to CIA staff (op. cit.) was also motivated in part as a response to these criticisms.

52 For a useful review of the controversy over the Soviet strategic estimate, see Anne Hessing Cahn, *Killing Detente: The Right Attacks the CIA* (University Park: Pennsylvania State University Press, 1998). Also see John Prados, *The Soviet Estimate* (New York: Dial, 1982); and Laurence Freedman, *U.S. Intelligence and the Soviet Strategic Threat* (London: Macmillan, 1977).

FOUR   The Problem of Analysis in the New Era

1 Peter Drucker, "The Coming of the New Organization," *Harvard Business Review* (January-February 1988), p. 101.

2 The CIA defines "intelligence" as "knowledge and foreknowledge of the world around us . . . that helps consumers, either civilian leaders or military commanders, to consider alternative options and outcomes." See Office of Public Affairs, *A Consumer's Guide to Intelligence* (Washington D.C.: Central Intelligence Agency, 1994), p. vii.

3 See, for example, CIA/NPIC Photographic Intelligence Report, "Regional Nuclear Weapons Storage Site Near Berdichev, USSR" (May 1963), in Kevin C. Ruffner, ed., *CORONA: America's First Satellite Program* (Washington, D.C.: Central Intelligence Agency, 1995), pp. 169–174.

4 James Risen, "U.S. Attacks Based on Strong Evidence Against Bin Laden Group," *New York Times,* August 21, 1998. For a discussion of prior knowledge of the Afghan bases by U.S. intelligence, see Tim Weiner, "Afghan Camps, Hidden in Hills, Stymied Soviet Attacks for Years," *New York Times,* August 24, 1998.

5 See Tim Weiner and Steven Lee Myer, "U.S. Defends Attack on Sudanese Drug Plant," *New York Times,* September 3, 1998. Also see Seymour M. Hersh, "Annals of National Security: The Missiles of August," *New Yorker,* October 12, 1998, pp. 34–41.

6 Tim Weiner and James Risen, "Decision to Strike Factory in Sudan Based on Surmise," *New York Times,* September 21, 1998. Also see Hersh, "National Security."

7 See John Ranelagh, *The Agency: The Rise and Decline of the CIA* (New York: Touchstone, 1986), p. 55. Also see, for example, President Truman's explanation for establishing the CIA in Harry S. Truman, *1946–1952: Years of Trial and Hope: Memoirs by Harry S. Truman* (New York: New American Library, 1956), chap. 4.

8 Lt. Gen. Patrick M. Hughes, USA, Statement before the Senate Select Committee on Intelligence, January 28, 1998, p. 19.

9 For a discussion of the difficulties of monitoring arms control—and how arms control becomes more difficult to monitor as successive agreements are adopted—see Bruce D. Berkowitz, *Calculated Risks: A Century of Arms Control, Why It Has Failed, and How to Make It Work* (New York: Simon and Schuster, 1987), chap. 4. The seminal discussion of the political problems linked with verification is probably Fred Charles Iklé, "After Detection, What?" *Foreign Affairs* (January 1961), 208–220.

10 See Freedom House Survey Team Staff, *Freedom In The World 1996* (New York: Freedom House, 1996). For a more measured view, see Thomas Carothers, "Democracy Without Illusions," *Foreign Affairs* (January-February 1997), 85–99.

11 Vaclav Havel, "The Need for Transcendence In the Postmodern World" Speech presented at Independence Hall in Philadelphia, Pennsylvania, July 4, 1994. President Havel gave the speech at a ceremony at which he was presented the Philadelphia Liberty Medal.

12 Charles F. Doran, a professor at Johns Hopkins University's School of Advanced International Studies, argues that this is exactly the kind of analysis on Canada that U.S. leaders require, although he acknowledges the potential controversy. See his "Will Canada Unravel?" *Foreign Affairs* (September-October 1996), 97–109.

13 Kim R. Holmes, Melanie Kirkpatrick, and Bryan T. Johnson, eds., *Index of Economic Freedom,* 1997 edition (Washington, D.C.: Heritage Foundation, 1996).

14 See Daniel Yergin and Joseph Stanislaw, *The Commanding Heights: The*

Battle Between Government and the Marketplace That Is Remaking the Modern World (New York: Simon and Schuster, 1998).

15 See, for example, William T. Lee, *The Estimation of Soviet Defense Expenditures for 1955–1975; An Unconventional Approach* (New York: Praeger, 1977); and David F. Burton, "Estimating Soviet Defense Spending," *Problems of Communism* (March 1983).

16 The specific shortcomings are well summarized in the companion background paper for the Aspin-Brown Commission developed by Philip Zelikow, "American Intelligence and the World Economy" (Draft manuscript provided by author). See especially Chapter 4 and the author's survey of the findings of the National Research Council of the National Academy of Sciences on the adequacy of existing data collection methods and systems. A revised version is included in Twentieth Century Fund Task Force on the Future of U.S. Intelligence, *In From the Cold* (New York: Twentieth Century Fund, 1996).

17 William Webster, Text of Remarks to the Los Angeles World Affairs Council, (September 19, 1989). One of his predecessors, Admiral Stansfield Turner, took a different view and has argued that the intelligence agencies can and should do more work on economic issues provided they can also improve analyst recruiting and training. See his article, "Intelligence for a New World Order," *Foreign Affairs* (Autumn 1991), 150–166.

18 See "Remarks by The President to Staff of the CIA and Intelligence Community," speech delivered by President Bill Clinton at the Central Intelligence Agency, Langley, Virginia, July 14, 1995. Also see "Remarks By The President At The United States Naval Academy Commencement," speech delivered by President Bill Clinton at the United States Naval Academy, Annapolis, Maryland, May 22, 1998.

19 See Jeffrey T. Richelson, "Scientists in Black," *Scientific American,* February 1998, pp. 48–55; John Deutch, "The Environment On The Intelligence Agenda," speech at World Affairs Council, Los Angeles, California, July 25, 1996; and William J. Broad, "U.S. Will Deploy Its Spy Satellites on Nature Mission," *New York Times,* November 27, 1995.

20 For a critical assessment of the role of military requirements in intelligence planning, the background paper by Gregory F. Treverton in Task Force, *In From the Cold.*

21 See Thomas F. Troy, *Donovan and the CIA: A History of the Establishment of the Central Intelligence Agency* (Frederick, Md,: University Publications of America, 1981); Thomas Powers, *The Man Who Kept the Secrets: Richard Helms and the CIA* (New York: Knopf, 1979); and Joseph E. Persico, *Casey: The Lives and Secrets of William J. Casey: From the OSS to the CIA* (New York: Viking, 1990).

22 See Allan E. Goodman, "The Future of U.S. Intelligence," *Intelligence and National Security* (October 1996), 645–656.

23 See Senate Committee on Armed Services, *United Nations Peacekeeping Operations* (Washington, D.C.: U.S. Government Printing Office, 1994), p. 11. PDD-25 was also described by the administration in a press briefing; see The White House, Office of the Press Secretary, "President Clinton Signs New Peacekeeping Policy" (May 5, 1994). The implementation of this guidance on intelligence sharing is governed by guidelines issued by the Director of Central Intelligence. The first was issued in November 1994; See U.S. Congress, House Permanent Select Committee on Intelligence, *Support to the United Nations,* Open Session (Washington, D.C.: U.S. Government Printing Office, 1996), p. 14.

FIVE   Covert Action in the Information Age

1 Office of Public Affairs, *A Consumer's Guide to Intelligence,* (Washington D.C.: Central Intelligence Agency, 1994), p. 38. Covert action is officially defined in Executive Order 12333, *United States Intelligence Activities* (December 4, 1981), Section 3.4h. This executive order, which serves as the charter of the intelligence community, refers to "special activities," which is understood to mean "covert action." The section defining covert action reads: "Special activities means activities conducted in support of national foreign policy objectives abroad which are planned and executed so that the role of the United States Government is not apparent or acknowledged publicly, and functions in support of such activities, but which are not intended to influence United States political processes, public opinion, policies, or media and do not include diplomatic activities or the collection and production of intelligence or related support functions."

2 See the account by Arthur B. Darling in his *The Central Intelligence Agency: An Instrument of Government, to 1950,* (University Park: Pennsylvania State University Press, 1990) pp. 245–81. Darling, the CIA's first historian, prepared this study of the early years of the agency for the director of central intelligence in 1952–1953. Parts were published during the 1960s in *Studies in Intelligence,* the CIA's in-house journal, but it remained classified until November 1989, when the CIA released it with a few minor deletions throughout the text. An annotated edition with references to the original documentation was published the following year. Also see Ludwell Lee Montague, *General Walter Bedell Smith as Director of Central Intelligence,* (University Park: Pennsylvania State University Press, 1992), pp. 217–227.

3 See Thomas Powers, *The Man Who Kept the Secrets: Richard Helms and the CIA* (New York: Alfred A. Knopf, 1979), pp. 34–35, 41–43.

4 Darling, *The Central Intelligence Agency,* pp. 256–262.

5 50 U.S.C. 403-3, *Responsibilities of the Director of Central Intelligence* (July 26, 1947).

6 For a history and analysis, see Stephen F. Knott, *Secret and Sanctioned: Covert Operations And The American Presidency* (New York: Oxford University Press, 1996); Loch Johnson, *Secret Agencies: U.S. Intelligence in a Hostile World* (New Haven: Yale University Press, 1996); John Prados, *Presidents' Secret Wars: CIA and Pentagon Covert Operations Since World War II* (New York: William Morrow and Company, 1986); and Evan Thomas, *The Very*

Best Men: Four Who Dared: The Early Years of the CIA (New York: Simon and Schuster 1995). For an argument supporting covert action as the "middle option," see Theodore Shackley, *The Third Option: An American View Of Counterinsurgency* (Pleasantville, N.Y.: Reader's Digest Press, 1981).

7 For example, see Darling, *The Central Intelligence Agency,* pp. 38-39. When President Truman was considering whether to preserve the OSS, the House Appropriations Committee asked top U.S. military leaders for their opinion. Their opinions were divided. General officers who directed operations in Southeast Asia, southern and central Europe, and China reported favorably. Those serving in the Pacific (in particular, Douglas MacArthur and Chester Nimitz) were less supportive. Dwight Eisenhower replied that the future value of the OSS in Europe would be "very high," but that it would be confined to intelligence gathering (i.e., he did not foresee a covert action role for the agency).

8 For example, see the views summarized in Roy Godson, *Dirty Tricks or Trump Cards: U.S. Covert Action and Counterintelligence* (Washington, D.C.: Brassey's, 1996).

9 See Allan E. Goodman and Bruce D. Berkowitz, *The Need to Know: The Report of the Twentieth Century Fund Task Force on Covert Action and American Democracy* (New York: Twentieth Century Fund Press, 1992). Also see Gregory F. Treverton, *Covert Action: The Limits of Intervention in the Postwar World* (New York: Basic, 1987); and John Prados, *Presidents' Secret Wars: CIA and Pentagon Covert Operations Since World War II* (New York: Morrow, 1986).

10 William Colby, *Honorable Men: My Life in CIA* (New York: Simon and Schuster, 1978), pp. 191-202; and Prados, *Presidents' Secret Wars* pp. 261-296.

11 See Jonathan Marshall, Peter Dale Scott, and Jane Hunter, *The Iran-Contra Connection: Secret Teams and Covert Operations in the Reagan Era* (Boston: South End, 1987); and National Security Archive, *The Chronology: The Documented Day-by-Day Account of the Secret Military Assistance to Iran and the Contras* (New York: Warner, 1987).

12 Prados, *Presidents' Secret Wars* pp. 354-363. Also see James Scott, *Deciding to Intervene: The Reagan Doctrine and American Foreign Policy* (Durham, N.C.: Duke University Press, 1996).

13 Victor Marchetti and John D. Marks, *The CIA and the Cult of Intelligence* (New York: Alfred Knopf, 1974), p. 54.

14 John Ranelagh, *The Agency: The Rise and Decline of the CIA* (New York: Touchstone, 1986), pp. 133, 513-520. For one of the earliest public accounts of these operations, see Powers, *The Man Who Kept the Secrets.*

15 Select Committee to Study Government Operations with Respect to Intelligence Activities ("Church Committee"), U.S. Senate, 94th Congress, *Alleged Assassination Plots Involving Foreign Leaders* (Washington, D.C.: U.S. Government Printing Office, November 20, 1975), pp. 110, 181-184.

16 See, for example, Francis X. Winters, *The Year of the Hare: America in*

Vietnam, January 25, 1963–February 15, 1964 (Athens: University of Georgia Press, 1997).

17 For an account, see Stephen Schlesinger and Stephen Kinzer, *Bitter Fruit: The Untold Story of the American Coup in Guatemala* (New York: Doubleday, 1982).

18 The standard account is Kermit Roosevelt, *Countercoup: The Struggle for the Control of Iran* (New York: McGraw-Hill, 1979).

19 For an overall analysis of Casey's views of covert action and its role in U.S. national security policy, see Joseph E. Persico, *Casey: The Lives and Secrets of William J. Casey: From the OSS to the CIA* (New York: Viking, 1990); and Bob Woodward, *Veil: The Secret Wars of the CIA, 1981–1987* (New York: Simon and Schuster, 1987). For an examination of how Casey's role in the Reagan administration and his views of covert action led to the Iran-Contra affair, see the analysis in Martin Anderson, *Revolution* (San Diego: Harcourt Brace Jovanovich, 1988), pp. 336–347.

20 The literature—especially criticism—about the CIA and covert operations that was generated during the 1970s is vast. Some of the more notable examples include Marchetti and Marks, *The CIA and the Cult of Intelligence;* John Stockwell, *In Search of Enemies* (New York: Norton, 1978); and Philip Agee, *Inside the Company: CIA Diary* (New York: Penguin, 1975). For a more favorable assessment, see Harry Rozitzke, *The CIA's Secret Operations: Espionage, Counterespionage, and Covert Action* (New York: Reader's Digest Press, 1977).

21 For an overview of the development of notification requirements and procedures, see Goodman and Berkowitz, *The Need to Know,* chap. 7.

22 See, for example, the "Dissenting View of Hodding Carter III" in Goodman and Berkowitz, *The Need to Know* p. 21.

23 For an analysis of the various tradeoffs between restrictive institutions and democratic rule, see Robert A. Dahl, *A Preface to Democratic Theory* (Chicago: University of Chicago Press 1956); Arend Lijphart, *Democracies in Plural Societies: A Comparative Exploration* (New Haven Yale University Press, 1977); and especially William H. Riker, *Liberalism Against Populism: A Confrontation Between the Theory of Democracy and the Theory of Social Choice* (San Francisco: W. H. Freeman, 1982).

24 See William S. Cohen and George Mitchell, *Men of Zeal: A Candid Inside Story of the Iran-Contra Hearings* (New York: Viking, 1988).

25 President Reagan appointed a commission headed by former senator John Tower to investigate the affair. See *Report of the President's Special Review Board* (Washington, D.C.: U.S. Government Printing Office, February 26, 1987). For the report of the special prosecutor, see *Report of the Independent Counsel for Iran/Contra Matters, Volume III: Comments and Materials Submitted by Individuals and Their Attorneys Responding to Volume I of the Final Report* (Washington, D.C.: U.S. Government Printing Office, December 3, 1993). For Walsh's own account, see *Firewall: The Iran-Contra Conspiracy and Cover-Up* (New York: W.W. Norton & Company, 1997).

26 See Public Law 102–88, August 14, 1991, 102d Congress. Also see the Conference Committee Report, *Intelligence Authorization Act, Fiscal Year 1991* (Washington, D.C.: U.S. Government Printing Office, July 25, 1991).

27 The following account is based on press reports and public testimony by U.S. officials. See in particular Jim Hoagland, "How CIA's Secret War on Saddam Collapsed," *Washington Post,* June 26, 1997. Also see R. Jeffrey Smith, "CIA-Backed Iraqi Dissidents Killed," *Washington Post,* September 10, 1996; and Bruce D. Berkowitz and Allan E. Goodman, "The Logic of Covert Action," *The National Interest* (Spring 1998), 38–46. Much of Hoagland's account was based on interviews with Warren Marik, a retired CIA case officer who had participated in the operation. The CIA later submitted a request for the Justice Department to investigate Marik's disclosure. See Walter Pincus, "Justice Asked to Investigate Leaks by CIA Ex-Officer," *Washington Post,* July 19, 1997.

28 For a history of the experience of the Kurds in regional and great power politics, see Jonathan C. Randal, *After Such Knowledge, What Forgiveness: My Encounters with Kurdistan* (New York: Farrar Straus Giroux, 1997); and Susan Meiselas, *Kurdistan: In the Shadow of History* (New York: Random House, 1998).

29 Hoagland, "Secret War."

30 See Tim Weiner, "Iraqi Offensive Disrupts Plot to Oust Saddam Hussein," *Washington Post,* September 7, 1996 and Robin Wright, "Hussein Torpedoes CIA Plot Against Him, Officials Say," *Los Angeles Times,* September 8, 1996.

31 Weiner, "Iraqi Offensive."

32 R. Jeffrey Smith "CIA-Backed Iraqi Dissidents Killed," *Washington Post,* September 10, 1996.

33 Robin Wright, "U.S. Failed to Assist Plan to Block Kurdish Infighting," *Los Angeles Times,* September 15, 1996.

34 See Hoagland, "Secret War." Hoagland reports that the order authorizing the operation was a "lethal finding."

35 This typology is adopted from a scheme proposed in a Defense Science Board study; see Office of the Under Secretary of Defense for Acquisition and Technology, *Report of The Defense Science Board Task Force on Information Warfare-Defense (IW-D)* (Washington, D.C.: U.S. Government Printing Office, January 1997). Also see Bruce D. Berkowitz, "Warfare in the Information Age," *Issues in Science and Technology* (Fall 1995), 59–67; John Arquilla and David Ronfeldt, eds., *In Athena's Camp: Preparing for Conflict in the Information Age* (Santa Monica, Calif.: RAND Corporation, 1997); L. Scott Johnson, "Toward a Functional Model of Information Warfare," *Studies in Intelligence,* 1 (1997); and Statement for the Record of Louis J. Freeh, Director, Federal Bureau of Investigation, before the Senate Select Committee Hearing on Intelligence hearing on Threats to U.S. National Security, January 28, 1998.

36 For an analysis of debates concerning targeting, tactics, and U.S. policy for IW, see David A. Flughum, "Cyberwar Plans Trigger Intelligence

Controversy," *Aviation Week and Space Technology,* January 19, 1998, pp. 52–58. For a discussion of policy discussions concerning U.S. vulnerabilities to an IW attack, see John T. Correll, "War in Cyberspace," *Air Force Magazine,* January 1998, pp. 33–36.

37 For example, the Senate Committee on Government Operations held hearings in 1996 in which witnesses warned of the potential threat from terrorists interfering with U.S. information systems; see Permanent Subcommittee on Investigations, U.S. Senate, "Opening Statement Of Senator Sam Nunn, Ranking Minority Member," Hearing On Security In Cyberspace (Washington, U.S. Government Printing Office, June 5, 1996); and "Statement by John Deutch, Director of U.S. Central Intelligence," *Hearing On Security In Cyberspace* (June 25, 1996). For an example of the reported use of offensive information warfare by the United States, see the article by Gregory L. Vistica, "Cyberwar and Sabotage," *Newsweek,* May 31, 1999." Vistica reported that U.S. intelligence used computer hacking to tamper with funds Serbian leader Slobodan Milosevic kept in foreign bank accounts.

SIX   The Intelligence Culture and the Future

1 For a discussion of the neglect of culture in international politics, see Daniel P. Moynihan, *Pandemonium: Ethnicity in International Politics.* (New York: Oxford University Press, 1993). Some early examples of this rethinking include Samuel P. Huntington, *Political Order in Changing Societies* (New Haven: Yale University Press, 1968); Alvin Rabushka and Kenneth A. Shepsle, *Politics in Plural Societies: A Theory of Democratic Instability* (Columbus, Ohio: Merrill, 1972); Eric Nordlinger, *Conflict Regulation in Divided Societies,* Occasional Papers in International Affairs, No. 29, (Cambridge, Mass.: Center for International Affairs, Harvard University, 1972); and Arend Lijphart, *Democracy in Plural Societies: A Comparative Exploration* (New Haven: Yale University Press, 1977).

2 Judges 12:5–6

3 Mariner S. Eccles, *Beckoning Frontiers* (New York: Knopf, 1951), p. 336.

4 For a recent discussion of secrecy in intelligence and other government affairs, see the *Report of the Commission on Protecting and Reducing Government Secrecy* (Washington, D.C.: U.S. Government Printing Office, 1997). For an expanded study of the subject, see the book by the commission's chairman, Daniel Patrick Moynihan, *Secrecy: The American Experience* (New Haven: Yale University Press, 1998). For a first-hand account of the problems caused by excessive secrecy in the analysis of the foreign ballistic missile threat, see Walter Pincus, "Rumsfeld: Intelligence 'Need to Know' Smacks of Not to Know," *Washington Post,* May 5, 1999.

5 George Kennan, "Spy and Counterspy," *New York Times,* May 18, 1997.

6 See Jeffrey T. Richelson, "Out of the Black: The Disclosure and Declassification of the National Reconnaissance Office," *International Journal of Intelligence and Counterintelligence* (Spring, 1998), 1–25. Richelson makes a compelling case by illustrating how secrecy requirements can be arbitrary. He cites, for instance, how the earliest U.S. reconnaissance satellites such as SAMOS were unclassified. Richelson also notes that most airborne collection systems operated by U.S. military services are unclassified, even though aircraft are much more vulnerable than satellites.

7 See Frederick P. Hitz, *The Aldrich H. Ames Case: An Assessment of CIA'S Role in Identifying Ames as an Intelligence Penetration of the Agency* (Washington, D.C.: Central Intelligence Agency, October 21, 1994). Although the official assessments of the Ames case did not identify the agents Ames betrayed, Ames himself has spoken freely on the subject. See, for example, the interviews with Ames cited in David Wise, *Nightmover* (New York: Harper Collins, 1995).

8 Frederick P. Hitz, *The Aldrich H. Ames Case.* Also see Select Committee on Intelligence, U.S. Senate, *An Assessment of the Aldrich H. Ames Espionage Case and Implications for U.S. Intelligence* (November 1, 1994); the quotation is from p. 83. Both provide overviews of Ames' career.

9 Senate Committee, *Assessment,* p. 113.

10 *Statement of Frederick P. Hitz, Inspector General, Central Intelligence Agency, Before the Select Committee on Intelligence, United States Senate* (November 9, 1995).

11 James Risen, "CIA Still Reeling From Ames Ties to Soviet Agents," *Los Angeles Times,* November 27, 1995. Risen provides an excellent summary and analysis of the controversy.

12 *Ibid.* One of the reports officers who worked on the Ames material recalled, in some cases, "[We] would get technical military information, [and we] would have to talk to the Air Force or Army and tell them what intelligence [we] had, because this was really arcane stuff that we didn't understand. . . . So the military people would know what we had even before we had released it to policy-makers—and they would always say: 'Put that stuff out.' If we said: 'We're not sure about the source,' they would say they wanted it anyway. And if we held it back, they might complain that we were suppressing intelligence."

13 Intelligence Oversight Board, *Report On The Guatemala Review* (June 28, 1996).

14 James Risen, "2 CIA Officers Ousted Over Guatemala Scandal," *Los Angeles Times,* September 30, 1995.

15 Henry de Wolfe Smyth, *Atomic Energy for Military Purposes: The Official Report in the Development of the Atomic Bomb Under the Auspices of the United States Government, 1940–1945.* (Washington, D.C.: U.S. Government Printing Office, 1945).

16 U.S. Congress, House of Representatives Report 105-135, *Intelligence Authorization Act for Fiscal Year 1998,* (Washington, D.C.: U.S. Government Printing Office, June 18, 1997), p. 17.

17 The background and findings of the estimate, NIE 95-19, were summarized in Senate Select Committee on Intelligence, "Opening Statement of Chairman Arlen Specter (R-Pa.), Hearing on Intelligence Analysis on the

Long-Range Missile Threat to the United States" (December 4, 1996). Estimates over foreign missile capabilities and related debates over missile defenses have a long history; see, for example, Kirsten Lundberg, "The SS-9 Controversy: Intelligence as Political Football," in *Case Book: Intelligence and Policy Project* (Cambridge: John F. Kennedy School of Government, Harvard University, May 1991).

18 The following draws on the prepared statements of former DCI Robert Gates; Richard Davis, director for national security analysis at the General Accounting Office; John E. McLaughlin, vice chairman of the National Intelligence Council; and former DCI R. James Woolsey before the Senate Select Committee on Intelligence, "Hearing on Intelligence Analysis on the Long-Range Missile Threat to the United States" (December 4, 1996).

19 As a result of the controversy over the NIE, Congress mandated in the FY 1998 Defense Authorization Act that a bipartisan commission be appointed to investigate the missile threat issue. The commission, headed by former defense secretary Donald Rumsfeld, concluded that the potential foreign missile threat was greater than that projected by the NIE. The commission argued that countries determined to acquire such weapons would likely use unconventional methods to develop them, and that these methods would be faster and more difficult to detect. See Bradley Graham, "Iran, N. Korea Missile Gains Spur Warning," *Washington Post*, July 16, 1998.

20 See R. Jeffrey Smith, "CIA Missed Signs Of India's Tests, U.S. Officials Say," *Washington Post*, May 13, 1998.

INDEX

accountability: controversial sources and, 159; deniability and, 130–36; Iraq operation and, 142; in new intelligence model, 93–94; secrecy and, 149–50, 159–60

adaptability: funding transfers and, 49–51; intelligence culture and, 98, 165–67; in intelligence process, 74–92; steps toward increasing, 49–57; traditional planning process and, 44–49

adaptive software, 20

Afghanistan: covert action in, 127, 130, 141, 142; threats by nonstate actors and, 10, 100

Africa, intelligence and CIA field stations in, 35–36, 177n.11

Albright, Madeleine, 62

Allied Force. *See* Operation Allied Force

allies, and intelligence planning, 115–16

Amanpour, Christiane, 43

American culture: controversy over intelligence in, 2–3, 26–29, 125, 175n.43; covert action and, 132, 145–46; Information Revolution and, 21–23; secrecy and, 28, 132, 150, 151

America Online (AOL), 37, 39n.

Ames, Aldrich, 36, 152–54, 156, 157n., 174n.43

AOL. *See* America Online

Apple Computer, 76–77

Aquino, Corazon, 128

arms control support: Cold War *vs.* post-Cold War, 102, 104–05; monitoring and, 105, 185n.9; treaties and, 104–05, 162

Asahara, Shoko, 87

Aspin, Les, 175n.1

Aspin-Brown Commission, 25, 34, 36, 37, 69, 78, 174n.4, 175n.1

assassination, 127–28

Atkins, Derek, 91

Aum Shinrikyo (cult), 87–88

ballistic missile defense (BMD), 162–65

Ballistic Missile Defense Organization (BMDO), 55

Barnes, Charles, 96

Barzani, Masoud, 138–39

"best truth," definition of, *xi*

bin Laden, Osama, 10, 100–101

biological weapons (BW) threat, 11, 104, 118–22

biosensors, 20

BMD. *See* ballistic missile defense

BMDO. *See* Ballistic Missile Defense Organization

Bomar Brain, 44

Bosnia, 65–67, 82–83

Brown, Harold, 175n.1

bureaucracy: adaptability and, 39–40, 165–67; breakthrough thinking and, 58–59; competition and, 54; concept of, 67–68, 71; traditional intelligence model and, 67–71

Bush, George, 138, 141

BW. *See* biological weapons threat

Carter, Jimmy, 31

Casey, William, 33, 129, 133, 134, 135

Castro, Fidel, 127–28

Central Intelligence Agency (CIA), 25, 26; adaptability and, 50–51; agency analysts and, 161; Ames affair and, 152–54, 156, 157n., 174n.43; budget and,